Beauty Treatments

Prepare to Meet Your King

Jodie Dye

5 Fold Media
Visit us at www.5foldmedia.com

Endorsements

"Jodie's passion for leading women on a journey toward uncovering their true beauty is inspiring. It's my hope that the words and Scripture in *Beauty Treatments* will help you draw close to the Creator and King, coming to rest in the truth that, in Him, you are fearfully and wonderfully made."

- Matt Hammitt, Lead Singer of Sanctus Real

"Jodie Dye is one of those rare individuals who inspires everyone around her with her boundless enthusiasm and love of life. I like to think of her as 'Jodie Joy.' While it was obvious that Jodie had a gift for touching people's lives with her spoken words and a smile, I didn't know she also had a gift for the written word until I read some of her book. I guess I shouldn't have been surprised that the same enthusiasm and joy that Jodie exudes in person also shines through on the pages she writes. I am excited about her first book, *Beauty Treatments*, and what it will do to bless those who read it, and I am certain that it is just the first of many life-changing and inspiring books to come from my friend, Jodie Joy."

- David Yonke, Author and Journalist

Acknowledgements

Thank You, King Jesus, for all that You have done to prepare me for You! I willfully give my life to You to do as You please. This book is Your baby, and I am thankful that by Your great mercy, and through Your Spirit, You chose me to birth it into existence.

Thank you, Sir William Thatcher Dye, Jr., my earthly king, for supporting and believing in me so that I could follow through with the calling to write this book. You are a truly royal husband—fit for the kingdom.

Thank you, Victoria, Isaac, and Daniel, my beautiful children, for your sacrifice and love during the time I received my beauty treatments, and for the times we all received them together. You are my royal gifts from God, and I treasure each one of you. You each have different talents that will bring God great glory as you pursue Him. I love you. You are all gems that are fit to adorn the hand of our King.

Thank you, Pastor Chad and Pastor Bill, of Calvary Assembly of God, for the Word of truth. As I waited on the Lord, the Word spoken from the pulpit helped me receive my beauty treatments from Jesus. Both of you have been like my spiritual fathers; you have given me "special food" and watched me grow, wanting only God's best for me. You helped prepare me for my earthly king.

Thank you, Jerry and Bill Sr., my "father-in-law," for bringing together our match made in heaven. In my opinion, you two are the best janitors that Christ has in His service.

Thank you, Christian, for being obedient to God—to pursue Him, and not me. As heartbreaking as it was, it brought about a beautiful heartfelt ministry—one I can offer to others. Those labor pains birthed this book.

Thank you, Jimmy White (a.k.a. Memucan), for seeing this work into fruition and for being my number one devoted fan. You're not only a faithful friend, committed in all your endeavors, but you are also a very talented and creative one too. Your character is all over this book. Your additions only made it more beautiful. I appreciate all the time and energy you spent, sometimes into the late hours of the night, editing this book. You were used mightily in "such a time as this."

Thank you, Carolyn, for your continued friendship throughout this journey. The "Jod-Esther grams" that you sent me were always timely and encouraging. Thank you for believing in me and doing your part to see this book become a reality.

Thanks to all my friends and family—too many to name—for your love and support. Each of you had your part in administering the beauty treatments that have prepared me for King Jesus!

Thank you to Andy and Cathy Sanders of 5 Fold Media for seeing the potential of this book, and offering me a publishing agreement that I could not refuse.

Contents

Foreword

$\mathcal{I}$ have the privilege to pastor a great church in Toledo, Ohio. Toledo is known as the Glass City because of the variety of glass industries that have been here over the years. It is a wonderful place to call home.

Not too long ago my wife and I were at an event that included a glass-blowing demonstration. We watched as the artist took the molten material, and through careful and skillful work, began to shape what appeared to be a melted mess into something valuable and beautiful. It is not a quick process. Rather, it takes time, heat, repetition, and experience. But, there is something special about knowing that it was the breath that a master creator breathed into that vessel that made it what it was. The process is fascinating to watch. The product is a treasure.

What you hold in your hands is also a treasure. As Jodie Dye's pastor over the last nine years, I have watched as God has been in the process of working in her life and the life of her family. It has not always been an easy process, as you will read in this book. It has, however, been the story of the Master Creator breathing life into a willing vessel, and shaping a priceless treasure.

This is not a book of theories or possible solutions. Jodie has lived the pages of this book. I remember when she first explained to me in the front of our sanctuary how she felt God was calling her to passionately seek to know Him for a year-long beauty treatment. It is amazing to see how God not only blessed Jodie through that time, but is now blessing you through this book.

Jodie's life has not been easy or perfect. She could easily have made excuses or poor choices based on life's circumstances and the things that came her way. Instead, she made a commitment to allow God to work His process in her life. The treatments that Jodie learned in this season and describes in this book are not necessarily pleasant. They can, however, create a beautiful product that God can use.

You are holding a treasure—how you allow God to use this in your life is your choice. My prayer is that through this work, God will speak to your heart. Allow the Master Creator to breathe new life into your world. Just like He did centuries ago for Queen Esther, and more recently for my friend, Jodie, God will create something more beautiful from your life than you could ever have imagined.

Pastor Chad Gilligan

Introduction

*A*fter years of procrastinating, I finally sat down and wrote the book that was laid upon my heart. Knowing how my daughter, and countless other women, have been left feeling empty due to relational issues, there was a burning desire to share with them the wisdom I received from going through my own intensely personal journey of emptiness. This emptiness inside me kept my eyes on man, with an ever-increasing desire to be filled with the love of a man. Going from relationship to relationship while looking for a man to make me feel better about myself only left me feeling emptier. This ultimately made me feel unattractive and downright ugly—inside and out. I realized the inner turmoil I was experiencing had to do with who I believed I was. My identity was shaken by rejection and abuse. I needed to get a true perspective of who I was from the Creator of my soul. I learned that the woman who loves herself has inner harmony with her Creator and herself. Because my past was full of distorted views of my identity, I found myself to be a woman who loved too quickly and held on too tightly—both of which put too much responsibility on the man to "make" me happy, and caused a wider chasm between me and my Creator. It was through this realization that I decided to anchor myself in the love of the Lord.

God's love is incomparable to any other. He created each one of us with a purpose. He designed us so beautifully; even before the creation of the world, He had our design in mind. The Bible says we are fearfully and wonderfully made. He is incredibly creative and beautiful Himself. There will never be enough days on this earth to really know all His beauty and all He created for His pleasure, but what splendor He has shown me is worth mentioning to others who may have struggled with their identity only to end up in a never ending cycle of bad relationships.

I have much to say to women who consistently look to others for their meaning and identity because I have done that too. I hated the thought of being alone. Since I was a teenager, I've always had a boyfriend. I looked for love in all the wrong places. I got married for the wrong reasons even after being warned not to. The stubborn part of me thought I knew best, and it wasn't until I fell flat on my face in anguish and abuse that I decided I wanted only what God had for me. The man I married found comfort in the arms of other women and would still come home to me, treating me like a vessel of no value and expecting me to give him some value because he also felt empty inside. It became an even uglier cycle of abuse. I would cry out to the Lord for help in my marriage, but I felt stuck. After our third child and many years of tears, he left with a woman he had been seeing and they moved away. He was gone and I felt relieved. I remained alone and faithful, but it was hard to get over him. I had prayed for his salvation and hoped he would come back a changed man. But it never happened.

Then I joined a ministry that expressed God's unfailing love in such tangible ways which gave me a desire for a godly man. Still, I wanted a man! The men that were a part of this ministry had a confidence in their own identity; they were not looking to women for their meaning. They looked to their Creator, and showed much adoration and love for Him. I still had a hard time understanding God's love for me, but I saw a different kind of love in a man—one that I desired and wanted badly. These men were different and I wanted one of them. Although I had been a Christian for sixteen years at this point in my life, I still hadn't surrendered this area in my life. I knew I still pursued and clung too tightly to what I thought was what God had in store for me.

There was a man I pursued who loved God with all his heart. We had wonderful moments of pure love, laughing, and sharing our stories and our lives. However, determined to know God's will for our relationship, he decided we both needed to spend time fasting and seeking confirmation apart from one another. It was during this time the Lord closed that door, *much* to my great disappointment. This man had not pursued me; I had pursued him. He loved me, but he loved me as a sister in the Lord and that was it. The longing inside for a godly man continued because, you see, I was still empty, and I thought a man would fill it. A few months later, after whining and pouting and standing at a closed door, I realized the door was not going to open. I cried out to the Lord until the early morning and He spoke to me (as you would hear a melody in your mind) and told me to read Isaiah 54; there were verses in that chapter that stopped my tears from flowing.

Isaiah 54:2-3 says, "Enlarge your house; build an addition. Spread out your home, and spare no expense! For you will soon be bursting at the seams. Your descendants will occupy other nations and resettle the ruined cities."

He was telling me that my pain had clouded my vision. I had focused on my lack—my lack of a husband and a father to my children. It was a matter of how I was seeing my situation. I could only see my little tent of self-pity.

God literally gave us an incredible treasure in this promise! In verse 4, He tells us to fear not for we will no longer live in shame. We will no longer remember the shame of our youth and the sorrows of widowhood. For our Maker is our Husband.

Verse 6 nearly jumped off the page and into my heart with its encouragement. "For the Lord has called you back from your grief— as though you were a young wife abandoned by her husband" (Isaiah 54:6). God opened my eyes at that moment to see Him as my first love. He desired my company under a larger tent so that I might expand His kingdom with Him. His vision became my vision of a greater purpose than just my small comfortable tent of pity; for even though it was dark and cramped with worthless and meaningless idols, it was that tent with which I was familiar. I realized and understood that my eyes had been opened to spiritual truths, just as Paul had described it in his letter to the church in 1 Corinthians chapter 2. For though my flesh was still rebelling against God and suffering the consequences of the sinful nature of my soul, my spirit had in reality been renewed the moment

I was born again, and therefore I could now know God and His will through my spirit.

Yes, I possess an imperfect soul, and I live in a body that is ever in decay. But who I am as a believer is a spiritual being created in the image of God—a new creation who has been given the mind of Christ so that God Himself can reveal to me all that He has given to me freely through the love of His Son. For it is only in discovering and receiving from Him all that He has prepared for us that we can finally do away with our own wisdom and understanding and begin, at last, our life's calling to share with others all we have ourselves received.

On April 16, 2008, spiritual truths awakened me in the middle of the night. God was calling me to give Him a year of my life. He spoke in my spirit that He wanted me to repent and return to Him. He was calling me to turn away from my self-sufficiency and surrender my will to Him. He wanted me to remain completely unavailable for any dating relationships for one year, and set aside this year for a purification process. God's Spirit spoke to me saying that just as Esther prepared herself for one year for King Xerxes, so must I be purified and prepared for the King of Kings. The Lord said He would give me grace to obey as He called on me to fast from food every other day for the entire year. I began to study the book of Esther to discover some spiritual truths for myself. Those spiritual truths will be revealed in the pages to come. Applying these spiritual truths to my life not only brought me closer to the throne of the King of Kings, they also changed my life and gave me an inner and radiant beauty that is more valuable than gold. I call these spiritual truths, "Beauty Treatments."

The struggle for inner peace is always in conflict with tangible outer circumstances—it becomes almost impossible to get quiet before the Lord and receive peace from Him. Therefore, I had to be disciplined; and though it wasn't easy at times, it was rewarding. I needed to cut out many activities, including my social life and ministry to others, to be able to hear from the Lord. He was faithful. I heard from Him. I have those words etched in my soul to share with you; and if you can get quiet before the Lord, you will hear from Him too. He has much to say to His bride. He wants to fill your hearts and your emptiness with His Spirit. He makes you feel like a lady when you truly make Him your priority. He has much beauty to reveal. I must be honest with you however; I believe the reason I have procrastinated in finishing this book is because it is not a popular teaching. It may hurt you to surrender areas of your life that need to undergo beauty treatments. I know it hurt me, but sincere are the wounds from a friend (Proverbs 27:6). And there is no greater friend than the friend we have in Jesus. With that in mind, find a quiet place, and begin your beauty treatments. Prepare yourself for the King of Kings.

Before we get started on those beauty treatments, we probably should get to know the King who orders them. We will also get to know the main characters who are in the book of Esther in the Bible. Someone who desires a makeover goes to great lengths to make sure that the person who is attending to them has the expertise, knowledge, and commitment to satisfy their client. They want to make sure this specialist knows what he or she is doing, and they want the assurance that he will do what he says he will do. Let me assure you, I found the perfect specialist in beauty treatments for the *inner* man. God himself specializes in making us beautiful from the inside out.

Now let's assume you don't know Jesus as your personal Savior; to know Him as Lord of Lords and King of Kings is foreign to you. My suggestion for you is to make it your ambition to find out what it means to know Him personally. Without this relationship with Jesus, this book will seem like foolishness to you—that is, until the Spirit of the Living God dwells in you. The Spirit of God only comes to those who invite Him in and He is the only one who can open your eyes to these spiritual truths. My friend, if you would like to know Jesus as your personal Savior, it is as easy as admitting that you are a sinner. We all have sinned. The Bible says there is no one righteous, not one who does what is right in His eyes (Romans 3:10). It is only by what Christ did on the cross, and by the grace that He extends to those who believe that truth, that anyone can be saved. My prayer is that after you come to know Jesus as your personal Savior, you will also know Him as the King of Kings.

Jesus is my personal Savior and has been since September 1, 1992. I was at the end of my rope. I hit bottom. The only way to look was up. God had a plan, a strategic plan, to get me where He wanted me so I would know He saved me from a life that was headed for destruction and defeat. He set my feet on a new path and gave me hope and purpose. Over the past twenty years, Jesus has become not only my King, but my everything. He did so much work in me over those years; I could go on and on about the changes He made as a result of giving Him my heart and my life. It is my desire that this book will inspire your surrender to the work He wants to do in you, and that He would also become your King.

Let me make myself clear: I am not a theologian or a historian. I am just a simple woman who wants to be used of God by the testimony of what I have been through, and what God has covered over with His blood. I can testify that the Specialist I surrendered to first opened my eyes to the splendor and majesty of His work in me and made me beautiful. I am not talking about physical beauty; inner beauty will radiate from the inward being out. Since this book is not about the physical body, I would appeal to you that you view this book from a spiritual standpoint. Your eyes may only be opened by the King Himself. I am praying that you have eyes to see amazing treasure in God's Word, that you can see His beauty treatments.

Chapter One: Meet the King

*K*ings are given kingdoms. They have power and strength. They are royalty and possess splendor and majesty. Some kings brought justice and good to their people and did what was right in the sight of God. There were others who did what was evil in the sight of God, and used the people for their own gain. However, not one kingdom has ever been established through the efforts of the king. God is sovereign in setting up each king that ever existed; there is no authority except that which God has established (Romans 13:1).

One king in particular that we will draw our attention to is King Xerxes because he is the king that made Esther, a commoner, his queen. He is the one who ordered the beauty treatments and special food for his queen. He is the king that I got to know well through my own personal study of him. He is the king that I discovered is very much like a picture of Christ and His church.

We will go back to the year 486 BC to find out what happened when mighty King Xerxes reigned. He ruled over 127 provinces in the Persian Empire. He was known to the people there as Xerxes the Great. Let's go a little bit farther back to find out how this man came to be king. His father was King Darius, but his father was not born into a royal family. His father married into royalty; his mother, Atossa, was the daughter of Cyrus the Great. Cyrus started the rebuilding of the temple of Jerusalem and set the exiles free (Isaiah 45:13). Darius married Atossa; this marriage strengthened his position as king, and he became a powerful ruler. He followed in his father-in-law's footsteps, continuing the rebuilding of the temple as God had commanded. Xerxes was crowned and succeeded as king after his father's death. He immediately took hold of the authority given him and suppressed a revolt that was taking place. He wasted no time in walking in his daddy's shoes, and I am sure that his granddaddy had a lot of influence in his life as well.

Each one of us has a history and everyone has a story to tell. You might have even heard stories from your parents and grandparents which directly impacted your life and helped form your belief system. A belief system provides a core set of values on which we base everything we do, say, or believe. Our past and the people of our past will shape our beliefs, whether we like it or not, and whether these beliefs are true or distorted. What we believe ultimately shapes the story of our lives.

My life is no exception. But, my history has become *His* story. This story of mine starts out a little like this: Once upon a time, in the days of the great and glorious Jesus, king of the vast empire of heaven and earth, there was a little girl who thought she was forgotten. Her name was Jodie, but the King called her "Star." This is the story of how she won His favor.

Throughout the coming pages, you will get to know me better as well as the characters from the book of Esther. The history of King Xerxes is given so that you might get a mental picture in your head of how this king came to be a king in the first place.

The book of Esther does not mention God, or any gods, for that matter. Nevertheless, God was all over this book. In the story of Esther, the belief system of the great King Xerxes is examined through the way he lived his life. We do know through Scripture that his grandfather, Cyrus the Great, feared God and walked in His ways. We also know that his father, Darius, was convinced of the truth of the God of Daniel (Ezra 6:14b; Daniel 6:25-27). We know through history that Xerxes' country had a belief system called Zoroastrianism. After doing my own research, I found that Zoroaster was the first to teach the doctrines of an individual judgment, heaven and hell, the future resurrection of the body, the general last judgment, and life everlasting for the reunited soul and body.[1] King Xerxes was a man

1. www.avesta.org Mary Boyce, Op. Cit. p. 29.

18

who believed in values. He had morals, even though it may seem as if he were impulsive and rash in his decision making. He believed in the same Creator as you and I; He believed there was a supreme Creator who ruled him. It is my opinion that he feared God and wanted God's wisdom in ruling. We will see that more clearly as the story unfolds. Many people who have read the book of Esther see King Xerxes as an egotistical man who sought only to please himself. Even though it may appear like that at first, we must remember that we can never judge a book by its cover. Let's really get to know this king as he is: as human as you and I. We can learn a few things about ourselves and the others around us. I personally have to give this king the benefit of the doubt, knowing how he believed. It may look like he was doing what was wrong, but there is a lesson to be learned from King Xerxes that we may all be wise to adhere to.

First of all, we learn that King Xerxes was not a self-proclaimed king. He was crowned king and he was given a kingdom to rule. Again, I want to establish and emphasize that he was indeed the king. He was ruler. It was his kingdom. He could do what he pleased in his kingdom. He was the man of his house. He had every right to summon his wife to the throne whenever he wanted. We will read later on that the king wanted his queen. According to the story, the reason the king called for his queen was that he might display her beauty for all to see. He had that right as king. After all, it was King Xerxes who made Vashti his queen: he gave her that crown. He was humiliated when she refused to come; his kingdom was divided. Jesus once said that every kingdom that is divided against itself will be ruined, and every city or household divided against itself will not stand (Matthew 12:25). He knew that if he allowed this division in his marriage, the entire empire that he ruled would be jeopardized. The verdict: banish the queen.

Wisdom is Supreme

Secondly, he had seven wise men that were close to him to help him govern. King Xerxes did not make decisions on his own. On the contrary, he sought wise counsel. Xerxes was getting ready to attack

Greece when he was in his third year ruling. He knew that in order to get cooperation from the nobles and military leaders, he needed to display his glory in order to gain their trust. He wanted to demonstrate that he had sufficient wealth to carry out his strategies for war. He knew if they got to know him, they could trust him to conquer whatever came against them. Xerxes knew the importance of relationship. He knew that he could not fight alone. The Bible says that there is wisdom in a multitude of counselors. The King James Version says it best, "Where no counsel is, the people fall: but in the multitude of counselors there is safety" (Proverbs 11:14). Wisdom tells us that fools think their own way is right, but the wise listen to others (Proverbs 12:15).

When you are experiencing a battle in your life, it is crucial to have a community of believers to give you mutual support in your difficult times. It is in these times that we need to turn to fellow believers for support by sharing our trials with them. Ask them to pray with you and stand in the gap for you. You will gain the strength and courage from the bond that is created from friendship in the kingdom. Additionally, seek out the counsel of those who have gone through battles before you; chances are they have learned a few strategies that could help you get through. The book of Proverbs is full of wisdom which will guide your every step and lead you along straight paths (Proverbs 4:11).

This king became lonely after he banished his queen. His personal attendants suggested that he make a search of all the beautiful young virgins for another queen. They further suggested they be given special beauty treatments before meeting him. Then from all the girls brought to the palace, the king was to choose the one that pleased him most. He thought this was wise and agreed. After twelve months of beauty treatments and special food, King Xerxes found himself attracted to Esther more than any of the other virgins, and, in the seventh year of his reign, he set a royal crown on her head and made her queen instead of Vashti.

The wisdom of this world is not the wisdom of the Word. If you think about the calling that Jesus Christ has given each one of us as individuals, you will realize that He too wants to display us before the world. He calls us to come wearing the fine linen that He provided.

20

He wants to show the world what is His. In His wisdom, He wants to display His splendor and majesty through the church. He is King and the church is His queen, His bride. He is so wise that He gives us the choice to come to Him; if we choose not to come, then He has to give our royal position to another more worthy of His calling.

There is something about the name of Jesus that endures forever, way past any king or kingdom. King Xerxes was the ruler of 127 provinces, but Jesus was, is, and will always be the wise ruler of this world. Jesus loves us so much; He came to earth to have a relationship with us. He wants to expand His kingdom with every one of us. He has called us to be different and set apart for His noble purposes. He created this universe and everything in it. That makes Him the ruler of what He created. He has a right to judge us and our actions. He is sovereign and that means He can do what He pleases with His creation. He is the potter and we are the clay. He chose us to be His people, a royal priesthood, a holy nation, a people belonging to Him so that we would declare the praises of Him Who called us out of darkness and into His beautiful light (1 Peter 2:9). Unlike King Xerxes who did not give Vashti the choice, our heavenly Father has given us a choice. In His sovereignty and wisdom, He gave us free will. It is up to us to accept the invitation to come.

Lord, grant us Your wisdom, for wisdom is more precious than rubies, and nothing we desire can compare with it. Lord, forgive us for choosing the wisdom of this world over Yours. Oh, Lord, I prefer Your wisdom to silver or gold. It is said in Your Word that he who acquires wisdom loves himself; and he who cherishes understanding prospers (Proverbs 19:8). Therefore, through Your Word I will acquire wisdom and understanding.

The Banquet Invitation

King Jesus is looking for willing hearts to dwell with Him in a larger tent to expand His kingdom. There can only be one king in each kingdom. We cannot rule alongside Him. If we want to partake in the feast of the kingdom of God, then it is time to stop making excuses and come to the banquet He has prepared. He wants us to sup with Him, to fellowship with Him, and to have relationship with Him. In order to trust that He is able to perform a good work in and through us, we have to *know* Him. We need to see His glory from His royal throne, so we will know He is in control. Like I said before, He will give us that choice—whether or not we choose to receive His gracious invitation. He will not force us, but the consequences of not surrendering are costly. Jesus is not only King, but He is the only way. He is the whole truth, and He is eternal life. He wants His life, His way, and His truth to live inside of us. This is the foundation for the concept of this book. The beauty treatments come from Jesus making an exchange with us. He wants us to give Him all of us, and He will exchange it with all of Him. Will you come? Will you enter into His royal chambers and have a taste of beauty? Or will you refuse, walk away, never taste and never know?

For a full 180 days, King Xerxes put on a show of the vast wealth of his kingdom and the splendor and glory of his majesty in an enclosed palace garden (Esther 1:2-5). Xerxes used this time to socialize and prepare for the war. I chose the same amount of time to not socialize, which was not easy for a social butterfly like me, but God in His majesty began to show me He was worth it. A full 180 days is six months. In August 2008, the Lord challenged me to a six-month social fast so that I could begin to feast in the Lord's heavenly garden, figuratively speaking—spending time in God's Word. As the Word came alive to me, it was like a sweet smelling aroma in that garden. He displayed the vast wealth of His kingdom to me. This is the kingdom that will never pass away. This is the kingdom that displays God's splendor, glory, and majesty. This is where I came boldly to the throne of grace to find help in my time of need. He invited me into the garden and spoke gently to me. With His loving-kindness, He brought me to repentance and to the end of my fleshly self. I became fully aware of my need to repent, and I responded to the Lord's rebuke because I had not made Him the priority, my first love.

Since I responded to His rebuke, the Lord has been faithful to pour out His heart to me as He promised in His Word (Proverbs 1:23)

In preparation to know my King's heart better, I learned I needed to respond to His rebuke every time I sinned. Even though I knew my sins were already forgiven, the act of repentance kept me in my place and the King in His.

On September 1st, I started this fast from seeing my friends; it lasted up until March 1st. The exciting part was a revelation that I received from the Lord that I believed He wanted me to act upon immediately following this six month fast. I had been studying the book of Esther since April 2008, and I got some new insights that put me on cloud nine. Look at the verses in Esther 1:1-3 and we'll discuss its application.

During the reign of Xerxes, he ruled over 127 provinces stretching from India to Cush. At this point in time, Greece was the only part of the world that wasn't already in his grasp, and he wanted Greece badly and needed the support of his officials to try to take it. King Xerxes reigned from his royal throne in the citadel of Susa, and in the third year of his reign he gave a banquet for all his nobles and officials. The military leaders of Persia and Media, the princes, and the nobles of the provinces were present.

The Lord told me that there is a part of His kingdom that is not yet in His grasp, and He needs the support of His royal priesthood and chosen generation (1 Peter 2:9) to go out there and win this battle for His glory. He said that just as Xerxes prepared his military leaders and chosen officials, so He was also preparing me and others for a battle that would bring souls into His kingdom. He reigns! Take note of this. This is important. That 180-day banquet was just for the ones he was preparing for this battle, building them up and strengthening their faith. The next banquet was for everyone.

When the 180 days were over, the king gave a banquet that lasted seven days in the enclosed garden of the king's palace for all the people from the least to the greatest who were in the citadel of Susa (Esther 1:4-5). The Lord opened my eyes to Luke 14. Oh, what a blessing it will be to attend a banquet in the kingdom of God!

In Luke14, Jesus shares a parable with His disciples about a man who had invited many people to join him at a great banquet, but who was amazed to find that each of his invited guest gave different excuses as to why they would not attend. Determined to have his banquet, he ordered his servants to go out and compel everyone that they could find to come freely and join him, and many did. But he assured that those who initially refused to attend would not share at all in his celebration. Sadly, this is an accurate depiction of God's offer of salvation to all mankind. Dear friends, as one who found every excuse in the book for not coming to Him sooner and who now understands the cost, I plead with you to make sure that you do not refuse Him now yourself.

As the application of this section of Scripture beat upon my heart, the Lord said to me that the six month time of preparation for me would end on March 1. So from March 1–March 8 (a seven-day gospel feast), I believed that He wanted me to get a team that was prepared and willing in mind, body, and spirit to go and evangelize everywhere. All kinds of places came to my mind—nursing homes, shelters, hospitals, jails, streets, and even different homes. As all these places were popping up in my head, a song I was listening to stilled my racing mind to hear the sweet words of Jesus, saying to me, "There are so many places I want to take you, My bride." His bride is the church, and He wants us to be prepared because He is sending us out to bring in the remnant of His kingdom that has not yet been found. Later as I looked on the calendar—I have a Jewish calendar—I discovered that the Feast of Purim was on March 9-10. This was the holiday the Jews celebrated because they had victory over their enemies in the book of Esther. Praise God! He will always give us the victory! With the team I had gathered, we went to many places, inviting people to a banquet that we had prepared for them; we fed them a nice dinner and gave them the dessert of God's Word.

Just as King Xerxes gave a banquet for the people in his province, God is also preparing a banquet for those least to greatest—one in which we will sup with Him, to eat of His flesh and die to ours. He wants to bring us to the table for fellowship, and He guarantees that, by the end of this feast, we will have had quite a hearty meal. He will have nourished our soul and spirit.

This was the point of the banquet: my King Jesus was letting me know that He is richer and more powerful than anything or anyone else. We can completely trust in Him. He has shown off the incredible wealth of His Word, and His promises will endure forever.

He is no respecters of persons. God has no favorites; He desires that no one perish, but that all would come (2 Peter 3:9). All the people from least to the greatest are invited. "Taste and see that the Lord is good" (Psalm 34:8a). Our thirst will be quenched as we taste, and our vision will be clear as we see Your splendor and majesty. Show us Your glory, Lord!

The Scepter of Mercy

Throughout the book of Esther, the mighty King Xerxes is often depicted as a type of Christ, although imperfect due to his humanity. When the queen was faced with a life-threatening situation, she knew she needed to go to the king. Only he could prevent what was about to take place. Esther knew that ultimately, the king's heart was in the hand of the Lord, and the Lord would direct it like a watercourse— wherever it pleased Him (Proverbs 21:1). God had placed Esther in this royal position "for such a time as this," just as God has placed us in the time in which we live. In our time, more than any other time in history, we see the signs of the end of time unfolding more clearly. The time of Christ's return and our final judgment is quickly approaching.

We need to cry out for mercy and remember our need for a Savior. These days that we are living in are short; it is a time to take seriously. Even if Christ should tarry, we must remember that our days here could be brief. In this time we need to go to the King. We can trust that the Lord will hear our cry for mercy, and the Lord will accept our prayer (Psalm 6:9).

In Esther 5:1-4, Queen Esther went to plead with the king, she knew that protocol would be broken because she came without being called;

she knew that could mean her death. But she trusted in her God. With faith and courage, she boldly went to the king, wearing her royal robes. She stood in the inner court that was in front of the king's hall. He was sitting on his royal throne, facing the entrance. When he saw her, he was pleased with her and welcomed her. So she walked through, approached the king, and touched the tip of his scepter. Then he asked, "What do you want, Queen Esther? What is your request? I will give it to you, even if it is half the kingdom!" (Esther 5:3).

Let's dig into this treasure a little deeper and apply it to our lives. First, we need to understand that unless God extends mercy to us, we will perish. All the good we have ever done won't save us, only His mercy can. The Bible declares that we all are guilty of sin, and that the wages of sin is death (Romans 6:23). But it also promises that King Jesus will extend mercy to us when we stand in judgment before Him. In this life, we must repent and trust what He has done for us on the cross. When we touch this scepter of His mercy, we are clothed with the royal robe of His righteousness. Then, dressed in this holy and royal robe, we can freely come before His throne at any time, to find mercy when we need it. Can you imagine Esther's relief when her earthly king extended mercy to her? How much more wonderful it is when our heavenly King does!

Because of what Christ did for us at the Cross, mercy was extended to us, and we can approach the throne with boldness and courage and receive the promises that are foretold according to His will. King Xerxes offered to the queen in that moment anything—even up to half of the kingdom. Jesus said in the book of John that He will do whatever we ask in His Name, so that the Son may bring glory to the Father. We can ask anything in His Name and He will do it (John 14:13-14). The key to this is pleasing our King. Esther said if it pleases the king, or if this petition is in line with your will. We must also believe that our cry for mercy will be heard for our loved ones just as Esther's was, because it is not the Lord's will that any should perish (Matthew 18:14). Esther knew that this was not a time that she could keep silent. She had to cry out for her own salvation and the salvation of her family. Her cousin Mordecai told her that if she remained silent at this time, relief and deliverance for the Jews would arise from another place, but she and her father's family would perish. However, when the king saw Queen Esther standing in the court, he was pleased with her and held out to her the gold scepter that was in his hand. So Esther approached and touched the tip of the scepter. He gave her mercy.

The Holy Vessels

*I*f you are like me, then you can relate to the fact that it is hard letting go and letting God handle the exchange. We want to have some kind of control, and when things don't go right, we take control. Later we want God to come and fix our mess. But we need to discover our inability to meet our own needs in our own fleshly strength. We need a King in our life who can rule our flesh well. The flesh is the way of living we learned before salvation; we were taught by the world how to live independent from God. Once we become a believer in Jesus Christ, the Bible says that we are no longer our own, but His. As it says in His Word, "Don't you realize that your body is the temple of the Holy Spirit, who lives in you and was given to you by God? You do not belong to yourself, for God bought you with a high price. So you must honor God with your body" (1 Corinthians 6:19-20). Once we give Him our bodies, He clothes us, fills us, and makes us ready! He gives us fine linen to wear, bright and clean, so we are prepared as a bride for the wedding of the Lamb (Revelation 19:7-8).

In the royal garden of King Xerxes, wine was served in goblets of gold, each one different from the other, and the royal wine was abundant. By the king's command, each guest was allowed to drink with no restrictions, for the king instructed all the wine stewards to serve each man what he wished (Esther 1:7-8). Just as the royal wine was abundant for each man as he desired, we too are to be empty vessels for God so He can fill us with as much of His life as we want. If you are thirsty, come and He will fill you up to overflowing so that it reaches everyone around you. Unfortunately, the king and his officials were not being filled up with the Spirit—they were getting drunk on wine.

Scripture tells us, "Don't be drunk with wine, because that will ruin your life. Instead, be filled with the Holy Spirit" (Ephesians 5:18). The Lord instructed me that I should not be so concerned with how much of the Holy Spirit I have, but instead how much of me does the Holy Spirit have. Even though Christ permits the proper use of wine, He does not do away with His own caution, which is, that our hearts be not at any time weighed down with drunkenness (Luke 21:34). This does not mean that we should be so legalistic that we hesitate to feast with our friends on occasion, with a glass of wine or a beer. We should just make sure that every social meeting should be so conducted, that we might invite the King to join us if He were now on earth. Therefore, if our King were present, would we act foolishly and consume more than we should and do things that could offend Him? Sometimes it is just better to avoid it altogether, as it can get out of control. Everything is permissible, but not everything is beneficial.

One of the first ways Jesus revealed His glory was when He turned the water into wine at a wedding that took place in Cana. When the wine was gone, Jesus' mother said to Him that they had no more wine, evidently expecting some display of His glory. Spiritually speaking, I believe that she was saying they are empty of God's power and anointing, and Mary knew that they could only be filled by Jesus. Jesus did indeed turn their water into wine that day, thereby replacing or exchanging the natural with the supernatural. He told the servants to fill the jars with water to the brim. But Jesus gives us living water (Jeremiah 17:13). If Jesus gives living water, we need to fill up our hearts to the brim with Him and Him alone. We do this by reading and applying His Word to our own heart. "As a face is reflected in water, so the heart reflects the real person" (Proverbs 27:19). Our hearts will reflect Jesus Christ as we fill up with more of Him.

At the wedding in Cana, the servants were then told to draw some water out and take it to the master of the banquet. When the master of the banquet had tasted the water that had been turned to wine, he complimented the bridegroom for saving the best for last (John 2:1-11).

When we run out of wine, or run out of our own resources, then do we finally turn to our Bridegroom?

Jesus said, "Anyone who believes in Me may come and drink" (John 7:38a). Revelations 22:17 says, "The Spirit and the bride say, 'Come.' Let anyone who hears this say, 'Come.' Let anyone who is thirsty come. Let anyone who desires drink freely from the water of life." Has He turned your water into wine? Has He given you knowledge and grace? That water—that grace—is meant to profit everyone. Draw it out and use it. It is time for the best wine.

The goblets of gold used in King Xerxes' banquet are a metaphor for God's vessels of honor which He chooses to dwell in. He wants His life to fill us and move through us. He wants to fill us with His Spirit. Wine is symbolic for His Spirit. Not one of the vessels was the same. Neither are God's children. We are all uniquely designed by God to be used differently. Not one of us will have the same calling.

If you have received Jesus Christ as your personal Savior, then you have become His holy vessel in the house of the Lord. The word translated "holy" is *hagios*, meaning "holy, sacred, most holy thing."[2] Something holy is that which has been brought into relationship with God and designated by Him as having a sacred purpose or special significance. It is marked as holy, or classified as belonging to God. Therefore we are marked as holy and belonging to God. And yet those of us who have used our bodies for unholy purposes, like sexual sin, have failed to regard ourselves with the honor we should always be mindful to do. For even a sacred vessel, set apart for special use, is only useful as long as it remains pure and consecrated towards its originally intended purpose. Therefore, having already received Christ, strive to be ever filled with His Holy Spirit; a sacred vessel unto God and a source of living waters to all those we meet.

2. Thayer and Smith. "Greek Lexicon entry for Hagios." "The NAS New Testament Greek Lexicon." 1999.

The Enclosed Garden

*T*he book of Esther begins with a vivid description of the enclosed garden within the king's palace in which a great banquet was held for all. At first glance I could not see a way this could be relevant to me; however, this garden put an image in my mind—a heavenly garden. In every garden, there are birds that come and rest on the branches of the trees. The couch was a place where I could picture myself laying down, being completely still. All of a sudden, a dove comes out of nowhere and rests on my shoulder.

John gave this testimony in John 1:32: "I saw the Holy Spirit descending like a dove from heaven and resting upon him." John gives the metaphor of a dove that comes down from heaven and remains. The dove is symbolic for the Holy Spirit. Doves are gentle in nature; however, they are shy, nervous and very sensitive. They will only remain if there is peace and no conflict. The Dove will not bend the rules; on the contrary, if we want the Dove to come and rest on us, we need to adjust to Him. The Bible tells us to not grieve the Holy Spirit of God. Since the Holy Spirit is very sensitive, we can trust that He will not stay if He is grieved. The Dove will just fly away. It is very easy to grieve the Holy Spirit: every time I lose my temper, anytime I am judgmental to another person, anytime I point the finger, anytime I am holding a grudge, or anytime I will not totally forgive. In any of these situations, I am grieving the Holy Spirit. It is not too long after the Dove flies away that you lose the sense of His presence; then a deep hunger sets in to fill the void. If we are not careful, we are tempted to fill the garden of our hearts with things that have no eternal value at all. I thought of this king trying to fill the void with this banquet, showing off his splendor and wealth. But instead of attracting the doves to his garden, he attracted the pigeons, and they are the complete opposite of their gentle kindred. They are boisterous, hostile, and always ready for a fight. Pigeons are symbolic of a counterfeit Holy Spirit. R.T. Kendall, a well-known Christian author, calls it "pigeon religion."

The enclosed garden is a metaphor for our hearts, a garden of true intimacy where the Lord desires to meet with us. He wants to speak to us, and He wants us to speak to Him. I am not talking about a temporary relationship with God where He flies in and out of our life. It's a place of wanting more of Him—a wanting and need for Him to remain on us, in us, with us, and for us. It is an eternal relationship with Him where we can see the unseen and eternal realm of His kingdom. We were created for this reason!

As I laid on the couch, I was also waiting on the Lord for the right earthly king for me. I would truly be blessed and I would be matched up with my soul mate, whoever it would be. While I waited there on the couch, resting in His peace, I wanted the Lord to prepare me to be the best wife that I could possibly be. I wanted to share the garden of my heart with one who also had his cup filled by the Holy Spirit—one who was peaceful so that the dove remained on him as well. Ladies, look for that one that has a dove resting on his shoulders. He will be sent to you. Just wait for him.

Pleasures of the King

*W*hat pleases a king? A queen who knows she's a queen, but never forgets who made her for that purpose, and why she was made to be queen. A queen who appreciates and trusts in her king. A queen who is a peaceful homemaker, and one who is not full of the drama of endless quarrels that stem from selfish motives. A queen who knows what is the right thing to do and does it gracefully. Queen Esther pleased her king in all that she said and did.

The time when Esther approached the king on behalf of her people, she fell down at his feet and begged him with tears in her eyes to stop the evil plot devised by Haman. The king held out the gold scepter to Esther so that she could rise and speak before him. Esther said, "If it please the king, and if I have found favor with him, and if he thinks it is right, and if I am pleasing to him, let there be a decree that reverses the orders of Haman…who ordered that Jews throughout all the king's provinces should be destroyed" (Esther 8:5).

Later, she was bold enough to ask, "If it please the king,…let the bodies of Haman's ten sons be impaled on a pole" (Esther 9:13).

When the Lord is pleased with us, He overrules the plans that the enemy has devised for us and our families, in order to destroy us. That is, if we are conformed to His plan, and that which pleases Him. We usually need to be tired of doing things our own way, and being frustrated with the results, before we conform to His plan. The Lord has the perfect plan for our life and we need to follow His blueprints for our futures. I realized that if I was to live by faith as God's Word commands, then I would need to follow the blueprints that God made for my future. He will not be pleased with us if we do not walk by faith (Hebrews 10:38). When He is pleased with us, as David the psalmist wrote, our enemy will not triumph over us (Psalm 41:11). I want to please the Lord in all I do. We cannot make anything happen by imagining it. We have to come to a place where we trust God in the present situation. Ultimately God knows our future, and we can trust Him because He knows what is going to happen. Our finite minds cannot fully understand the infinite aspects of God's nature, so we need to leave our untold future in the hands of a God who will reveal what we need to know at the time that He knows we will understand it. We do not know the thoughts of the Lord; we do not understand His plan, as yet.

In John 21, Jesus was asking Peter a series of questions which grieved Peter because he felt as though Jesus was questioning his loyalty to Him. Actually, Jesus was simply teaching him that, although the road they had traveled together had been at times difficult, the road that was yet to come for Peter would hold even greater challenges. But He wanted Peter to hear, directly from Him, that although this would happen, Peter's life would greatly glorify God as long as he remained focused on sharing Christ's love with the world. Despite what Peter's future held, Jesus told him to follow Him. We may be totally uncertain and fearful about our future, but if we know God is in control, we can confidently follow Christ. To follow Him, you must be willing to go the narrow way that leads to life. Too many people are taking the easy way (the broad road). People tend to follow the flock instead of the Shepherd. There are many obstacles the enemy has in his mind designed to get you on an easy track—resist him and keep your eyes on our eternal King. Resolve in your heart today that, regardless of how circumstances may appear for the moment, you are determined to live a life of love guided by the Word of God and led by His Holy Spirit. The fruit of such devotion will always please God and lead you into His perfect will for your life.

Chapter Two: Meet the Queen

Queen Vashti

Queen Vashti was considered the most beautiful woman in the Persian Empire. It is said that one look upon her left a person breathless. Her Persian name even meant beautiful. She was the kind of woman who turned every head. But before you are swept away by her beauty and start wishing you looked like her or could have her as your queen, let's remember that although man looks upon the outward appearance, the Lord always looks at our hearts. The heart of Jesus was clear when He spoke to the Pharisees: "What sorrow awaits you teachers of religious law and you Pharisees. Hypocrites! For you are like whitewashed tombs—beautiful on the outside but filled on the inside with dead people's bones and all sorts of impurity. Outwardly you look like righteous people, but inwardly your hearts are filled with hypocrisy and lawlessness" (Matthew 23:27-28).

History tells us that Vashti was the daughter of King Belshazzar of Babylon and the great-granddaughter of King Nebuchadnezzar, the man who destroyed the first temple in Jerusalem. The night her father was murdered by King Darius (Daniel 5:30-31), Vashti was captured by him, the succeeding king. Darius took pity on the young Vashti and gave her to his son, Xerxes, as a wife. When Xerxes became king over Persia, he and Vashti ruled over 127 provinces. In the third year of their reign, the king gave a banquet for all his royal officials. They were married only a short time at this point. Her blood must have been boiling as he indulged himself the way he did. After drinking a great deal of wine for seven days, King Xerxes was in high spirits. He told the seven eunuchs who attended him to bring Queen Vashti to him with the royal crown on her head. He wanted to show off his queen, for she was a very beautiful woman. For whatever reason, she did not see it the way the king did. She had another agenda. So what did she do? She decided she was going to have a banquet too, but for all the women. Oh, the drama! Get the women together and the effect is multiplied. I can just hear her now and how it might have sounded: "I hate him. I can't stand to even look at him. Ladies, we need to put an end to how they treat us. They treat us as mere objects—made for passion and pleasure. I am tired of being used. I am tired of him only thinking of himself. I am tired of being second best in his world. What about me? What about my feelings? Does he not care that I am queen?" The women cheer her on, making the nagging feelings inside her become so strong that she begins to allow her soul to dictate how she will respond. And so, when her husband called her to come, she refused (Esther 1:9-12).

In reference to the text in Esther that the king sent for the queen under the influence of alcohol, Bob Deffinbaugh, Th.M. says, "We should be careful not to read too much into this text. Nevertheless, it was when the king's heart was 'merry' that he sent for Vashti to appear before the men who were gathered with him. From all I can tell, he planned this as the grand finale. From what we are told, she was not instructed with regard to her dress other than she should appear wearing her royal crown. She was summoned to display her royal beauty, not to entertain the troops with some kind of burlesque show. Remember, the purpose of the celebration is for the king to display his 'royal glory and the splendor of his great majesty.' The king was not asking; he was summoning his queen. But neither was he demanding she do anything demeaning to herself. She was to appear in all her glory to bring glory to the king. Many commentators and most Christians seem to read a great deal into this text. They suppose the king has commanded the queen to disgrace herself by acting in an unseemly way or by performing to a crowd of drunks (I wonder how much more sober the women were)."[3]

3. Bob Deffinbaugh, *Esther, A Study on Divine Providence*, http://bible.org/seriespage/miss-persia-esther-11-218 (accessed April 10th, 2013).

Scripture tells us that she was lovely to look upon and the king wanted to display her beauty to the people and nobles. Scripture goes on to say that she refused to come when the king summoned her. After consulting the experts in matters of law and justice about what should be done to the queen for not obeying the command of the king, the wise men replied to the king, "Queen Vashti has wronged not only the king but also every noble and citizen throughout your empire. Women everywhere will begin to despise their husbands when they learn that Queen Vashti has refused to appear before the king. Before this day is out, the wives of all the king's nobles throughout Persia and Media will hear what the queen did and will start treating their husbands the same way. There will be no end to their contempt and anger" (Esther 1:16-18).

Queen Vashti was never allowed to enter the king's presence again; her royal position was to be given to someone else who was more worthy of the position. A law was passed in Persia that all women would respect their husbands from the least to the greatest and that every man should be ruler of his own household.

I Timothy 3:4-5 makes it clear that any man who is unwilling or unable to control his own household can hardly be considered fit to serve as a leader in the church. It was wise for the king to have the rule over his household.

Today rebellion in our homes—with wives who will not obey their husbands—is, to a great extent, destroying our nation. We need to return to following God's Word in the home. The king divorced Vashti, his disobedient wife, and I'm convinced this is one of the greatest underlining causes of the high divorce rate in our country. We have far too many disobedient wives who are following the Jezebel spirit. Jezebel was the wife of King Ahab; she was a wicked bossy queen of Israel, who in truth ruled the kingdom from behind the scenes. Instead of King Ahab making the decisions, Jezebel did—Ahab was nothing but a wimp (1 Kings 21).

We have lost the beauty of the Scriptures that help govern the household. The Bible is very clear in many places that it is God's will for women to respect their husbands and submit to their authority in all ways that are not in and of themselves in direct violation to the Word of God. It is equally clear that it is God's will that the man love and cherish his wife, even as Christ Himself cherishes the church. As more and more men fail to abide by this, women have become increasing deceived into believing that they are no longer bound by their responsibility toward God in their marriage. However, obedience to God's commands is always first and foremost between God and that person, and we all need to submit to Him with the assurance that He will take care of everything else.

This queen represents many wives today. There is no end to the disrespect many show their husbands. Households are divided. Divorce is rampant. Don't get me wrong though, the blame does not fall on women alone. Men need to take their stand and be the king of their homes. But this chapters focus is not on the king, it is on the queen that disobeyed. "Such things were written in the Scriptures long ago to teach us. And the Scriptures give us hope and encouragement as we wait patiently for God's promises to be fulfilled" (Romans 15:4).

Queen Vashti represents the old creation in me as well. Before I asked Jesus to become my personal Savior, I was a Vashti too. I wanted nothing to do with God. I was like this partly because I was never brought up in the knowledge of who God is, but also because darkness surrounded me and clouded my vision of a redeemer—someone who could save me from myself. I was, and did, just about everything described in Galatians 5:19-21: I followed the desires of my flesh, or in other words, my sinful nature, in sexual immorality, impurity, lustful pleasures, idolatry, sorcery, hostility, quarreling, jealousy, outbursts of anger, selfish ambition, dissension, division, envy, drunkenness, wild parties, and other sins like these.

The definition for the flesh, or self-life, is the condition where my focus is primarily on myself—one in which I am living out of my own resources in order to cope and deal with life, solve my problems, meet my needs, and become a success. It is all that I am apart from Christ; as I function in self-sufficiency, establishing my own strategy for living while trying to find an identity and victory by means of the law.

When I realized that I wasn't capable of handling life's problems on my own, I actually wanted to take my own life. I hated who I was and who I had become. I didn't know who I was and I didn't know how I could find out. I felt lost in depression; I knew I needed help, but didn't know where to find it. Then one day God sent someone my way to offer me an invitation to church. My first reaction was no, I didn't have time for the whole God thing. I am so glad that God strategically set up a divine appointment for me to have another opportunity, and to accept that time. If I had refused then, perhaps I would have died never knowing the eternal life that I now have in Christ.

So, according to the law, what must be done to Queen Vashti? Vashti was not given another opportunity to accept like I was. She was, in a sense, put to death. She was never allowed to enter the king's presence again. No mercy, no second chance, no divine appointment for another opportunity. She has no testimony and we cannot point to any transformation that happened in her life. There was no power of God displayed.

In the same way Queen Vashti was no longer allowed in the kings' presence, so the old flesh in me had to be banished as well. No flesh shall glory in His presence (1 Corinthians 1:29). "This means that anyone who belongs to Christ has become a new person. The old life is gone; a new life has begun!" (2 Corinthians 5:17). The newness of life in me is further expressed through the life of Queen Esther. She represents the Spirit-filled life rather than the life I once lived in the flesh apart from Christ. The difference between Queen Vashti and Queen Esther is a beautiful picture of law versus grace. Romans 6 illuminates the way to live for Christ under grace, as He is our Master, our King. In it, Paul encourages the church to embrace the freedom they have gained through their union with Christ, and to live their lives wholly submitting their hearts and all their bodily members as servants to righteousness, rather than living as slaves to sin as they had been. This was now possible through the grace of God ruling their lives.

Not only is Queen Vashti a portrait of the women of today's culture and who I was before salvation, but she is also a representation of the church of today. The church, as a whole, is not submissive. The church has its own agenda and will only come to the King of heaven on its own terms. I am not talking about denominations. We, ladies and gentlemen, are the church. We, who call ourselves Christians and followers of Christ, are the church. We call the shots. We say when it is time to pray, worship, and preach. We make purposeful plans, but only follow through when it is easy or convenient. We don't like to get out of our comfort zones.

Just as Vashti chose to remain busy entertaining her own guests, we, as the church, become so busy trying to entertain the people that we have come to regard the calling of the King as a trivial thing—something we can disregard. But the Bridegroom desires us. He has called us! He has called us to live a life of reverence that puts Him first. He desires that we are His first love. In Revelation 2, God acknowledges how zealous and determined the church in Ephesus had been in persevering through hardship for His name and His sake. But He immediately warns them that if they do not return to the strong love they initially displayed, He will remove the light of His presence from their midst.

In essence, Vashti may have been so consumed with the wickedness of others that she failed to see her own shortcomings. The same is true of the church. We have deceived ourselves into thinking we are holier than everyone else, that we are somehow better than they are, or that we have it all together. We compare ourselves with other churches by the law and according to the law, but the King has declared that no one is righteous (Ephesians 2:8-9). Paul exhorts us in Ephesians, that we should never be so foolish as to commend ourselves for our own glory, but that our only boast should be that we have been called into the service of Christ as fellow laborers with all believers. It is by His grace that we boldly come to the throne as He calls, but with this strong warning: if we don't come when He calls, He will come and remove our lampstand from its place, just as King Xerxes removed Vashti from her place as queen.

Knowing that we all, men and women alike, are called by the King to come and show off His splendor in us, is foundational in preparation for the beauty treatments ahead. We need to be the chosen people, the royal priesthood that is pleasing to Him. We are to believe the Bible, and do what the Bible has commanded us to do out of love and not duty. We are not saved by what we do; but doing all that we believe to be His will for us will keep us on the straight and narrow path that very few find. Dear bride of Christ, love your King, listen to His voice, do what He commands, and you will find yourself in a very favorable place in His kingdom.

Queen Esther

*W*hat a beautiful queen! But she was more than just a pretty face. Queen Esther is a beautiful picture of grace filled with surrender and submission. She was lovely in form and feature, but there was something about Queen Esther that made her radiant. She was the kind of woman every man dreams of. She was submissive and respectful; she prepared herself for her king; she was someone who did not allow the beauty treatments and special food go to her head; she gave humility and grace; she let the inward change happen as she waited on the possibilities of her future. She was not obsessed with her beauty—the character inside is what mattered to her. She knew that God looked at the heart, and outward appearance would fade. She knew God had a plan and a purpose for her; she trusted not in her beauty but in the promises of God. Queen Esther was a Proverbs 31 woman: "There are many virtuous and capable women in the world, but you surpass them all! Charm is deceptive, and beauty does not last; but a woman who fears the Lord will be greatly praised" (Proverbs 31:29-30).

Esther was not born of royal descent; in fact, she was an orphan who had neither mother nor father. She was raised by her cousin Mordecai, who brought her up in the way a child should go, for he was a scribe. He taught her about the Law so that she knew what sin was, but she was a woman who found comfort in that Law. She was a woman who was taught the fear of the Lord. She felt secure in having boundaries, for she knew that Mordecai had her best interests at heart. She felt loved and accepted. She was not under the Law; instead, she lived and loved the principles taught in the Law. She modeled the fruit that was spoken of through the Apostle Paul, which is love, joy, peace, patience, kindness, goodness, faithfulness, gentleness, and self-control.

Since Esther knew the Law of God, she also knew His promises. Although there is no mention of God in her story, she lived a life that spoke loudly of God's love and grace. You have heard the saying, "You may be the only Bible some people may ever read." Esther was a living testimony of God's grace. She knew she was created in His image and that she was fearfully and wonderfully made. She learned, at some point in her life—probably during the hard and lonely times of not having her mother and father—that true beauty comes from within. Her example and her life speak to us of the importance of finding that true beauty for ourselves as well as knowing who we are in Christ. She must have had this character developed in her even before she arrived in the palace because the head eunuch was very impressed with her. This is how that story goes:

After King Xerxes missed having a queen, he desired one again. So the king's officials proposed that a search be made for beautiful young virgins for the king. They went on to suggest that "the king appoint agents in each province to bring these beautiful young women into the royal harem at the fortress of Susa. Hegai, the king's eunuch in charge of the harem, will see that they are all given beauty treatments. After that, the young woman who most pleases the king will be made queen instead of Vashti" (Esther 2:3-4).

"As a result of the king's decree, Esther, along with many other young women, was brought to the king's harem at the fortress of Susa and placed in Hegai's care. Hegai was very impressed with Esther and treated her kindly. He quickly ordered a special menu for her and provided her with beauty treatments. He also assigned her seven maids specially chosen from the king's palace, and he moved her and her maids into the best place in the harem" (Esther 2:8-9).

Many women were brought into the palace that day, and through the following year, they were given beauty treatments and special food. All the women that were chosen to receive beauty treatments were already quite beautiful on the outside. Women are, by their nature, very strong. And as they continue growing into maturity and wisdom, they are constantly confronted with the desire to experience and develop their sense of self-determination and independence. However, in the kingdom of God, those qualities have to be broken so that we are weak and dependent on Christ alone. The women in that harem were no different from the women of today. They were manipulative and competitive. They were competing for the throne. They were self-seeking and deceitful. Esther did not need to prove herself, because God saw her heart, and it was God who gave Esther favor with the eunuchs. Esther pleased Hegai, and was immediately given beauty treatments and special food. He assigned to her seven maids selected from the king's palace, and moved her and her maids into the best place in the harem. (Esther 2:9) God's Word assures us that if we do not forget His teachings and keep His commands in our hearts, it will win us favor and a good name in the sight of God and man (Proverbs 3:3-4).

Now before we get our minds wrapped around the idea that we are just talking about women, allow me to say that I beg to differ. If we were talking about outer beauty and the things of this world, then I could see that standpoint. However, in God's kingdom we are all, men and women alike, made in His image (Genesis 1:27). We are all called to be His bride, His queen. So for men, this book applies to you too.

Before Esther was found and taken to the king's palace to be prepared to meet the king, she was a young virgin named Hadassah (Esther 2:7). Mordecai gave her a new name, a new identity. She was now being prepared for royalty. It was her time to walk in the newness of life. She was given a new quality of life—the one Christ has intended for all His children. He came to give us life and life abundantly (John 10:10). When we take on His life, our lives change. After making the decision that I was no longer going to live the way I was living on my own, I exchanged my old life, in the spiritual sense, and received the newness of the life that Christ had for me. He gave us the perfect example as He actually died on our behalf and was physically resurrected, so that we could spiritually rise from the dead. I was dead in my trespasses before I knew this life, and I was on a highway to hell. Now my sweet King Jesus has set me on a different path—from peasant to princess and from commoner to queen. He prepared me for royalty, for His royal kingdom that is set apart for His glory.

So what was it that set Esther apart from all the other women? What is it that separates the church from the world? Was her physical beauty so superior to the other women of the harem? Or did her beauty come from a different source? I believe she made herself ready by purifying and cultivating the inner beauty of her heart.

Unlike our outward appearance, inner beauty does not wrinkle, gray, or diminish with age. It only radiates stronger as you cultivate it. Today, the media pressures us with their ideas about good looks more than ever before. Outer beauty is emphasized to a great extent in our world today. Seasonal fashions, makeup, diets, plastic surgery, injection of chemicals to reduce wrinkles, exercise programs, you name it—it is all centered on making yourself look more beautiful than you ever were before. The media has imprinted the idea of a perfect body and a perfect face in the minds of us all, pressuring us to be like this perfect image. This pressure has led to eating disorders, obsessions with exercise, addictions to diet pills, deaths, and countless other things. The imagination of the human mind, focused upon what we consider to be perfect beauty, has left in its path a mess of confused and unhappy minds and bodies. God's children are faced with the dilemma of not knowing who they are. Their judgment is based on comparison to someone else, and they do not realize or remember that they are created in God's image. In Him is all fullness, and when we get our perspective on that truth, we find that we lack nothing of value. We compare ourselves to our daddy in heaven, and we find that we are becoming just like Him.

Ultimately, all this preparation is to prepare us as a bride for our Bridegroom. Hallelujah! Yes, our Lord God Almighty reigns! Let us be glad and give Him all the glory. The wedding of the Lamb has come, and His bride has made herself ready for His return (Revelation 19:6-7).

How does the bride get ready? The bride needs to make herself ready much like a garden is made ready for the planting of seeds. The ground must be broken up, any hardness removed, and it has to be tilled and hoed to make it soft and pliable. So it is with our hearts. We need to ready ourselves with a pliable and teachable spirit. Then we need to cultivate a willingness of heart to let the Lord do the work to make us beautiful. The beauty of the princess bride of Christ will not be just skin-deep, it will also be Spirit-deep—a harvest of loveliness deeply rooted in God's own beauty.

The beauty treatments of Christ bring forth life and wholeness in the inner man, until finally we are so beautifully refined on the inside that we actually glow and radiate on the outside as well. But neglecting the outer man was not something these women did either. These women not only prepared their heart for the king, but they also prepared their bodies. The Bible says that Esther was lovely in form and feature.

Although it is not known exactly how these women prepared their bodies, it is said that they soaked in oils for six months and fragrances for the remaining six months (Esther 2:12). As I was on this journey to find my own inner beauty, I was pretty literal in refining my outward walk as well. I fasted from food every other day for the entire year. On the nights of my fast, I would end the night with a very long bath, sometimes for two to three hours, soaking in oils of myrrh and frankincense, and other scents like lavender and jasmine, depending upon what I had. I even made my own bath salts. I would just soak in a candlelit room with soft music playing in the background that was soothing to my mind. In my soaking times, I felt very close to the Lord. I was anointing myself to meet with the King. After I bathed in the oils, I would apply olive oil to my skin and my hair to moisturize it.

In my desire to be consecrated, I followed the law of Moses to a degree. When God consecrated the priests for service to the Lord, He told them to pour anointing oil over their heads (Exodus 29:7). He further instructed them to take some of the blood and some of the anointing oil and sprinkle it on Aaron, his sons, and their garments to set them apart as holy (Exodus 29:21). I pictured the blood of Jesus and what He did for me at the cross, and then I meditated on what the psalmist says in Psalm 104—a little wine gladdens the heart, oil can rejuvenate the countenance, and bread can refresh and sustain the heart. Spiritually applying this prescription for my life meant that the Lord would fill my heart with His Spirit, making my heart glad. After anointing and moisturizing me for His purposes, He fed me His Word to sustain my heart.

My hair was another area of focus during this year. There once was a woman who had lived a sinful life yet wanted so badly to be forgiven of her sins. Upon hearing that the Messiah was in town, she made her way through the crowd holding an alabaster jar tightly to her chest until she finally found Him at a Pharisee's house. Upon entering the home, she fell to the ground behind Him, crying her heart out as her tears wet His feet. She wiped the tears with her hair, kissing His feet and then proceeded to pour the perfume from her jar upon them (Luke 7:37-38). If she was behind Jesus, she must have been up against a wall. But she didn't stay up against the wall; she had one more move. She fell to His feet with her hair down. A woman's hair is her glory. By letting her hair down, she was saying that she was His. Women in that culture never showed their hair to the public; they always wore a covering. During this consecrated year, I chose to put my hair up in a ponytail to symbolize that I would be available and committed to only one man— Jesus. When I was alone at home with Jesus, my hair came down. I fell to my knees and symbolically wiped His feet with my tears, and my prayer life became an aroma to my King.

In order for the women to remain lovely in form and feature while they were pampered and did not have to do anything, they had to have done some kind of exercise to keep their muscles looking lean and toned. It is not possible that they did nothing. If they were sitting around all day long, they would surely have gained some weight. Those women had to exercise. They probably walked around the garden several times a day. I have heard that dancing may have played a huge role in the lives of these women as well. So I exercised too.

Working out in the gym during my year of consecration was for the Lord and for no other reason. Since I believe that my body belongs to the Lord, I must take care of it and be devoted to the Lord in both body and Spirit (1 Corinthians 7:34). By being devoted to the Lord in this manner, I was also preparing for marriage. I hoped that the Lord would favor me by giving me to a man that ran after the mysteries of the Lord. If I were to marry again, my body would not belong to me alone, but would also belong to my husband (1 Corinthians 7:4). I had allowed my body to become saggy and droopy; toning was the best thing for that. My body was unattractive. I understood where I went wrong. I thought, "This is just the way I am made and there is nothing I can do about it." Wrong! There was something that I could do about it, and I was going to do it. The fasting pulled a lot of weight off me, even though I was not fasting for that reason. I fasted in obedience to the Lord and He was the one sustaining me through the fast. I now eat healthier; I want this body to last the time needed to be a blessing to this world.

Not just the form, but also the features. My nails needed to be manicured, and my skin needs to be cared for too. I don't want to focus on these things too much, but we are not called to neglect them either. We need to glorify God with our whole being. It is only God Himself, the God of Peace, who can make us holy so that our entire spirit, soul, and body would be kept blameless at the coming of our Lord Jesus Christ (1 Thessalonians 5:23). Again, the emphasis was not to focus overmuch on the outer appearance. On the contrary, the beauty treatments are for the inner man, where we are so beautifully refined until we really do glow on the outside.

The Bible says that blessed are the pure in heart for they will see God (Matthew 5:8). If our hearts are pure, then this is a promise that we will see God. I do not believe we have to wait until we get to heaven either. I believe that we can see God in the minute details of our lives right now. As He is purifying my heart, I notice Him much more than I ever did before. I see God in the sunrise; I see God in the people around me; I see Him in the steps that I take; I see Him in the choices that I make. By golly, I can see Him in me. He is incredibly beautiful as He increases in me. He shines through me and I can see Him as I look in the mirror. When I look in the mirror and I don't see Jesus, I usually spot all my flaws—my pimples, my wrinkles, my dark spots, and my weight gain. These things become my focus, and I lose sight of what God sees. I realize that I am once again increasing and He is decreasing. So I get back on my face and pray until He purifies my heart because when I look in the mirror I want to see God and His radiant beauty. When my focus is on me I can't see His beauty. I want to see God in everything I do. When I see God in what I do, He gently reminds me of the desire I have to lead a quiet life that is marked with patience—He'll remind me of this even as I am just about to lose my patience. Then I thank Him for the gentle reminders that are always there to transform me into to His image.

My friends have commented that they see Jesus in me. One of my closest friends sent these verses to me in the middle of my year and said when she read them she thought of me. "Oh most beautiful of women," she said to me, "I know where the Lord is, He is browsing for lilies!" She led me to read this passage in the Song of Songs 6:1-3 as if she was the young women of Jerusalem, I was the young woman, or the beloved, and the lover is our King:

"**Young Women of Jerusalem:** Where has your lover gone, O woman of rare beauty? Which way did He turn so we can help you find him?

Young Woman: My lover has gone down to his garden, to his spice beds, to browse in the gardens and gather the lilies. I am my lover's, and my lover is mine. He browses among the lilies."

My friend was saying to me that I was, in fact, radiating the Son—it inspired her to find the beauty of God in the garden of her heart as well. My prayer is that your hearts will also become part of the ground spring of love as you immerse yourself in the beauty treatments that go deeper than the natural eye can detect.

Chapter Three: The Harem

*I*n the ancient Far East, palaces contained harems, where the women lived. Originally from the Arabic for "forbidden," the word came into common usage to describe the women's quarters of the home that were forbidden to all males outside the family. In the book of Esther, we learned that the king's personal attendants proposed that the king should provide for himself a new bride, and that all of the women deemed eligible should receive one year of beauty treatments in preparation before the king chose from among them.

Get ready then, for a move into the harem, the place where the beauty treatments begin. The harem is the place of change and new beginnings. It's time to start packing and cleaning and organizing and removing the junk. Get rid of clutter. On this journey, take only the necessities needed for this season. Get rid of everything else. Start in the shed, the place where we hardly ever go, a place of cobwebs and filth. Get organized, put things in order. Get things in line with God's Word. Disorder brings confusion and double mindedness. For example, my house was always a scattered mess. I once heard someone say that a messy house is a reflection of a messy heart. I needed to clean up the inside—to get rid of bitterness and unforgiveness, to clean up and stay clean. I don't like it when people see my mess. It is so embarrassing. No one wants others to see the disorder in their houses, let alone their hearts. Being exposed is a humiliating, yet beautiful, thing when the Lord is exchanging our mess for His character.

I had some friends named James and John who wanted to come over and fix one of my son's dressers, but their room was so messy that my friends couldn't even get to it. I realized that sometimes people want to help fix us, but they can't because we are just not getting to the root of our problems. As we try to help with the surface issues, the root problems are buried deep amidst the huge mess.

A couple of weeks after starting my year-long sabbatical, the Lord spoke to my heart that He was going to move me into the best place. I had no idea that the next day I would be let go from my job as a computer programmer. I had finished the project that I was hired to complete, but they didn't have the money to keep me. Being let go from a job is humiliating. I needed to trust God that He would take care of me and my children. It was then that I realized that the best place—the place God was moving me into—was the Holy of Holies. I believe that being fired from this job brought me into position to be able to receive all that He had for me, a place where I could grow and mature in my faith and love for Him. It was also a perfect place for dying to my flesh. I rejoiced, knowing that God was in control. I felt in my heart that I was going to remain jobless, yet, at the same time, I also knew that I would not be physically moving until the Lord brought me my earthly king. There were many people that did not agree that the projects of Toledo were the best place for me and my family, but it was okay in my heart. Sometimes you just have to trust that what looks like a humiliating circumstance is actually the best place in the harem.

Being in the best place also meant homeschooling my children, even if I had to do it without a husband to support me. I could teach them all that the Lord was teaching me, passing down the inheritance of kingdom royalty. There are many moms who feel overwhelmed with the responsibilities of the home, and if you're single, the burden doubles. However, the Lord assured me that he was moving me into position. My goal was to train my children up in the way that they should go. My desire was to be able to remain at home for as long as they were with me. They are my highest ministry and top priority until they are of the age of accountability before God. I desired to reach others for Christ as well though, and if given the opportunity to minister to others, it was my desire that I would be obedient to that calling. I would go anywhere and everywhere for the cause of Christ. I would take my children with me so they could be a part of ministering God's unfailing love to the lost and dying world.

During this year, I remember needing a "move of God" in my life. My heart's desire was to go where His glory belongs. One of my friends was reading from the book of Joshua and he said to me, "If God is in the camp, don't you go off trying to fight a battle." The harem was, for me, like a call to stay in the camp because it was not yet my season to be in battle.

Scripture teaches us that there is a time for everything and a season for every activity under heaven. Sometimes we need to remain silent, even when man invites us to speak. God may be saying wait. Remaining silent before the Lord in hopeful expectation is never an act of fear, but rather an affirmation of meekness and humility.

If we do not wait upon the Lord, we will not fulfill our destinies. Wait for the Holy Spirit's power to come before you go. The book of Acts, appropriately named because it chronicles all the activity that took place during the earliest days of the church, begins with Jesus instructing His disciples to stay where they were—not go anywhere, but rather to wait in Jerusalem a few days until after they had received the Holy Spirit. If we are to succeed in our endeavors, we must realize that it is not by power, nor by might, that we will gain the victory, but rather by His Spirit.

It was not my season to be in ministry; it was a time for me to get ready. From the harem camp, the Lord would move me to take possession of the land the He was giving me. The time frame for me, though, was not three days like it was for Joshua. God spoke to Joshua before he led the people into the Promised Land and instructed him to get their supplies ready for the move. He would lead them in three days' time.

It was at the camp that the Lord commanded Joshua to be strong and courageous. Moses had just died. The leader he had loved and followed for many years had just been taken from him. What was next? Like Joshua, Esther was taken from her only relative, Mordecai. She needed to be strong and courageous as well. Joshua knew what it was like to grieve over loss in his life, just as we sometimes do. We have to allow ourselves the grieving time at the camp. But when the Lord says, "Get ready," we must prepare our hearts because He is taking us into battle. Just like God said to Joshua, He is telling us, "Get ready to cross the river into the land I am about to give you. Your territory will extend from here to there. No one will be able to stand against you for I will never leave you nor forsake you" (see Joshua 1:2-5).

In Joshua 1:7-9, God didn't just encourage us, He commanded us to be strong and courageous and trust that He has us in the best place right now. Joshua had to have faced depression and discouragement to have to be first commanded, and then reminded. We often need to be reminded as well. So get your supplies ready. For this journey to inner beauty, you will need only what the Holy Spirit suggests. When the time came for Esther to go to the king, she asked for nothing other than what Hegai suggested.

You might ask, what are our supplies? Food, armor, and fragrances are the only items needed.

You will need your daily bread. Just as you eat physically three times a day, partaking of the living Bread is just as crucial to this journey. His Word will feed your spirit and will make you ready for battle over all the areas of your heart in which He wants you to receive victory. For example, it is a battle and a struggle to defeat the enemy of pride in my heart. Feeding upon God's Word gives me the strength to combat that enemy. The Lord showed me that is where we gain new spiritual territory—in the heart. The Lord will give you rest and grant you victory in this land of pride. When the enemy is defeated, beauty will rest in that part of your heart. The Promised Land is a place where there is an end of striving; it is a place of resting in who you are, and in what the Lord does through you.

Another supply that you will need is your armor. Every single morning for the past couple of years, my son Daniel put his armor on religiously before he walked out the door for school. It has become a part of his daily routine. He says, "I've got my peace shoes on my feet; I've got my breastplate of righteousness; I've got my helmet of salvation; I've put my belt of truth on to hold it all in place; I've got my shield of faith. The shield says, 'God is who He says He is. God can do what He says He can do. I am who God says I am. I can do what God says I can do. God's Word is alive and active in me, and I got my sword right here.'" As he pretends to bring out a sword from his side, he declares, "I am ready to go out in the mighty power of the Lord." (We learned about the "5 Statement Pledge of Faith" from Beth Moore's *Believing God* Bible study and my son has never forgotten it.)[4] The armor spoken about in Ephesians 6 is more important to our journey than many realize. We don't have to declare it out loud as Daniel does, but, by faith, knowing that we have that armor on protects us more than we can imagine.

Finally, the supplies needed while camped in the harem are the fragrances and oils, which are symbolic for prayer and fasting. The sweet smelling fragrance of prayer and the aroma of the anointing oils will make this journey more pleasurable and sweet to the soul. Prayer makes dying to self attainable. I learned to operate in all three realms of prayer during the time I attended a Tim Enloe Holy Spirit conference. The speaker taught about the three realms of prayer: natural, prophetic, and supernatural. As he did, I started to see how all three realms of prayer were evident in the book of Esther, even though there is no mention of God. Prayer is crucial to all believers in our intimate walk with Him. Let me share with you what I learned about operating in the three realms of prayer.

The natural realm of prayer is when we pray out of our own understanding. We know that some of our families and close friends are perishing, and so, in our understanding, we pray for their salvation. We ask God for mercy on their behalf. When Mordecai heard the news of the king's edict to annihilate the Jews, he sent word to explain to Esther what was happening and urged her to go into the king's presence to beg for mercy and plead with him for her people. We carry that same urgency inside our hearts to go into the King's presence and plead with

---

4. Beth Moore, *Believing God*, (Nashville, TN: B & H *Publishing* Group, 2004) used by permission.

Him for our lost loved ones. We know that without God they are lost and on the highway to hell. Not only is it a natural tendency to cry out for our loved ones, but the natural body that we live in has needs and we pray spontaneously throughout the day for those needs in a natural way. For example, "Lord, heal; Lord, help; Lord, save; Lord, provide; Lord, change; and Lord bless" are among some of our natural prayers. We are promised through God's Word that He will do whatever we ask in His name, so that He may bring glory to the Father (John 14:13).

The prophetic realm of prayer happens when our prayer is the result of prophetic prompting. For example, Mordecai's words to Esther were a prophetic prompting: "Don't think for a moment that because you're in the palace you will escape when all other Jews are killed. If you keep quiet at a time like this, deliverance and relief for the Jews will arise from some other place, but you and your relatives will die. Who knows if perhaps you were made queen for just such a time as this?" (Esther 4:13-14). This is when God gives us a glimpse of what could take place, and often warns us through a prophetic word that we are heading in the wrong direction.

I have experienced both the receiving end and the giving end of a prophetic word. Going into my year of consecration, I received a prophetic warning from a friend. She warned me that I was standing at a closed door, and that if I didn't turn around, I would miss out on what God truly had for me. She said there was an open window of opportunity right next to this closed door. She did not know what that window represented because God did not reveal that to her, but God did reveal to her that there was, in fact, an opportunity for me to walk right into my promise, if I would just walk away from the closed door. God may have tried to speak to me personally, but because I wanted what was behind the closed door so badly, my ears were dull to the whisper of the wind. Instead He sent a friend my way who was listening to God to help me shift my gaze toward the open window.

The prophetic realm of prayer is often manifested in churches when God wants to speak to His children all at once as well. The Bible is full of prayers that have come from prophets as they foretold the coming of our Messiah, as well as the warnings that the prophets spoke to the children of Israel about their wandering. This realm of prayer is where we connect the natural to the supernatural—it's where we see what God sees, and hear what God is saying to us. In writing this book, I am operating out of the prophetic realm of prayer. My intent is to deliver what I have received to the church—everything God implanted in me. There is a King within me, and He is kicking with life in my spirit. He placed within me the seed of tomorrow that will produce a great harvest. I submit it to you.

The natural realm of prayer is when we talk, the prophetic realm of prayer is when God speaks to us, and the supernatural realm of prayer is when God intercedes for us. The supernatural realm of prayer is when we pray in the language of the Spirit. When we do not know how to pray or what to pray, we can use our heavenly language to touch the throne. This is where the Spirit helps us in our weakness. We do not know what we ought to pray, but the Spirit Himself intercedes for us with groans that words cannot express. And He who searches our hearts knows the mind of the Spirit, because the Spirit intercedes for the saints in accordance with God's will (Romans 8:26-27). This language originates in the Spirit, and therefore it is only by the Spirit that we can operate in this realm.

Esther operated in the supernatural realm of prayer when she sent a reply back to Mordecai. She said, "Go and gather together all the Jews of Susa and fast for me. Do not eat or drink for three days, night or day. My maids and I will do the same. And then, though it is against the law, I will go in to see the king. If I must die, I must die" (Esther 4:16). When we operate in this realm, we have absolutely no natural explanation. We literally put aside the natural to gain access to the supernatural. It is a natural thing to eat three times a day, or even more in some cases. But to fast from food, to give up the natural, we put ourselves in a realm that is supernatural and cannot be naturally explained. We starve our flesh so that our spirit man is fed by the living Bread. Jesus calls Himself the Manna, our daily Bread. God called me to fast from food every other day for the entire year. In those days of fasting, God supernaturally fed me the words of this book.

Prayer is where we get our minds off ourselves and temporary things. Prayer is when we align ourselves with God's Word. Prayer is communion with God. Just being in His presence is a sweet-smelling fragrance. Spending time with God will permeate our very being like perfume does. Praying while we wait prepares us for the unknown.

One whole year Esther waited, and the other ladies in the harem waited that long as well. I can only imagine the many different states they were in—some waited in desperation, some waited in expectation, some waited for restoration, and still others waited for an invitation. They really couldn't have known what they were waiting for, and yet there they sat, waiting. As they waited, they received beauty treatments. Beauty treatments may find you while you are waiting in desperation for who knows what.

Imagine the life of the harem. Those who waited in desperation probably operated out of that sense. They felt that they needed to take desperate measures to win the approval of the king. "Desperate times call for desperate measures" was the perspective of some, and now was that time. Some of the young women who found themselves taken from their familiar surroundings and placed in an unknown and unwelcoming atmosphere felt they had no hope. And we know that when hope is gone, you feel like you have nothing. Change is scary. But the promise is just around the corner. You know that you have something to look forward to; it's just not here yet. Everyone is waiting on the same thing, but each of them has a different history, each of them has a different expectation, and each of them has a different need. However, when desperation meets faith, the results are miraculous. Desperation gives us the chance to wait on God to do something. What are you desperate for? What do you need from God that you could not get anywhere else?

Next there were those who were waiting with expectation. They expected to have the throne by the time the year was up. This was the scenario I found myself relating to the most. Similarly, we read in the first chapter of Acts that after the suffering of Jesus, He showed Himself to the apostles He had chosen and gave them many convincing proofs that He was alive. The disciples asked Him if He was about to restore the kingdom to Israel, but He told them that it was not for them to concern themselves with knowing the timing of God's choosing.

My question was just a little different, "Lord, when my year is up, will You release someone to pursue me, to be their bride?" My expectations were challenged because I realized I could be disappointed if I focused on that. I tried hard to remember what Jesus said to His chosen ones: it is not for us to know what He has in store.

James, one of the sons of thunder, could also relate to this as he and his brother sat with Jesus. James wanted things done his way. He wanted the kingdom to come the way that he perceived it should come. James wanted to sit at Jesus' right hand and be His right hand man (Mark 10:35-37). James had to change his idea regarding Jesus' plan. In the same way, we have to stop making Jesus what He never intended to be. He is not a magician whose purpose it is to make things happen the way we want. As for James, he and his brother John both asked to be seated next to Jesus in places of glory, having expressed confidence that they were prepared to share even Jesus' suffering. He assured them that they would share His suffering, but that it was God alone who would decide whom He wanted seated there.

Beauty treatments will challenge your expectations. I guess I can relate to James in that I had a picture for how the end of my year would look. I imagined having my fairy tale dream—Prince Charming coming to my door at midnight to sweep me off into the moonlight. It sounds silly, but realistically it is how many woman think. The Lord needed to change the way I perceived Him and His plan. My heart had to get to a point where it didn't matter what happened or who it happened with—just as long as I was in His perfect will. I came to understand that God will endue you with power, even for the things that you never wanted to do and yet find are a part of His plan for your life. I never wanted to be single; yet I knew that if the Lord called me to be single for the rest of my life, He would endue me with the power to be content in that singleness.

Beauty treatments also bring you to a point of powerful restoration. When Esther was taken from her only relative, it could have been devastating to her. I can only imagine her hoping that she would one day be with Mordecai again as she prepared herself for the king.

Finally, beauty treatments are your invitation to join God in the time of your life. As hard as it was to leave their families and surroundings, these women were entering into a life full of surprises. Think about it— one whole year of days spent soaking in oils and fragrances, hot tubs, massages, and being pampered and served day in and day out. This was the life. Who wouldn't want to be pampered? It had to have made the waiting a little bit easier.

When the day of Pentecost came in Acts 2, everything that was at the root of the apostles waiting had been resolved. All of them were filled with the Holy Spirit and their desperation was answered, their expectation was met, their restoration was received, and their invitation was accepted.

At the end of the year, the day finally came when Esther's desperate need for God was answered, her waiting through expectations were met, her restoration with Mordecai was received, and her invitation to the throne was accepted. She was invited into the palace and the king chose her to be queen. Then, with the beauty that she possessed, she became an example to the women around her. She became an example that the woman of today can follow. She also became a picture of what Christ desires in His bride, the church.

So it was that I too waited with expectations, but waiting was not easy for a girl like me, a girl that was nicknamed by one of her best friends, "Jump the gun, Jackie." She called everyone Jackie, but she added "jump the gun" to my name because I was known to run ahead of God. The real lesson that she taught me relates to the pride that causes many Christians to fall. Not willing to wait on the Lord, we run ahead and attempt to take the reins. We forget who is in control and make unsound financial decisions or foolish choices based on our emotions, not expecting to be hurt in the process. God may even tell us no, but we ignore Him and let our pride tell us we can handle it. We run into problems and pain we could have avoided if we had just waited on the Lord.

Are you struggling with waiting on God today? Is your anxious attitude becoming like the worlds? They say, "I can't take this anymore. I'll take care of it myself!" Be careful! Running ahead of God may find you lying on your back someday as you struggle to pray and ask Him for help. Why not dedicate yourself today to experiencing the goodness of the Lord by deciding to walk with Him, rather than running from Him?

Heavenly Harem

The ultimate place in the harem is where our hearts become His Heavenly dwelling. As God moves us from our earthly tent into the best place, we can be sure that He will provide us with the beauty treatments and special food that will prepare us for royalty in His eternal kingdom.

God blessed Esther with great favor in Hegai's eyes. He not only provided her with beauty treatments and special food, he also provided seven maids for her. Each of them were handpicked from the king's palace, which I consider to be a metaphor for the earthly tent. Together they went into the best place in the harem, or in other words, our heavenly dwelling (Esther 2:9).

While we were estranged from God, our souls roamed about like dead men, trapped in bodies of decay while our spirits languished in their alienation from the Lord. But once we accepted Jesus Christ as our Lord and Savior, our minds were renewed by the Word of God and our spirits were born again into the fullness of life that only His Holy Spirit can provide. And even though our earthly bodies continue to decay, and we die daily in our souls as we strive to overcome the habits of the flesh we formerly embraced, we now do so with the knowledge that God has provided a home for Himself within our spirits and a heavenly dwelling for each of us where we can find refuge and seek His unfailing love. We have God's holy presence abiding in our spirits and healing us in our hearts.

The harem that Esther was in was at the citadel of Susa. A citadel is a stronghold into which people could go for shelter during a battle. God will provide the shelter that you need while He Himself beautifies every area of your life. He will give you everything that you need to follow Him. In His unfailing love for us, He will lead the people He has redeemed. In His mighty strength, He will guide us to our holy dwelling (Exodus 15:13).

Christ has blessed us in the heavenly realms with every spiritual blessing that we need in order to be united in Christ. He chose us (just as King Xerxes chose Esther) before even the creation of the world to be holy and without fault in His eyes. God decided a long time ago that we would be adopted as His offspring through Jesus Christ. This is what He wanted to do. This gave the Father great pleasure (Ephesians 1:3-6).

There have been numerous times in my forty years of living that I have moved. From city to city, from mom's house to dad's, to foster homes and group homes, living in someone else's house, to living in the projects, to being in my own place, and the list goes on. But in all my moving, I have found that there is no greater place than in His presence—there is nothing better than His dwelling within me.

These are the words I spoke to the Lord as I waited on Him, "Oh, Lord, hear my prayer: Since I am a garden enclosed, come and rest in me, oh, Lord! I am Your locked garden, and I am Your sealed fountain. I have prepared a place for You to dwell in the reservoir of my heart. I want to fellowship with You in the deepest part of me. I am Your resting place, Lord—just as You are my resting place."

Hopes of the Harem

If you are a single man or woman waiting on the Lord to bring you a mate, then you need to prepare yourself for that mate. This preparation will be different according to your genders, and because I am a woman, I will speak mostly to women. However, since I know what I was looking for in a man, I can say that much of your preparation will be focused on making Christ your example of what a great man should look like.

For women, the Proverbs 31 woman gives us an example of what a woman should look like as she prepares. She is a wife of noble character and her husband has full confidence in her. In order for her to have her husband's full trust, she needs to prepare herself to be one who can be trusted. She needs to be able to keep herself pure for the man she marries. Waiting for sex before marriage is not a popular teaching anymore. Women are pressured into thinking that it is sex that will attract and keep a man; however, this is a lie from the enemy. It is time for women to get old fashioned in their thinking again and bring purity back into relationships. Men are not exempt in this concept, but it is the women that allow it. Women have made it way too easy for men, allowing ungodly sexual relationships when God has called women to be locked gardens. When we as women are determined and committed to be a locked garden and sealed up sexually until the day we are taken as brides, we give our mate full confidence in a lifelong relationship. That is priceless.

She brings him good all the days of her life. The Proverbs 31 woman prepared her heart to be purposeful in all her doings. The Bible said that she worked eagerly with her hands: she prepared food for her family, she was a wise steward of her earnings, she planted a vineyard, her arms were open to the poor, and her hands reached out to the needy. All of these skills need practice and preparation. In order for me to learn how to cook, I had to go and learn from a cook. In order for me to be a wise steward of my earnings, I had to sit under those who have learned how to do that. I had to put my hand to the plow by putting into practice what I had learned. This is, of course, common sense. However, women today are not preparing themselves in this way. When I asked some women, Christian and non-Christian, how they were preparing themselves for their mate should God bring him their way, many of them responded to the question with a focus on their outward appearance, saying, "I'm losing weight, and I'm going to look so good." Although they were willing to devote themselves to becoming more attractive physically, they failed to understand the need to prepare spiritually.

Not only did I desire to be like the Proverbs 31 woman, but I also desired to be like the Shulammite woman in the Song of Songs. She intimately reflects my desire to love and be loved. I am a passionate woman who desires the physical touch of a man and I love to reciprocate that touch. However, knowing this was not the time for me, I cried out to the Lord for a touch from Him. I wanted to make good use of the time I had and I wanted to better know what type of man would coincide with my style of love. If you were to think that it was easy for me and I went the whole year without the temptation of being unfaithful to the Lord, you would be thinking more highly of me than you should. In fact, there were times that I stayed up all night thinking about the men I thought God might have in store for me. I even wrote a letter to a man I thought was the one—even though I knew I was supposed to remain unavailable for the entire year. What woman doesn't dream or daydream of becoming a wife? Will it be so and so? Or maybe it's…? Will it be someone I haven't even met yet? Whoever it is, our hope is that he looks just like Jesus! Until then, we have to learn to stop occupying our thoughts with the unknown. I knew I wasn't ready yet. There was still so much in me that needed to immerse in the beauty of my King. My consecration had to go deeper with my King. The King of Kings is who I lived for—available for whatever He wanted from, and for, me. He makes me and molds me into His perfect vessel. Just as I prepared my heart for the King of Kings first, I also prepared my heart to give myself to the one who would take me as his wife.

The Lord used the longing in my heart that I had for a husband and He began to teach me. Through the sacrifice of making myself unavailable, I learned that I really was the kind of woman that a man would pursue, that I did not need to be too easily available. I realized that I was too precious to be predictable and available to every onlooker who looked at me with interest. My eyes could finally see that I was rare and sacred. I always had a hard time seeing how valuable I was in the past because of all my previous experience. I learned that a positive self-image was not arrogance. On the contrary, it was a necessary part of any relationship. The Lord was giving me a fresh start and revealing to me how special I was. In the same way that God would wipe out the memory of Amalek for the Israelites, He was wiping out the memory of my past. He spoke clearly to my heart that history would not repeat itself any longer, and that after I had sacrificed the time needed to prepare myself, I would be pursued by an exceptional man chosen by Him. The Lord showed me that I was too valuable to settle for anything less than what He had for me.

While we wait for God to take us to the Promised Land, we need to allow Him to make us ready for the move. Some think of their promised land as dreams fulfilled and visions that have come to pass. There are still many dreams and desires that I have that I believe God gave me that have not yet come to pass. We have to want it. We have to desire more. God loves us hungry! I am asking for more in this season than I did last season. Last year was good, but today I am dreaming bigger. I have tasted an awesome breakthrough, but I am craving more. If I get a taste of something I like, I want more and I won't quit until I get it. How about you?

I desire to write books and be a public speaker, traveling to the nations with a message of inner beauty for the women of this century. The art of inner beauty has been diminishing over recent years, and women are faced with a dilemma—a true identity crisis. Many do not know who they are. They are looking at themselves, finding all their flaws based on their comparison to someone else. However, we are created in God's image, and God is beautiful. So is everyone that He created. By the time you are reading this book, I may be presenting this message in another country. Who knows but God? I will go where He sends me, and His timing is perfect.

The benefits of persevering and waiting on what God releases to you are many. Primarily, you become a person who is not tossed to and fro, not moved by the words of man, not moved by your circumstances, but so deeply rooted and anchored in the love of God that you cannot be moved! Someone who cannot be moved by circumstances or others is a person firmly planted and drenched by His grace. In short, this is the ammunition of one who overcomes! But there's one more thing of which we can sure. That is, that we will be glad. Let God arise and be glad!

The House of Beauty

Another unfulfilled dream that I have, and continue to wait on God for, is establishing a woman's home. I had been searching my heart to discover what my passion was, and how I could fulfill my God-given purpose in life. In April of 2008, the Lord woke me up in the middle of the night to speak to me and tell me about the year-long commitment to him and fast that I have already described. I knew after nine months of this particular fast that it was no doubt from God because He sustained me through it all. He has given me revelation after revelation on the book of Esther and has birthed this book within me. I write this to you to share a vision that the Lord gave to me in my quiet time with Him. I was talking with the Lord and asked Him to share with me the purpose of this year that I had consecrated to Him. I had sacrificed my meals and my fellowship with other believers so that I could hear God more clearly regarding His direction in my life. After He quieted my soul, He reminded me of the words He had spoken to me on October 15, 1994. I had totally forgotten my passion and purpose that He had given me so long ago. He said I would be the director of a women's discipleship home, and in the ninth month of my fast, I believe He gave me the name for it: the House of Beauty.

I believe God revealed to me that I will have this home that has been in my heart for so many years. I believe the House of Beauty is where God exchanges beauty for ashes. A heavenly harem could also describe this home, as it will serve as a refuge and offer year-long beauty treatments to the hurting world of women. This home will be a hiding place for women to go: to escape unhealthy relationships and to allow a woman the chance to beautify herself before she enters into a relationship. She will be made whole inside and out during this year of intense treatment. It will be a disciplined home in order to break a rebellious spirit, but one that will help a woman know that she is valuable. This home will be for any single or married woman who has a desire to exchange their life for His. It will have at least five bathtubs for soaking in His presence, and some family units as well. Single girls without children will share a room and families will be another area. This home will also be able to serve children of all ages as long as the parents agree to homeschooling. This will make sure that outside influences do not interfere with the program. A program would also be in place to provide discipline to unruly children of the mothers coming in off the street. It will be patterned after the Hannah House that my daughter and I moved into back in September of 1993.

The Hannah House was a women's discipleship home directed by Pastor Kelly and Jackie Hartman. It was similar to that of Teen Challenge. A commitment of one whole year was necessary in order to graduate from the program. The Teen Challenge program is known for offering a true cure for any addiction. Their mission is to disciple men and women in the knowledge of Jesus Christ and to help build a foundation for a true relationship with Him. The difference between Teen Challenge and the Hannah House was that I was able to keep my daughter with me. Hannah House was equipped to care for children if they were under the age of four. It was during this year at Hannah House that a series of wonderful changes began to take place. We began to grow and heal through the daily dose of God's Word. We grew in our understanding of God in a real and tangible way, and we learned how to apply God's teachings to our daily living. We were in an intense Bible college, but without the credits. We had strict rules that helped us become more disciplined adults. Since we lived in this home with other women, we learned to live together in harmony—even though we were different in every way. We learned to love each other and care for each other. We learned the importance of fellowship and the breaking of bread together. We lived the days of Acts and it was the best year of my life. My daughter and I graduated the program on October 15, 1994. On my graduation day, the Lord spoke to my heart and confirmed it ten minutes later through the director of the women's home. The Lord said, "You will be the director of a women's home." The Lord gave me purpose that day and a hope to make a difference in the world that I live in.

Over the past twenty years, the Lord has done some pretty amazing things in my life and I have continued to grow in the grace of the Lord despite the obstacles I have faced. Hannah House equipped me with the tools I needed to become all God wanted me to become. However, one thing I lacked was a sense of acceptance. After graduation, I had many dreams that I wanted to achieve. However, as so many young women do, I desired a man to share those dreams with me. At that time, to me any man would do. Prior to Hannah House, I left an unhealthy relationship for good reason, but when I graduated I went right back to the same unhealthy relationship and my children and I suffered much abuse because of it. I ended up marrying because I believed it to be God's will. In doing this, I jumped ahead of God. Years passed and the feeling of being stuck in an abusive situation overwhelmed me. I felt that, as a Christian woman, I just needed to be a doormat. I allowed the abuse and prayed that God would deliver me. God did deliver me from this relationship, but the pain that had caused me to believe that I needed to submit to that remained and stole years from my life. It wasn't until I attended a "God's Unfailing Love" retreat in May 2006 that I felt accepted by God for the first time in my life. I received so much pure love that weekend—from men and woman alike—that my life has been changed ever since. For the past six years, the men and woman of that retreat ministry have continued to be the best friends that I ever had. The men from that team have shown me that love is not lust, and they have accepted me and loved me in Christ. They have encouraged the cultivation of my inner beauty, and have challenged me to live a pure life devoted to Christ with no compromise. They are men who truly love God and will not settle for anything less than the best. They have encouraged me in my walk to live radically for God and not settle for anything less.

Women today are "looking for love in all the wrong places" as the saying goes. The beauty treatments I am going to share have been my focus in my time of consecration; they bring the beauty that comes only from above, the beauty that is referred to in 1 Peter 3:4b: "the unfading beauty of a gentle and quiet spirit, which is so precious to God."

This place will be like a heavenly harem, in which all the needs of the women are provided for. It will have an added emphasis on inner beauty and making women into vessels of honor. Just as Esther was given beauty treatments and special food, that will also be the intent of this home. Just as the eunuch assigned Esther her seven maids selected from the king's palace and moved her and her maids into the best place in the harem, it is my prayer that men and women of God would come alongside wounded and needy women and usher them into the presence of the King.

This home will be a testimony to all who are waiting as well. It is time to bring the old-fashioned woman back home: a woman that finds her place as a helpmate and a mother first, then she can minister the same to other women and teach them that they are worth waiting for. We need to be women who can be content with little or with abundance. We need to take back what the enemy has stolen from us. These women will learn that being a Christian woman is fun, appealing, and beautiful—inside and out. I am so excited about this, and I believe God will make it happen. As He leads me, I will follow.

During my soaking times—in my soothing and quiet candlelit baths—I put a lot of effort into being still and listening to what the Holy Spirit was speaking to me. This is when I disciplined my mind to be steady and calm, and found it to be the most refreshing time of the day. It was like allowing the Lord to write whatever He wanted on a blank sheet of paper. There is nothing more peaceful than resting and being still, and just knowing that He is God and God alone. He needs no help from me in planning my future. He just wants me to be emptied of myself, to be available for His work in my life. As I was listening to the Lord, He said to me, "You can't earn the gift of salvation, you can't earn My undying love, you can't earn the gifts of the Spirit, but you can earn the blessings that you receive. You earn blessings by obedience. Obeying My Word releases wealth." If we obey, in His time, He will reward everyone who diligently seeks Him.

Never in our wait is God inactive. Something is always happening. Xerxes will have insomnia, and Haman will build a gallows. Esther is preparing a banquet, and I am preparing for a King.

I must not be silent. I must speak to you as one who has received from God. It is not just for me; on the contrary, it is for all believers in Christ. He says, "It is a time to raise the standard, My royal priesthood, for such is the time that I have prepared you. Come boldly before the throne and redefine who you are. Come and examine yourself with faith, with hope, and with joy, and surely I shall bring you forth. For this reason I came to the world: to defeat the enemy who is set against you and bring you victory. Join with Me in this time. Raise the standard of your faith. Raise those things that I have brought you by way of revelation, and cause them to be a complete chapter in your book of destiny. Come boldly, I say, for indeed I am raising the standard in these days, and I shall come to you in stronger ways than ever before and with greater purpose. I will reveal Myself more perfectly with stronger impressions of My being. Come and dwell in the standard of My peace. Be one with Me, for I am the Lord of glory; and in this place, I will bring you through into the glory of My purposes, says the Lord."

This is a word of knowledge—I believe that the present challenge that some of you are going through is for the purpose of removing your need for honor among men. You cannot be a man-pleaser. You can't worry about your reputation. You have to come to grips with your stature, pride, and feelings. The cross was a place of shame for Jesus Christ, but also a place of victory—it is not who we are, but who He is in us. We must decrease so that He can increase in us.

Be ready for a move into the best place.

Chapter Four: Meet Mordecai

*M*ordecai was a Jew from the tribe of Benjamin and was among those who were taken captive by King Nebuchadnezzar. He lived as an exile, but he also lived to see freedom from captivity when King Darius came to reign. Mordecai had a cousin named Hadassah, whom he had brought up because she had neither father nor mother. Mordecai had taken her as his own daughter when her father and mother died, and she later became known as Esther.

Mordecai was a single parent. He was training Hadassah for royalty and didn't even know it. All he knew was that he needed to give her God's Word and instruct her in His ways. I can picture Mordecai as a peaceful man who taught Hadassah in patience. For a man to raise a girl requires patience and understanding. After Hadassah was taken, Mordecai would walk the temple gates back and forth, wondering how his princess was doing. He cared deeply for her and he never left her. He stayed near the palace the entire time she was there, just like the Holy Spirit never leaves us. God has said "I will never leave you nor forsake you" (Hebrews 13:5b NKJV). He will be with us always! Though my father and mother forsake me, the Lord will receive me. I could relate to Esther as I too was raised without a mother.

My mother left home when I was a child. At the age of seven, I became the mother of my younger siblings. My father became a single parent and he would remain single, at least for the next six years, but four kids were really more than he could handle on his own. We were divided up among relatives and separated from each other. Even the seven years I did have with my mom are a distant blur, with no memory of her touch, her smell, how she looked, or any words that she said. The only words I remember that she spoke to me were on the day she abandoned me. I remember being in the front yard playing when I heard my mom call to me from across the street. Our house was in a new subdivision and it was the first house on the block. Across the street adjacent to our house was the back of a business building. She was in the alley calling me to come to her. She knelt down to my level and told me she was leaving and did not know when she would return. She told me there was no sense crying about it; instead, I needed to be strong for my brother and sisters. She told me that I needed to be the mother now and help my dad take care of my brother and sisters. That was the only memory I had of my mom until she came back when I was thirteen years old. Some people say that those years must have been blacked out because of the trauma of losing my mother at such a young age. I am not sure what happened. All I know is that from that time on, at the age of seven, I became the mother—a very young mother with no memory of a childhood. I have no memory of playing dolls and dressing up, nor all the things that little girls do. I have no memory even of the pain I must have felt to lose my mother.

The memories I have of my father and I, after she left, are themselves very vague at best. It is almost like I was born and jumped right into adolescence. My dad often worked twelve hour shifts, and his shifts were always changing. When he worked the afternoon shifts, we hardly saw him at all. When he worked the midnight shift, he slept before he went to work so we didn't see much of him then either. He worked all the time, so most of the memories I have are only sparked by the photos that he has of us when we were little. My dad was an alcoholic, and it was very rare that he was not without a beer in hand. We were practically raised in the bar. We went there for dinner many nights and most weekends. My dad's closest friends came over often to drink with him. They were around so much that we grew up thinking of them as uncles. I know my dad loved me, however, he wasn't very good at expressing his love for us. In fact, I don't remember ever feeling loved. He never physically harmed me, and I can remember an occasional kiss goodnight, but mostly I have memories of my dad yelling at me or giving me dirty looks.

When I first read the book of Esther, I immediately connected with her. I could feel the heartache she must have felt with the loss of her parents. She was an orphan. She was raised by her cousin, her only living relative. Even if Esther had never even known her parents, she would still have the void of being without a mother. She had no one to show her how to care for herself in the way that a woman should. She was raised by a man; and even though a man may be godly, he might still find it difficult to put himself in a woman's shoes. Nevertheless, Mordecai raised Hadassah in the way he thought best. He instructed her in the ways of the Lord. He was a scribe. A scribe wrote down the Law, read the Law, and lived by the Law. Because she was raised by a scribe, it is likely that Esther knew how to read; this would have helped to set her apart from the other women. In those days, most women didn't read. They learned how to take care of the household. They learned from their mothers how to cook, clean, and care for the men and other children. They didn't need to read because they stayed home. However, Mordecai had to teach Hadassah in the way he knew best.

The story ultimately has a happy ending as good triumphs over evil. King Xerxes ended up giving Queen Esther the estate of Haman, the enemy of the Jews. And Mordecai came into the presence of the king, for Esther had told him how he was related to her (Esther 8:1). Just as Esther was restored to her cousin, Mordecai, in a powerful way, God brought about a powerful restoration with my mom and me as well. My mother is now saved and living for the King of Kings. Her life has real beauty now that she has come to Him wholly, not holding back as the Lord touches every part of her heart. My mom is a tremendous help and support to me now. She helps with my children. She teaches me about living and making a home. Were it not for Jesus, she would have vanished from my story, even as Vashti vanished. She has been freed from the bondage that held her captive, and now ministers to the people in her community who desperately need to know the Jesus that came to open the eyes of the blind and make the lame to walk the walk of faith.

She is writing a book as well about how her hardships made her into the woman she is today. I am so glad that God got a hold of her—she is a miracle and a testimony to all. My dad and I have also had restoration come to our lives, and I am cherishing the moments that make us closer.

Single Parenting

*M*y childhood has definitely affected the way I parent my children. I have three beautiful children named Victoria, Isaac, and Daniel. They are all seven years apart. Their father left to live in a different state with another woman when Daniel was just a baby, and I became a single parent. Not only do I relate to Esther being raised without a mother, but I also relate to Mordecai in that I too, was entrusted with the lives of these three precious gifts to train them up in the ways of the Lord as a single parent. And it has been a rough journey. Raising one child is hard, but raising three is even harder. Just when I got over the hump of the traumatic teenage years, I took a deep breath and went through it again. Every parent has their ups and downs, but I probably had more downs than ups. I felt like a failure in my parenting more than once. My children are all different and unique and hard to understand. I hated the way I responded to the whining and complaining, as well as the arguing and fighting. At times I ended up looking like a child myself, especially when I allowed myself to become entangled in arguments and conflicts. Sometimes, in an effort to quickly end the whining and insubordination, I just cleaned up after them myself. Although at the time I felt it was easier to do it myself, I now realize that those were opportunities where I failed to teach them important lessons about responsibility and proper submission to authority.

But how could I teach my children? How could I help them when I was clueless to their needs? How could I help my depressed teenager?

The best thing I could do was seek the guidance of others, because I had nothing to fall back on. I had no parental guidance growing up, so I had to seek wisdom from my pastors and people who mentored me in the faith.

During my year of consecration and preparation, the Lord gave me practical truths that helped me to truthfully evaluate the way I had been parenting my children. Let's face it; these children did not come with manuals. These are some truths that became my pillars for parenting. I hope that you can also benefit from them, and that they will help you prepare your children for the King.

I learned to always affirm my love by being happy when my children are happy, and being sad when they are sad. I try to give positive affirmation and never negative. For every negative word that I spoke, I found that I needed ten positive words to counteract that one, because negative words are more easily believed.

After having learned that unconditional acceptance will bring much security to your relationships, I realized that I needed to show them that my love is not based on what they do, but who they are, and I accept them just the way they are and nothing they do can change that. I had never really accepted Victoria—I had always pushed her away until I learned this. Don't wait until your children are almost out of the house before you realize that this is happening. It is heartbreaking to me that I had pushed her away for so many years; those years can never be regained.

When your loved ones do not feel appreciated, they do less because they do not feel like they are important. Catch them being good. Make it a goal to look for instances of them being good, and verbally appreciate them when you do. You will find the more that you catch them being good, the less you will catch them being bad. They will desire to please you.

One area that I really messed up in parenting was I always put others, and other things, before my family, and my actions spoke loud and clear that they were not important to me. Being available means that when they come to talk to you, you drop everything else and give them your full attention. Being a mother and a wife is sacrificial and it will always be that way. If we want to raise children that are above the status quo, we must sacrifice our "important" things so that our family knows that they are most important.

Give your loved ones a sense of lovability. You can be sure that, if they don't get all they need from mom and dad, they will look elsewhere for it. Young children desperately need love and affection. Never refuse to give it, even if you do not feel like it. Express it verbally. Everyone in the house needs to hear "I love you" ten times a day. Give appropriate physical affection constantly.

Come in close to their world. If they want to play with dolls, get down on the floor and play dolls. This was something I really struggled to overcome because I never grew up with dolls. But I realized how important it is. If they want to play hide and seek, play with them. Never underestimate the power of playing in their world. Let them make the rules in playtime. Ask them how they want to play, and no matter how you feel, just do it. This will actually be helping them to learn to play independently and securely. If you play with them at home, they will not require you to play with them when you are with friends. Let the housecleaning go and just play. Try it; it is freeing!

I think the next thing I learned applies most to teenagers, but a child learns a sense of responsibility when they have rules. If they have boundaries, they feel more loved because they know that they are cared about.

These are the ingredients to parenting that I learned create a sweet-smelling fragrance. I practice them on a daily basis with my children. Another thing I learned is that rules without relationship will lead to rebellion. Your children may be young enough to shape them, and give them a good foundation for their future. I am not the perfect parent, and I do not claim to have all the answers, but I do know that I have some very special children and they are worth me trying to be the best mom that I could possibly be. I mess up all the time, but I humble myself before God and ask their forgiveness. I try to learn from my mistakes so that I don't continue to walk in the same pattern. I hope that you can learn from my mistakes.

Let's face it: no one just has kids and knows what to do. We all have to learn how to be good parents. If you take heed to what I am saying, you will have a better chance of shaping your children for a successful future. We make our kids who they are. They become exactly what we tell them to become. If we tell them they are lazy and good for nothing, then that is what they become. If we tell them that they are going to be kings and queens made for royalty, that is what they will be.

How we discipline our children may be controversial to some, but the Bible is clear when it says that if you spare the rod, you spoil the child. Here is a partial list of Scriptures from just the book of Proverbs that support this position: Proverbs 13:24; 22:15; 23:13-14; 29:15. There are countless others throughout the Bible. Study what the Bible says; it will be beneficial for you.

We are not talking child abuse either. There has to be a balance and the parent must be in total control. We are not to discipline out of our anger. Instead, we need to take a deep breath and think clearly. We discipline them because we love them and do not want them to be spoiled.

When my daughter was about three-years old, we were in the Hannah House program. My daughter ran the show. She was always in charge, and I gave her everything she wanted. She caused a lot of chaos in the house because she demanded her way, and everyone in the house got tired of this toddler's temper tantrums. The director of the women's home took me and my daughter into the office one day and counseled us on the importance of discipline. The director, with a completely caring demeanor, kindly took Victoria and placed her over her knees and spanked her. Then she firmly held her as she looked into her eyes and began to tell her that she was loved. This home began to show me how to correctly discipline my children. I have a spoon that I use to spank my children if they are being disobedient. I call the spoon "The Motivator" because it is going to motivate them to do what is right with the hope that they will never forget.

I am committed to train my children up in the way that they should go, believing the Lord's promise that they will not depart from it in the end, for my children have all been brought up in the Word. I spent many years homeschooling them. My children needed extra attention. Most children do need a little extra love when they feel a void from an absent parent, so it is wise that single men and women that are parents take advantage of the time they have to train up and instruct their little ones for royalty. You never know, your child may become king or queen, president, or even a pastor. Your little one may one day lead others into the royal way of God's kingdom.

Even though parenting my children has been quite challenging at times, it has actually been an incredible blessing to me because the challenges I faced pushed me closer to the Lord. They drove me to my knees. They have been my training ground, and if God used me to reach into their stubborn hearts, then I could be used of God with others too! One of the rewards He gave me was the ability to homeschool. What an honor! The public school was just not an option in the neighborhood in which we lived. I had nothing against the public school. Homeschooling was just my personal preference to protect my children from the negative influences found there. Public schools do have positive traits, but I felt for my family, homeschooling was best. I didn't have a teaching degree, and everything I taught my children I had to first teach myself.

Every morning I wondered what new discoveries lay ahead for my children as we homeschooled. Although I had the day's schedule planned, God always seemed to lead with His divine lessons. As my son and I walked alongside a path in the park one spring morning, we noticed several cocoons hidden beneath a bench located on a trail. The cocoons were large, and as we examined one of them more closely, we saw a slight movement. Slowly, the cocoon began to crack open, and we could see something struggling to get out. "Mom, what is it?" cried my son. "Let's cut the rest of the cocoon so it can get out!"

"No, sweetheart," I replied. "You don't want to do that. If we interfere, the living thing inside that cocoon will be injured. We have to let it struggle on its own." As we watched the struggling moth, I understood how my past actions had interfered with our homeschooling. I realized that I needed to be firm and expect my children to do their own schoolwork without asking for help on every question.

Do you ever find yourself trying to "help" your children more than you should? Your children's education can suffer if you don't learn to balance the dual role you play as teacher and parent. Spelling out every answer will be damaging to the development of their reasoning and thinking processes. Be careful. Don't destroy the new life God is using you to shape. Instead direct your children onto the right path. We have the promise that when they are older, they will not leave it (Proverbs 22:6). We need to allow the Lord to show us how to educate them with a healthy balance of love and discipline, and to not remove the struggles that will cause them to grow in knowledge.

There were, of course, days that I felt as though I accomplished very little at the end of our homeschooling day. I looked around and saw more projects to finish and messes to clean up than when we had when we started our day. I had the joyous days when my child learned a new set of multiplication tables, but the frustration of him forgetting entirely all the historical facts he had learned about George Washington the day before. Some days I wondered if I could be my children's teacher. I thought maybe they would be better off if they went to school. I could hear my friend Carolyn, who also home-schooled her children, say to me, "Stop! Think about what just went through your mind. Where are those thoughts coming from? From the One who called you to teach your children and promised you the strength to do it, or from the one who would see you fail?"

Every homeschooling mother second guesses herself from time to time. After a difficult day, we all question whether we heard God right when He asked us to homeschool our children. We're not alone. Even great men of God faced similar doubts when God called them to difficult tasks. Men like David, Moses, and Mordecai struggled with their anxieties in serving God, too. Once Mordecai learned of the enemies plot to destroy all the Jews, what did he do? He tore his clothing, put on sackcloth, covered himself with ashes, and went into town crying passionately and bitterly (Esther 4:1). But God knew the hearts of these great men of God and He provided the confirmation and the assurance they needed to remain faithful in doing what He asked.

David said, "In my distress I prayed to the Lord, and the Lord answered me and set me free" (Psalm 118:5). God is waiting to do the same for you today. If you're wondering how you are going to get through homeschooling or another challenge today, ask the Lord to fill you with His presence and confirm to you that you are doing His will. Whether you homeschool or send your child to school, we still need the Lord to strengthen us to follow Him in obedience as we instruct them through teachable moments.

During the year that I set aside for the Lord, I allowed my boys to go and visit their dad in Tennessee for the summer. But things got out of hand there and I had to go and get them a month early. The children told me all sorts of things that made me believe that it was a mistake to ever send them there in the first place. Later when I learned my sons were being exposed to drinking and drugs, I felt a strong conviction to not allow them to go back there. God's wisdom for the prudent is that they give thought to their ways and their steps. (Proverbs 14:8,15) For a long time, I believed everything I heard their dad say to me—that he was clean and sober and that he had changed. But his foolish lifestyle was often hidden and I was deceived. My sons have been hurt by this. Isaac cried with tears that fell like a waterfall, wishing that he could have what he had with his dad before. He said that when he went down there to see him, he didn't even know the man he was calling dad. He said, "What happened to the dad that used to play with me and cared about me?" It was up to me to bring him the comfort that he needed; he felt fatherless.

My youngest son, Daniel, once told me that I was the best mom and dad. I was trying to be both parents and I often felt as though I failed at both, but to hear my son say that was encouraging to me. However, there were other times that, as a mother, I got very irritated in having to be both the mother and the father, which was never God's perfect plan for any family. It is hard to be both. But God sustained me as He gave me this promise in Isaiah, "I will teach all your children, and they will enjoy great peace" (Isaiah 54:13).

Another instance when parenting is difficult is when your children do not take heed to the decrees that God has given us for our own protection. It hurts to watch your children making mistakes that could ultimately affect their future. There is something natural that takes place within a mother to want to control their destiny and make them understand the importance of their choices. But ultimately, they are God's. This is not a cop-out; we do what we can, but then we leave the rest to God.

My Children

*M*y firstborn baby girl—how precious she was when I first laid eyes on her. She was born three days after my nineteenth birthday. I was a young mother who knew absolutely nothing about babies. Learning how to feed a baby, change diapers, discern which cry meant what, and get the sleep patterns down pat was quite a stretch for me, as it would be for any new mom. Unfortunately, I was not a good mom in the beginning. I often left Victoria with babysitters to raise her. It was too early for me to be a mom. I wasn't done partying, so I neglected the responsibility that I was given, and failed to cherish the gift that God had placed in my womb. When there was no one available to watch her, I took her in the stroller out on the streets with me until the wee hours of the night. Inside the stroller was a bundle of joy who laughed about everything. She giggled and giggled, and was easy to please. She really was precious. But I was selfish, and I wanted "me time."

I wasn't ready to sit down and have kids. Her dad was in and out of my life, so I got involved in other relationships as well. One guy in particular was a gang leader. Getting involved with him meant leaving my child in someone else's care even more. She was cared for most of the time by a wonderful couple on her dad's side of the family, whom she referred to as her mamaw and papaw. They loved her dearly, and I am so grateful for the time that they invested in her. It wasn't until she was two years old that I started to care. After I gave my life to the Lord

Jesus Christ and moved in with a Christian couple, I decided I needed to grow up and be a mom.

From that time on, I began to learn how to be a good one through the Christian women of the church. I decided that I would be the mom that this precious daughter needed. I cuddled and played with her. I trained her in the Word as I was taught. I prayed for her and spoke Scripture over her. I took her to church every time the door was open. I went to every event that she was involved in. I tried homeschooling her a few times, and when the challenges overwhelmed me, I sent her to public school. I remember helping a lot with homework, and I read a lot of books to her.

Apparently though, what I had taught my daughter about her value in God's eyes wasn't working. Satan's lies convinced her to identify herself with the world's definition of beauty. I cried as I thought of the depression she seemed to display each morning. "No wonder," I said to myself. "Who could compare to each of the air-brushed beauties we see every day in the media?" How could I teach her that Proverbs 31:30 was true? "Charm is deceptive, and beauty does not last; but a woman who fears the Lord will be greatly praised." I wanted her to receive the beauty treatments I was receiving. I wanted her to identify with Esther.

If there ever was a beauty in the Old Testament, Esther was it. Chosen from the most beautiful women in Persia to be the wife of King Xerxes, the meaning of her name came true: she was a "star." Although she wasn't in a major motion picture, God cast her for a part that would save the entire Jewish nation. The true beauty of her character, which lay in her faithfulness to God and His people, was revealed when she chose to listen to God instead of her fears and claimed, "If I must die, I must die" (Esther 4:16b). My daughter has a huge calling on her life as well. It started off on a rough road, but I did train her up in the way that she should go, and have placed her into the hands of the King. Praise God for the wisdom to teach our children the truth, and for the mighty power of His Holy Word that is tested and sure, never returning void or without the promised fruit of God's purpose fulfilled. I stand on that promise for my daughter. She is chosen to be a queen. My Queen Victoria!

My son, Isaac, was actually promised to me in my dreams before he was even conceived. When he was born, he brought light to everyone around. It was Isaac that brought my own mom back to her senses. Her life began to change once she laid eyes on this special son of mine. Isaac had always been a very compliant child. He was not one that required much attention. My other two children were always demanding, so he was actually a breath of fresh air. Isaac had always been an obedient child and very sensitive to discipline. In fact, he was so sensitive that he would often tell on himself if he did something wrong.

It was with much wonder and great expectation that I watched as this precious son of mine grew from a child into a young man. I watched to see the fulfillment of the promise God had granted me through him. But as he grew, he managed to grow apart from me. Though I fought desperately to hold him in that place where I knew he would be safe and protected, he had set his eyes upon other places, as young men often do, places where no mother's heart can bear to see their child wander. Perhaps I, much like Abraham, had grown to cling a little too tightly to the promise of God He had spoken to me, even as Abraham clung to his own son, Isaac. As it says in Genesis 22, the day came when God told Abraham to take his son, whom he loved, and entrust him back into the hands of the Lord.

As any parent knows, it is extremely difficult to seemingly let go of your child and allow him to go to a place of danger. God not only told Abraham to prepare to let go of his son, but He also told him to take the boy to the altar of sacrifice himself. And if that wasn't enough, Abraham was instructed to take a knife with him and actually sacrifice the boy there to the Lord. As we read of how Abraham responded, we see that he never hesitated to do all that the Lord had required of him, and that he was truly prepared to obey the Lord right to the end. But we also see how, even in the face of such apparent contradiction, he never once doubted that God would remain true to His Word. And of course, God did.

As I write this book today, I do so standing in such a place of faith myself. I know the promise the Lord spoke to my heart concerning my own son, Isaac. I know that the decisions he has made lately in his life, and the places he has chosen to dwell in, are not at all what I would choose for him if I could. But I can't. He is at the age where a young man is determined to make his own decisions, and I too, find myself releasing my son, whom I love, into the ever watchful hands of the Lord. But all these things, as difficult as they may be for my heart to bear, have not caused me to doubt for a moment that God is faithful. And the knife I now hold in my hand is nothing short of the two-edged sword that is the Word of God, in which I rejoice and place my trust. In Genesis 22:12, we are told that the Angel of the Lord, whom I believe to be Jesus Himself, called out to Abraham from heaven and said now I know that you love Me, because you have not withheld from Me your son.

We know that God loves us, because He did not withhold His only begotten Son from you and I. I pray constantly for the health and protection of my beloved Isaac. I yearn for the day that our relationship is restored and renewed. I share these things with you now so that you might know that God is good and He is faithful, even in the midst of trials and tribulation. And I confidently entrust the life of my beautiful little boy into the loving hands of our God, assured that His perfect will shall come to pass.

"Children are a gift from the Lord; they are a reward from him. Children born to a young man are like arrows in a warrior's hands. How joyful is the man whose quiver is full of them! He will not be put to shame when he confronts his accusers at the city gates" (Psalm 127:3-5). The Lord told me that Isaac was an arrow in my quiver that would shoot out into the darkness and spread light. The Lord will make His mouth like a sharpened sword. He hides Isaac in the shadow of His hand; He will make him into a polished arrow and hide him in His Almighty quiver. It was this promise that helped me to realize that the darkness Isaac has found would one day serve as a territory in which he would enjoy God's victory.

Daniel is my little miracle baby. He was born with a heart defect called "transposition of the great arteries." He needed open heart surgery when he was one week old. He fought for his life from the beginning.

He reminds me of a mighty warrior. He is very strong. He is also a bit strong willed, and parents of strong-willed children know what I mean when I say that we need to be stronger. However, Daniel has been a sponge in the sense that he soaks everything up that I have taught him. He may go through some hardships as he approaches different seasons in life, but it is my promise from God that Daniel will be more than a conqueror through Christ in everything that He does. He gets picked on and teased by his older brother, but it seems to only make him stronger. He has learned to put on his armor every time that happens. Daniel loves Jesus with his whole heart. He loves reading the Bible, and he loves talking to God. He prays every night before he goes to bed. I am reminded of a conversation I once had with my boys. I told them I wanted to be a world changer, and Daniel said to me, "Momma, you will change the world a little bit, but I am going to change the world a lot through Jesus." I knew that his words were prophetic and time will surely bring it to pass.

Disrespectful actions of children, no matter their age, are abhorred by God. This serious offense robs parents of their authority to teach, and destroys the family unit. Repeatedly, God warns children to honor their parents with loving and obedient hearts (Exodus 20:12; Ephesians 6:2). Mouthy and sarcastic children who belittle their parent's leadership and decision making are clearly on a path to destruction.

King David's son, Adonijah, is one such example in the Bible. He put himself forward and said, "I will be king." The tragic story of this young man's disrespect toward his father is recorded in 1 Kings 1-2. Adonijah was known as a handsome boy. He had external beauty, and he won the favor of many because of it. But his fame was short-lived. Adonijah was not only disrespectful of his father by defying him, but he also attempted to take over David's reign as king. David failed to intervene in his son's folly, nor did he prudently question his motives and actions. Fortunately, Solomon, David's wise son, put a stop to his foolish brother, but at the cost of Adonijah's life.

My children are no exception. As cute as they are, we have dealt with this area many times and, as I still have children under my roof,

Deuteronomy 5:16a is a continuous beauty treatment that I must give to them. "Honor your father and your mother, as the Lord your God has commanded you" (NKJV). My children have paid the consequences for their actions and it has not been pretty. But the Lord commands us to discipline them.

I will be the first to admit that sometimes it seems easier to look the other way or laugh it off when my children fail to respect me. But I had to realize the importance that God placed on correcting this problem when my children challenged me in ways that were inappropriate. After all, if children cannot learn to respect their parents, they will also have difficulty respecting the Lord.

Whether you're single or married, it is important to always be mindful that when Jesus gave us His great commission, as found in Matthew 28:19, to go out and make disciples of all nations, instructing them to obey His teachings, He was not simply speaking to foreign missionaries. The Great Commission starts in our own homes; "all nations" includes our own nation, our own family.

When the beauty of the glory of the Lord is upon you, your children will notice. Embrace them, teach them, and move them into the best place possible as they prepare for the seemingly unknown. Their promised land awaits. Glory hallelujah to our Father God!

Father God

There have been so many days that I have felt like a failure as a child of God because of all the sin exposed in my life. I would find myself thinking that God could never use a screw-up like me. All the pastors I knew had been brought up in the church and appeared to have their lives in good order. In comparing myself to them, I couldn't help but wonder if it wasn't already too late for God to use me. When I had those doubts, I prayed and sought the Lord until I could clearly hear Him say that, no matter what I had done, or did, it could not change His plans He had or what He wanted to accomplish in me. I could rest in the knowledge that He is the Maker of heaven and earth; He is just too big for me to worry whether or not I could mess things up. It is my heart's desire to obey and act on what the Lord is saying, but if at times I fail to obey. I do not need to fall under condemnation because He is God, and He will still accomplish what He desires in me. I am His workmanship, created in Christ Jesus before the world began (Ephesians 2:10). I do not need to give in to worry about whether or not I am doing what He wants because I am His child! He wants me to just keep going, knowing that He is ordering my steps. He is my Daddy! The more time I spend with my Daddy, the more I want to be just like Him.

On Father's Day of 2008, I specifically celebrated the day with my great Dad in heaven. God is the greatest dad, and the best example for all dads to follow. I read how Mordecai adopted Hadassah and made her one of his own. Our adoption with Christ is also pictured through what Mordecai did for Hadassah when he took her in as his own. As I read this, I was flooded with overwhelming gratefulness in my heart and soul; I was indeed a child of God, adopted into His royal family. I praised and worshiped the Lord for being unto us a Father who would never leave us orphaned (Romans 8:14-17). As I consecrated this year to receiving my Daddy's provisions and His manna in a protected harem free of outside cares or worries, He fed me, cared for me, sustained me, stuck by me, taught me, and loved me deeply.

God's Children

Almost every year, I attend a family reunion where we set up tents and stay the night or even the weekend. One year, somewhere in the area near where I had pitched my tent, I could hear the sounds of someone vomiting for much of the night; I noticed he was without a tent and just lying on the ground. He had been drinking. My heart grieved and broke for him, and I went and got my blankets to give to him. But he refused them. When Esther heard that the people, including Mordecai, were weeping and wailing and lying in sackcloth and ashes, she sent Mordecai a covering, but he refused it. She was trying to find out what was troubling him. Scripture says that Esther was in great distress. She sent clothes for him to put on instead of his sackcloth, but he would not accept them (Esther 4:5).

Our Father in heaven grieves over lost souls, over His children who are called by His name. As Mordecai grieved for His people, we must also grieve for those who are dead in their trespasses. We must grieve for our loved ones too, and lay down our lives for the Father's kingdom, for purposes greater than our own. Our loved one's lives are at stake here. We need to find out what is troubling them, and go to the King on their behalf.

There may be those who, for whatever reason, continue to reject God's offer of deliverance and salvation. My friend, Jimmy White, wrote an amazing piece that not only connects with me because of my own prodigal son, but will touch your heart as well. May it bring to remembrance the Father's love for you and your loved ones.

"The Bible contains a priceless wealth of insight into family life, and not only lessons of how God created families to abide and prosper as an intimate community, but also countless glimpses into the hearts and minds of real families who struggled to understand, endure, forgive, support, and love one another. It is difficult for me to think of even one family mentioned in the Bible that did not have more than its rightful share of drama, whether you examine the relationships between two spouses, or between siblings, or extended families, or in-laws, or especially between parents and their children. Even Jesus Himself had to put up with His siblings bringing their mother to try and grab Him by the ear and take Him home because they all believed He was 'a few fish sticks shy of a full order,' as found in Mark 3.

"As a matter of fact, if you really wanted to do a thorough study on these things, your search would have to begin right near the start of the Bible with the very first family. Blame, shame, fault-finding and jealousy: Adam and the gang had it all. After all, why did Cain murder his brother? It wasn't just because he was Abel; it was because they were brothers, and brothers have been putting the old saying 'brotherly love' to the test right from the dawn of creation. There is another story of a family in crisis—a story of a father and his two sons. It is a story of loss, and hope, and forgiveness, and redemption. It is one of my favorite Bible family stories of all. Luke15 records the story—the parable of the lost son. Many, many people have related to and come to love this story, and interestingly enough, there are many different opinions as to who the main character really is. Some identify with the son who left his family, only to discover that the dreams he believed he was destined to pursue had deceived him and cost him everything he had. Others relate to the son who instead remained home, working hard and keeping a record of every moment of it. There are also other characters as well: a foreign land owner, the father's servants, and even an unfortunate, fattened calf.

"But my favorite perspective to view this story from is by looking at it from the father's point of view. He was a man of wealth who had not only one, but two sons and an inheritance he desired to leave them both. The younger son decided one day that he had better places to see and better people to see them with, so he hit his father up for the money he knew he'd need in order to go and do his own thing, and then he left. Eventually, he makes his way back home, having prepared a statement that I guess he figured would be sufficient to at least get him in the door. As for the older brother, his reaction to the news that his little brother had returned makes me wonder if perhaps he wasn't at least part of the reason why the kid left in the first place. But it is the father's reaction that truly captures my heart. Yes, he had allowed his child to grab his things and go, when told that was how it was going to be. Yes, he had even given him the means to finance a journey he surely must have known would only end in bitterness and loss. But there is so much more revealed about the fathers' heart, hidden in plain sight within the few simple words it took to tell his reaction. He must have spent time every day straining his eyes in hopes of spotting his son on the distant horizon, because he managed to see him that day while his son was still a long way off. He apparently couldn't possibly wait any longer to reclaim his child because, instead of waiting there for him to return, he ran out to meet him right where he was. The son was obviously determined to deliver his well-planned speech because he tried, but I don't think the father heard a single word. He was too busy hugging him, and kissing him, and calling the servants to tell them to finally get ready for that big celebration he always knew one day he'd have, because his beloved son, who once was lost, was now found once again.

"But the father had one more family fire to try and put out that night as well. His elder son was none too happy about the warm reception his sibling was receiving, and he wasn't at all shy about letting his father know it. Still, the father, listening patiently to his dear child and without judgment, simply tried to comfort him by showing him the way he felt his son needed to see things. He never scolded him for his attitude, nor did he even command him to get inside and join the party. But what he did do was to explain to him why they had to celebrate, why they had to be glad, why they had to be together. This was the true inheritance his father had always longed to leave his sons. This was his most precious gift—family."[5]

---

5. Jimmy White, e-mail message to author, November 11, 2012.

Chapter Five: Meet the Eunuchs, Maidservants, and their Ministry

The Eunuchs

Although it was King Xerxes who ordered the beauty treatments, the actual process was administered under the care of the eunuchs and maidservants. The eunuchs, in particular, were servants to the king, and even if they were made eunuchs by force, they were committed and loyal to the king. They were close enough to the king that they knew what would please him. They knew what qualities the king was looking for, and they were dedicated to teaching and preparing the women who entered the harem to please the king.

King Xerxes had seven eunuchs who attended him. When I did a word search on the eunuchs that directly served the king, I found that each eunuch's name was symbolic and served their king much like Jesus came to serve the church. The Lord has a special place in His heart for those who serve in this way. "Don't let foreigners who commit themselves to the Lord say, 'The Lord will never let me be part of His people.' And don't let the eunuchs say, 'I'm a dried-up tree with no children and no future.' For this is what the Lord says: I will bless those eunuchs who keep my Sabbath days holy and who choose to do what pleases me and commit their lives to me. I will give them—within the walls of my house—a memorial and a name far greater than sons and daughters could give. For the name I give them is an everlasting one. It will never disappear" (Isaiah 56:3-5).

The names of the seven eunuchs who served the king were Mehuman, Biztha, Harbona, Bigtha, Abagtha, Zethar and Carcas. The Lord said He would give to the eunuchs a name better than sons and daughters, an everlasting name that would endure forever, and yet the names they already had were considered important enough to be included in the book itself. This caused me to wonder what exactly each name represented. As I did, it struck me how similar they are to the attributes of Christ.

Mehuman means "faithful" and that sums up Christ and what He came to do for us. [6]

Biztha means "bound," hence "eunuch," which Romans 7:4-6 sums up the meaning of his name (Revelation 1:4-5). [7]

Harbona means "ass-driver". [8] Harbona is the one who suggested Haman be hung on the gallows that he had erected for Mordecai (Esther 7:9). Jesus rode a donkey on His way into Jerusalem (Zechariah 9:9).

Rev. D. Rebecca Dinovo says that "this symbolized that Jesus came on a mission of peace. The donkey revealed Jesus to be a humble peasant on a peace mission, not a military warrior. This donkey becomes the sacred throne for, not only a King, but the very Son of God." [9]

Bigtha means "in the wine press" which symbolizes the blood of Christ [10] (Isaiah 63:3; Revelation 19:13).

Abagtha means "God-given," and also "father of the wine press." [11] It was profound to me to think that through the study of this name, the Lord led me to the very first verse I had learned in kindergarten. In my years as a Christian, I have found it to be true that most people hear this verse early in their Christian walk and it becomes the foundation that serves in building our faith. "For God loved the

---

6. *Smith's Bible Dictionary*, c 1884, (Madison, WI: Porter and Coates), 393.
7. Ibid., 94.
8. Ibid., 92.
9. Quote by Rebecca D. Dinovo.
10. J. B. Jackson, *A Dictionary of Scripture Proper Names*, (Loizeaux Brothers, c 1909), 19.
11. *Smith's Bible Dictionary*, c 1884, (Madison, WI: Porter and Coates), 9.

world so much that he gave his one and only Son, so that everyone who believes in Him will not perish but have eternal Life" (John 3:16).

Zethar means "star" and also "he that examines or beholds."[12]

Carcas means "severe"[13] and also "as the (bound) one."[14] In the Old Testament, the Law was given to Moses. Every year a lamb was bound and sacrificed at Passover to show how God had faithfully delivered the Israelites from the Egyptians. The blood was sprinkled on hyssop and brushed over the door post, and when the angel of death passed by, he passed over the houses which were covered by the blood. This is a type and shadow of Jesus Christ. Jesus Christ was born into our world, He was fully God and fully man. He offered Himself as our Passover Lamb. He was sinless—tempted in every way, yet without sin. It is fascinating that God allowed Himself to take on human flesh, to suffer through human temptations, just so that He could empathize and sympathize with His creation. Jesus went to the cross, and as He hung there, He took upon Himself the sin of all humanity. He is referred to as the Lamb of God who takes away the sin of the world (John 1:29).

The king was blessed to have been served by such meek and humble men. These eunuchs held great purposes in their hearts. They wanted to prepare the women for someone great—someone they held in high respect. They themselves were subject to authority, and they knew that they would be blessed through faithfully accomplishing their responsibilities. There was no sense fighting against the king—then they would be fighting against what God instituted. Their consciences were clear; they were doing what was right, and in so doing, they were able to teach the women about submission to the king by their own example. This is what Paul was referring to in Romans 13:1 when he instructed the church to be mindful to submit to governing authorities, because in

---

12. *Smith's Bible Dictionary*, c 1884, (Madison, WI: Porter and Coates), 764.
13. Net Bible Study Dictionary Online. http://classic.net.bible.org/dictionary. php?word=Zethar (accessed July 11, 2013). Used by permission.
14. Net Bible Study Dictionary Online. http://classic.net.bible.org/dictionary. php?word=Carcas (accessed July 11, 2013). Used by permission.

doing so we honor God's authority over all earthly rulers. As obedient followers of Christ, doing this will not only enable us to live with clean consciences before the Lord, but it will also help us to avoid reproach and trouble in our daily lives, even as we teach others a better way to live through our example.

The ladies that were being prepared for the king were also served by faithful and humble servants called eunuchs, as mentioned in Esther 2:3.

When the king's order and edict had been proclaimed, many young women including Esther were brought to the citadel, the royal city of Susa (*Susa* means "lily"[15]) and they were put under the care of Hegai. *Hegai* means "my meditation."[16]

The young women had to leave their families and their homes, as well as their way of doing things. They had to surrender their independence and be placed under the care of a eunuch whose very name meant groaning or separation.

Separation for me meant separating myself from the world of men. It was like being placed under the care of a pure eunuch in order to meditate on God's Word, to be brought into the royal city of joy, roses, and lilies. For me, this required groaning of the flesh and dying to my self-life; I was being set apart as a tree planted deep in intimacy with the King in a heavenly harem.

Hegai knew what pleased the king, and when Esther received favor with the head eunuch, he taught Esther how to please the king. He filled her in on the secrets that would win her the heart of this king. She listened and received. And when the time came for her to go to the king, she accepted the advice of Hegai, and asked for nothing except what he suggested (Esther 2:15).

In the evening she was be taken to the king's private rooms and in the morning she went to a second harem under the care of Shaashgaz. He was the king's eunuch in charge of the concubines (Esther 2:14).

---

15. J. B. Jackson, A Dictionary of Scripture Proper Names, (Loizeaux Brothers, c 1909), 90.
16. Ibid., 40.

Here we have the name of another eunuch who walked beside Esther and taught her.

Shaashgaz means "servant of the beautiful."[17] Studying this eunuch gave me a whole new meaning to service. During the time that I had separated myself from my social life and ministry, I felt that the Lord wanted me to commit to serving at my church in whatever capacity was needed. The church for me was another part of the harem in which I would receive care—a place where my character would be built and strengthened. I sat down with my pastors and told them I wanted to do a job in the church that no one else wanted to do. One of the pastors almost looked embarrassed by the job he suggested. He asked that I clean the toilets in the women's restroom after the first service every Sunday. I said I would love to, and so I committed to doing this job for one year. Cleaning toilets for me meant I was a servant of the beautiful King of Kings! I cleaned those toilets with joy! I knew that I was serving Him, and I had great satisfaction in pleasing the one who saw my every move and who knows me by name. This verse came alive to me in those toilet times, "You must have the same attitude that Christ Jesus had. Though he was God, he did not think of equality with God as something to cling to. Instead, he gave up his divine privileges; he took the humble position of a slave and was born as a human being" (Philippians 2:5-7).

Jerry, the janitor, became a great man to me. Throughout the toilet-cleaning year, my friend, Jerry, listened intently to everything God was revealing to me in my time alone with Him. He was not only a great listener, but he also gave me great advice. Jerry would tell me that it's more important to make an effort at something than to see the results of what you do. He would say that we shouldn't do things for others just to feel good about ourselves; it's not about us! That was one of his pet peeves. He also advised me to keep a journal of all that God was sharing with me, and when my year was over Jerry advised me not to rush into anything. Janitors tend to see things that others don't see, and they are not always recognized by those with a "higher calling." However, Jesus notices them. And He said in Mark 10:43-44, "But among you it will

17. Smith's Bible Dictionary, c 1884, (Madison, WI: Porter and Coates), 608.

be different. Whoever wants to be a leader among you must be your servant, and whoever wants to be first among you must be the slave of everyone else."

Eunuchs knew suffering much like Jesus did. "For even the Son of Man came not to be served but to serve others and to give his life as a ransom for many" (Mark 10:45). The point here is that this kind of serving results in dying—a giving up of one's life. Jesus shows the disciples the way to greatness; He gives His own death as an example: the Son of Man came to give His life as a ransom for many. Jesus gave His death as an example of the kind of suffering and service that the eunuchs were called to undergo.

This is a radical call to discipleship. In essence, Jesus was saying "If you want to follow Me and seek the glory of the kingdom, be prepared to suffer. That is the way I go, and those who follow Me go the same way. I don't take the hard road while you take the easy road. The road that leads to life is hard and very few will find it" (Matthew 7:14). We take the same road—the road that is straight and narrow. On this road, we must leave the baggage of our selfish ways behind, take up our cross, and follow Him.

There is one more eunuch that we will look at in this chapter. He was the eunuch assigned to Esther when she became queen. His name was Hathak. His name means "verily."[18] This is an old word meaning "truthfully." Interestingly, his name matched his character too. Esther wanted to hear the truth, no matter how hard it was to hear. This eunuch was to find and seek out the truth. "Then Esther sent for Hathach, one of the king's eunuchs who had been appointed as her attendant. She ordered him to go to Mordecai and find out what was troubling him and why he was in mourning" (Esther 4:5).

The truth is that there are a lot of things that we would like to cover up. We often hear the truth, and it makes us squirm in our seats. This eunuch represents truth in the inner parts.

18. Smith's Bible Dictionary, c 1884, (Madison, WI: Porter and Coates), 235.

"So Hathach went out to Mordecai in the square in front of the palace gate. Mordecai told him the whole story, including the exact amount of money Haman had promised to pay into the royal treasury for the destruction of the Jews. Mordecai gave Hathach a copy of the decree issued in Susa that called for the death of all Jews. He asked Hathach to show it to Esther and explain the situation to her. He also asked Hathach to direct her to go to the king to beg for mercy and plead for her people" (Esther 4:6-8).

Sometimes we just need someone who will tell us the truth—the truth that is written in the text of God's Word. Sometimes we need someone who will show it to us and explain it to us—the whole story, leaving nothing unsaid. Society says truth is whatever you make it to be, but Jesus said He is the Truth, and the truth will set us all free. When we don't receive the truth that God laid out for us in His Word, then we become a people who only listen when our ears are tickled (2 Timothy 4:3).

As you can see, there is more in a name than meets the eye. Names and numbers can be symbolic in the Bible. Each of the eunuchs I covered had a name that qualified them in administering beauty treatments. Now let's look at the ministry of the maidservants.

The Seven Maidservants

The use of the number seven is symbolic throughout the Scriptures, and signifies completion. There are a few different aspects of the number seven which hold special meaning for me.

On July 7, 2007, a group of friends accompanied me on a trip to Nashville, Tennessee to attend "The Call." The Call was a call to fast and pray. It lasted from ten in the morning until ten in the evening. After spending the whole day in prayer and fasting from food, I was given some insight into the life of my children's father. He left me for another woman in 2003. Still, my heart was filled with hope that he would leave her, get his life together, and return to his family. My sister-in-law told me that the news that my husband was in a Christian rehabilitation center during the years I had not heard from him was a lie. The truth

Beauty Treatments

was that he was still with the same woman and they were living it up in Mexico with the insurance money from her dead husband. That night, I cried out to the Lord from the depths of my heart. The pain I felt from accepting the truth about my situation brought me to my knees in the hope that God would rescue me.

That night the Lord answered me, and said in my heart "It is finished." I cannot explain how I felt at that moment; an incredible peace filled my heart as I sensed God releasing me from the soul ties that had held me bound for so long. God gave me a spiritual divorce. It was complete in the Spirit that very moment. Two days later, I received a letter in the mail from a lawyer who had previously denied my request for a divorce because I was not battered at the time of inquiry. In the letter, it said I was approved on some kind of new program that started July 1, and that if I was still interested in getting a divorce then I could come in and file. I did file, and three months later I was divorced by law. No hassles, no battles, just completely divorced. To me, the number seven became symbolic for me on that day.

God created everything in creation during the first six days, and on the seventh day He rested, declaring it was complete.

God said in His Word that the Holy Spirit is sevenfold as well—the sevenfold Spirits who are before His throne (Revelation 1:4-5). Isaiah 11:2 says, "The Spirit of the Lord shall rest upon Him, the Spirit of wisdom and understanding, the Spirit of counsel and might, the Spirit of knowledge and of the fear of the Lord" (NKJV). We can break this down as follows:

1. The Spirit of the Lord
2. The Spirit of Wisdom
3. The Spirit of Understanding
4. The Spirit of Counsel
5. The Spirit of Might
6. The Spirit of Knowledge
7. The Spirit of the Fear of the Lord

Chapter Five: Meet the Eunuchs, Maidservants, and their Ministry

The sevenfold Spirit of God reminds me of the seven maids that were brought in to complete Esther. Esther was not only blessed with the loyal and faithful eunuchs who served the king, but she was also highly favored to have beautiful maidservants that came directly from the palace of the king to help usher her to the throne (Esther 2:14). It was as if Esther had angels by her side at every moment, helping her to make every move that she made.

There are serving angels that have specific purposes. It is my belief that we all have angels that serve us and help move us into our destiny. I once felt the touch of angels when I went camping with some friends. I had decided to leave my troublesome burdens behind and I threw off all my anxieties like so many bad habits. I wanted to focus on my incredibly courageous King instead. We went camping at the Sleeping Bear National Park in Empire, Michigan. Inside the state park they have many sand dunes; one in particular had a 450-foot drop, at its bottom was Lake Michigan. It was an absolutely stunning view. We ran down this amazing dune quite easily; it was almost as if we were jumping in midair as we tumbled down towards the bottom. Once we got down there, the climb back up looked unexpectedly difficult. It was an incredibly steep climb and we knew it was not going to be easy. But it was the only way back up unless we wanted to pay for a helicopter ride, and that was not an option for me and my friends. We began climbing this steep hill, and occasionally I just turned around and rested in the dune as I looked out on the breathtaking view of the lake. My friends were right there alongside me the whole way up; at times I felt like they were angels who helped me climb.

One of them offered me water when I wished I had some with me. About one third of the way up, another friend dug out a seat for me to sit in and rest for a bit. Yet another friend, who had already made it to the top, ran down a second time to check on me and encourage me in my climb. Finally, when I got almost to the top and it felt like I was never going to make it, another friend tried to give me a piggy back ride; although that didn't work, but it was the thought that counted. As I was climbing, I thought of a message I had heard about living in high places. As climbers were going up, they had to be acclimated to positive thinking. They were all on the same rope, and so if anyone was negative, they had to turn around and go back because they were putting everyone else in danger. I realized that altogether, there were seven climbers that surrounded me. These friends of mine were like the seven maids that went with Esther into the best place. My friends were going with me to the best place, the best place in Him. After our climb, we gathered for praise and worship around a campfire and reflected on all of God's beauty.

My best friend, Jodi, was like a ministering angel to me. Before I met Jodi, I would say I had no friends. I went to church and met some great people that helped me through some rough times. They were all great people that I really loved, and those great people I had in my life gave me many blessed opportunities to feel welcomed and appreciated, but I never felt close enough with them to truly share life together. That is, until one day when God sent me an exceptionally good Christian friend. I met Jodi Lubas in a care group at our church for single women. I loved her right away. We had so much in common. Our names were the same, we both had daughters about the same age, we went to the same church, and we both loved Jesus with all our heart. She saw me at church one day. I had been having a rough week, and Jodi invited me to go on a retreat with her; I was ecstatic! I could hardly wait to go. It was a two-hour drive and Jodi and I rode together. I shared my testimony and she told me hers. We knew that we were going to be the best of friends after that. The connection that Jodi and I shared was priceless.

Jodi and I spent six years ministering in our neighborhood outreaches as well as going on missions' trips to New Orleans, Cincinnati, Jamaica, and Albania. We shared sleepovers and girl's nights of giggling and playing board games. We laughed so hard together, and we cried together. Many Wednesday nights were spent praying together on our faces for the retreats. We got mad at each other and then we forgave each other. Jodi's friendship to me was a picture of God's unfailing love. She made me a part of the A.S.K. ministry team. Today I have many friends that I know I can really count on. Jodi was my mentor, my accountability partner, and a friend who spoke the truth to me even if I didn't want to hear it. She was the kind of friend spoken about in Proverbs 27:6: "Wounds from a sincere friend are better than many kisses from an enemy." Jodi did not tickle my ears and allow me to act on emotions. She was a crucial part in my Christian growth, as she encouraged me to stay single. She was an awesome example. She never dated recklessly; instead she chose to wait for eighteen years for the right man. She did not get wrapped up in feel-good relationships. She encouraged me to wait at least one year to be in a relationship after my divorce. It was then that I was inspired to take a year off from my social life and really focus on God and His love and friendship towards me. In that year, I didn't even have much contact with Jodi except when I saw her at church, but I really felt like I needed to get closer to God and have a deeper understanding of Him, so I abandoned all to that calling. I got to know the Lord very personally and felt His friendship towards me was what I needed as I waited for Him to provide me with the friend and companion that I would marry. Jodi was like one of those maidservants who ushered me into the presence of the King.

Jodi was such an incredible support to me in this journey. She was also encouraged by the stand that I took, and one day she called me and told me that she was going to try and do the same fast I was doing, and start journaling everything God would show her too. I told her I believed she was going to have the greatest breakthrough of her life as she hungered for more of Him.

She was a true friend that I could count on and who I could share my life with. She died recently. She wanted to be a friend to a stranger in trouble. As Jodi got out of her car to go and help the stranger, she was struck by an oncoming truck and lost her life in an attempt to save another. I would not expect anything less of my best friend. She was the kind of person who would give you the shirt off her own back, and many testify to her doing so. Jesus said, "There is no greater love than to lay down one's life for one's friends" (John 15:13). Jodi left a legacy of true friendship. She was God's friendship to me through human hands and through human feet.

God also wants to be our friend. He gave His life so we could live. John 15:15-17 says, "I no longer call you slaves, because a master doesn't confide in his slaves. Now you are my friends, since I have told you everything the Father told me. You didn't choose me. I chose you. I appointed you to go and produce lasting fruit, so that the Father will give you whatever you ask for, using my name. This is my command: Love each other."

There are other times when the Lord has used me to help usher my friends into the best place as well—to come alongside them and administer the beauty treatments that I myself have received (2 Corinthians 1:4-5). One day while visiting a friend, I noticed she was really happy to see me and acted differently with me than with her own family. With me she was kind, but with her children she was cold and aloof. She pushed her children away and, out of frustration, she began to give her children dirty looks. Wow, if looks could kill, that surely would have done it. Seconds later, she turned to me with a smile, acting as if nothing ever happened. Has that ever happened to you? Did you feel like you should say something to your friend, and yet thought maybe you should mind your own business?

I wanted to talk to her about it and I hoped that she would receive it. I pondered how I could talk to her about this. My first thought was to just forget about it because she might get upset with me. I was afraid she might think I was judging her or that I didn't really understand what she was going through. But I woke up one morning remembering what great friends I have had, and how none of them were afraid to speak the truth to me, no matter what. They cared about me so much that they wanted to spare me from going down the wrong path that leads to destruction. I knew in my heart that a true friend would tell you the truth, even if it hurt. A false friend will tell you what you want to hear to make you feel better. False gratification is temporary. The truth will set us free to live a life that is pleasing to our Creator; this will give us eternal gratification. The truth that I wanted to tell her was about her response to her family. Don't get me wrong, I had also seen the love and the beautiful bond that she had with her children. I just wanted to point out a common problem in an area in which many parents struggle. Whenever a child is clingy, it is because they do not feel secure, and the worst thing we can do is refuse their hug. Unfortunately, this only causes them to be clingier. A simple hug that lasts five minutes, that says I love and accept you, can save you years of heartache.

Jesus said that you must first remove the plank in your own eye before you can remove the splinter in your brother's eye. So I spoke to her from my own experience—not judging her, but helping her find a way that would benefit their whole family.

I learned this through my clingy child. I had failed in many ways with her, and I am not afraid to admit it because it is an area that I have since received victory over. I am glad that I had friends who helped me to see that I had never really given Victoria the love she needed. I gave the love that I thought she needed when in truth, she needed that extra touch. She needed more than I gave her, so she looked for it in other avenues. Truly, I wish I would have known this when she was younger because I could of saved her from many of the issues that she has faced. Now I understand this. When my boys become clingy, I stop everything I am doing, no matter how pressing; and it doesn't matter if my own relaxation time is interrupted. If I just stop, hold back my irritation, and give them the hug that they need, they are able to go back to their play with the confidence that they are loved. However, if I push them away (which I have done) and yell at them by saying, "Will you stop clinging to me?" or "Leave me alone," I send them the message that they are not loved and that they are a burden to me. This makes them insecure in the relationship; in fact, the reason they are clingy in the first place is because they have lost the security that is found in unconditional love.

In observing my friend with her husband, I loved it when she affirmed him, saying, "Look at my man!" He was glowing when he got that positive affirmation from her. But I also noticed that she had a tendency to belittle him in front of others as well, and I had to tell her that she was cutting him deeply when she joked about him in front of others, especially people he was close to. When I was married, I needed to hear that as well; I was very grateful to my friends for pointing it out to me, thereby helping me to become a better mother, wife, and friend. These friends are the kind of maidservants Esther had.

Even the king had seven wise men (royal officials) who were close to him; if they were close to the king, it is safe to assume they were considered his friends (Esther 1:13-14). I have many acquaintances, but those whom I call friends are the ones I allow so close that they can see my human flaws and still love me.

Since I am fascinated with the meaning of names, I did a word study on each of the names of those closest to the king. It was exciting to see the character of God in each one of them.

Carshena: "illustrious."[19] This spoke of his character and dignity which shone clearly in his actions.

Shethar: "a star."[20] To be named thus, spoke of excellence of character.

Admatha: "given by the highest."[21]

Tarshish: "established."[22]

Meres: "lofty,"[23] which spoke of one who had risen to a great height.

Marsena: "worthy."[24]

Memucan: "dignified."[25] This speaks of someone who is greatly esteemed by his peers.

"These men were seven princes of Persia who were considered 'wise man who knew the times' which saw the king's face and sat first in the kingdom."[26]

In my personal journey, I related these royal officials to the Spirit-filled men and women of God who have mentored me in the faith. Some

19. Smith's Bible Dictionary, c 1884, (Madison, WI: Porter and Coates), 235.
20. Ibid., 619.
21. Ibid., 19.
22. Ibid., 19.
23. Ibid., 398.
24. Ibid., 385.
25. Ibid., 396.
26. Ibid., 619.

of the names of those who have directly impacted my journey are Pastor Chad Gilligan, Pastor Bill McGinnis, Pastor Kelly and Jackie Hartman, Patricia Monahan, Jodi Lubas, James Hooper, William Grassley, Pastor Daniel Martin, Christian Wetzel, Kevin Sardiga, Jimmy White, and Carolyn Bell. These are among those who were close enough to see the real me. Not only that, these were men and women who had the wisdom of God, and in my opinion, were experts in matters of the law of God, justice, and understanding the times.

Everyone needs friends that will serve and help them in their journey to inner beauty. I want to be your friend as well. I want to tell you the truth so that you can be free and experience victory.

Now that we know the king, queen, Mordecai, the eunuchs, and the seven maidservants, let's get to know ourselves a little better as we soak in, and soak up, all the beauty within. We will get to know Haman after we have first dealt with self. There are many beauty treatments in which we will immerse ourselves, but the foundation of all of them is this: God desires to make an exchange with you. You give Him whatever it is you are ashamed of, and He gives you what it is you need the most; and what we need the most is to see ourselves as God sees us. In this way, He is creating for Himself a people who can worship Him in the beauty of holiness. It's really that simple. Instead of _____ (you fill in the blank), God will give you beauty. The more we can look at ourselves and see the beauty of God, the more the world will be able to look at us and see the beauty of Jesus Christ.

Chapter Six: The Beauty Treatments

Treatment 1: A Crucified Life

The Lord inspired me to set aside one year for a purification process. Just as Esther prepared herself for one year for the king, I was purified and made to please the King of Kings. During the year that I had set aside to be beautified from the inside out, the Lord poured out His favor on me as well. It was during this time that He told me that I was chosen to write this book about beauty treatments. The process of building character in my life had started twenty years ago; however, it was now time for me to immerse myself in the beauty treatments that the King was providing for me. This is meant to be literal in my case. The beauty treatments for these women were six months soaking in the oil of myrrh and six months soaking in perfumes and cosmetics. Myrrh was a fragrant gum that was used for embalming, and it was one of the compounds used in the sacred anointing oil in the temple. In my attempt to follow the example of those women of the past, I found some myrrh in a health food store and I made up some of my own bath salts, using myrrh and a couple of other fragrances. Symbolically speaking, myrrh signified death. It became clear to me that there were areas in my life that had not been surrendered to the Lord. I needed to die daily to the desires of my sinful nature; this turned out to be my first beauty treatment—that my flesh life be crucified so that I might have the King's life instead.

I began a fast. Fasting is the best way to crucify the flesh life because food is more appealing to the natural eye than any other thing. I fasted every other day for the entire year, making it a six-month fast from food. On the days I fasted, I was given "special food" from the Scriptures; it became my manna (an Old Testament word for bread) for the day. It was truly a fast that God ordained for me because He sustained me for the entire fast, and not once did I slip. There were moments in which I was tempted to eat a wonderful home cooked meal, but no temptation seized me except that which is common to man. And God provided for me a way to escape temptation and focus on Him. At this point in my life, I wanted more of God, more than I wanted food. I wanted to be fed living Bread—true Bread from heaven. The true Bread gives life to the world (John 6:32-35).

The Lord impressed it upon my heart to keep a journal of all that He was feeding me. Everything He told me would be very significant for His plan and purpose in my life. This journey of death to self in my life would prove to be beneficial to me and everyone around me. The New Testament equivalent of death is repentance, brokenness, and humility before the Lord; it is where the Lord increases in our Spirit life and we decrease in our sinful nature. In 1 Corinthians 1:29, the NKJV says, "That no flesh should glory in his presence."

If there is flesh present when the glory of God is revealed, it will have to be dead flesh, because nothing can live in His presence. Only dead men can truly see His face. Our flesh life must die in His presence. Our flesh holds us back from the glory of God. The eternal part of our being desires, and can, live forever in His presence; but only when the flesh inside of you and me has decreased, just as John the Baptist said of Jesus.

"John replied, 'No one can receive anything unless God gives it from heaven. You yourselves know how plainly I told you, "I am not the Messiah. I am only here to prepare the way for him." It is the bridegroom who marries the bride, and the best man is simply glad to stand with him and hear his vows. Therefore, I am filled with joy at his success. He must become greater and greater, and I must become less and less'" (John 3:27-30).

Chapter Six: The Beauty Treatments

Let me repeat that in case you missed it the first time. "He must become great, but I must become less."

The King is in search of a people that will run after His heart and scream "not my will, but Your will, oh, Lord." This breakthrough only comes to broken people who are not pursuing their own ambition, but who are wholeheartedly running after the purposes of God. I'm sure Esther had many desires of her own, and I could also bet that she never imagined that she would be taken captive by the king's men. I can picture her as a young woman already planning out her fairy tale wedding, and suddenly she is faced with a choice in her attitude. She is left to embrace the change or become bitter in the ordeal. Since she immediately won the eunuchs favor, I can only assume that Esther was one who chose to embrace her future in being left in the hands of the king.

We do not know what our futures hold for us, but our heavenly King knows it all and has it all planned out. I willfully laid my life down; and all my dreams and ambitions of having a godly husband were crucified at the altar of sacrifice, the outcome of which only God Himself knew. It is my prayer, that by my testimony and by the blood of the Lamb, you may come to know the King and that you might have life and life abundantly in and through Him. However, in order to know His resurrected life, we must also taste of the suffering in His death. "And they have defeated him by the blood of the Lamb and by their testimony. And they did not love their lives so much that they were afraid to die" (Revelation 12:11).

In the book of Genesis, my attention was drawn to the land of Havilah; so I did a little research on the name. There was a river that flowed from the land of Eden; it was divided into four branches. The first branch flowed around the entire land of Havilah, where gold was found. The gold of that land was exceptionally pure; aromatic resin and onyx stone were also found there (Genesis 2:10-12). I found it interesting that the land the rivers ran through was called Havilah, a name derived from the a word meaning "that suffers pain" and "that brings forth,"[27] because throughout God's Word I saw that suffering

27. The Net Bible Study Dictionary Online, http://classic.net.bible.org/dictionary. php?word=Havilah (accessed April 22, 2013). Used by permission.

or refinement always brought forth precious jewels. Gold and incense are symbolic for the prayers of the saints. Myrrh, which is an aromatic resin, represents the death of self and has a correlation to the refiner's fire which purifies gold and other precious gems with which we are spiritually adorned. We have the image of God living in us—He came and made His dwelling among us and we are the eternal beings that He created. We were there in Eden (Ezekiel 28:13) and now we are seated in the heavenly realms with Him as well (Ephesians 2:4). I have suffered much this past year, but I believe the next year will bring forth the riches of His glorious inheritance. I looked back and examined my life to see how I fared through the refinement process, through suffering, so that God could bring forth the rare jewel that I was born to be. Those of us who have tasted suffering of any kind know that it is only temporary. We are diamonds in the rough, and through our hardships, He polishes us up for His purposes.

The beauty of the Lord is not comparable to any other. He is incredibly beautiful and marvelous in all He does. Only He has the sovereign power and anointing to bestow a crown of beauty on those He chooses. God's plan is to plant us in Him. It is only in Him that we can start the process of His beauty treatments. These treatments may be painful because it hurts to die to self, and there is no anesthesia to numb the pain. It is drastic soul surgery. However, God wants us to allow our pain and hurts to rise so He can comfort and heal. He administers these treatments according to His loving kindness. He will not treat more than one ailment at a time. He is patient; it is His job as the Great Physician to bring about His desired effect.

Beauty treatments begin by laying our lives down for the King of Kings, and Lord of Lords. If you want to see a crown of beauty instead of ashes in your life, please permit the Anointed One to deal with every part of your heart. Allow Him to put all the broken pieces back together again. Consent to the Spirit of God's power to set you free from captivity, and allow Him to bring you into the Light where everything is exposed and nothing is hidden. He will provide for you and you will see the beauty He has placed in you. You, beloved, are beautiful! You are fearfully and wonderfully created for a purpose.

My prayer throughout the year was "Find it; expose it; kill it. Crucify everything in me that is not of You." I hope you have made that your prayer as well. Your beauty treatments have begun.

Treatment 2: His Branding

The next treatment for me dealt strongly with understanding the difference between outward and inward beauty. I am an attractive woman outwardly; unfortunately I have used my beauty for my earthly advantage. Killing this area in my life was my heartfelt prayer. I was convicted in my spirit about using my outward beauty to sway men, to make them like me, and pursue me. I decided that I needed a change. I asked God to give me a beauty treatment that would make me feel beautiful on the inside. I quickly learned that it was not going to be a pretty process, as the Lord called for a refiner to burn that sin out of me. Not literally of course. As I told you before, I am talking spiritually, so picture the blacksmith at work. He takes a tool and works with it in the coals. The hot coals came in the form of hardship for me. He will begin with a blazing fire—hot enough to soften and refine metal. He sits like a refiner of silver, burning away the impurity. God will purify me and refine me like gold and silver (Malachi 3:2-3).

When I first heard the word "branding," I thought of how cattle herders take a hot iron and burn a mark into the cattle as a sign of ownership. The world tries to place its mark on us from birth too.

Paul reminds us in Acts that we must go through many hardships to enter the kingdom of God (Acts 14:22). No one likes hardship or pain. I will be the first to tell you that I have not had an easy road, and I am sure that I am not alone. There is a lot of pain in this world. My mother left home when I was seven, leaving me to help raise my younger siblings, and thereby forcing me to abandon the little girl that I wanted to be. I had to be the mom, and I just wasn't ready. The rejection that I felt of growing up without a mom scarred me for most of my life. I took on the label. I became everyone's mom. I got real good at taking care of everyone but, of course, myself. The pressure became unbearable to take care of everyone, and drugs became my escape. Drugs led to sex, and sex led to shame. I wanted attention. I wore short skirts and low halter tops. I put on makeup and curled my hair. I put on high heels, as uncomfortable as they were, and I got attention. I had a nice shape. I was lovely in form and feature. I was raped. I was molested by my stepfather. I was marked with a deep scar. Now, taking on yet another label in my life, I was known as promiscuous and easy. Anyone could walk all over me, and I didn't have the courage or the know-how to get out of it. I thought, "This is who I am and this is who I will always be so live with it." I lived with the pain of being used and abused. Living with the thought that I would never have a good guy, because I was not a good girl, was also something that branded me for most of my young life. I didn't have hope and didn't know that the one who created me was there with me through it all. So why didn't He stop it? Why did He allow those men to continuously scar me with abuse into adulthood?

Jesus was there, even if I didn't know it. He had an answer to give me when I sought Him out and asked Him those hard questions. He said to me, "If any nation comes to fight you, it is not because I sent them. Whoever attacks you will go down in defeat. 'I have created the blacksmith who fans the coals beneath the forge and makes the weapons of destruction. And I have created the armies that destroy. But in that coming day no weapon turned against you will succeed. You will silence every voice raised up to accuse you. These benefits are enjoyed by the servants of the Lord; their vindication will come from me. I, the Lord, have spoken!'" (Isaiah 54:15-17).

He continued to comfort me with the following verses:

"Can anything ever separate us from Christ's love? Does it mean he no longer loves us if we have trouble or calamity, or are persecuted, or hungry, or destitute, or in danger, or threatened with death? (As the Scriptures say, 'For your sake we are killed every day; we are being slaughtered like sheep.') No, despite all these things, overwhelming victory is ours through Christ, who loved us. And I am convinced that nothing can ever separate us from God's love. Neither death nor life, neither angels nor demons, neither our fears for today nor our worries about tomorrow—not even the powers of hell can separate us from God's love. No power in the sky above or in the earth below—indeed, nothing in all creation will ever be able to separate us from the love of God that is revealed in Christ Jesus our Lord" (Romans 8:35-39).

God started to change my perspective on my identity. I started to see clearly that I was a new creation. I was forgiven. I was predestined to be conformed to the likeness of His Son. My scars began to heal, but it was painful for the Lord to bring those willfully hidden hurts to the surface because I had buried the root of the way I behaved. Now that I was a Christian, I wasn't sleeping around anymore. I wasn't using drugs. I had found freedom from smoking and drinking. He had changed the way I spoke and looked. Basically, I was cleaned up on the outside. Outwardly, I was a white-washed tomb. Uh-oh! Inwardly, I needed a deep cleansing scrub. The Lord had beauty in mind for me—a beauty I could recognize and, most importantly, a beauty the world could recognize. But before He could give me that beauty, He needed to treat my heart. My heart had to undergo surgery. To do this, the Lord did some personal branding, burning away the sin in me. "And so it shall be: Instead of a sweet smell there will be a stench; instead of a sash, a rope; instead of well-set hair, baldness; instead of a rich robe, a girding of sackcloth; and branding instead of beauty" (Isaiah 3:24 NKJV).

My heart agonized over all the sin that had taken root in my heart. There was a godly sorrow that brought about repentance in me. The secret things of my heart were being revealed. The Lord showed me that my heart was still very much wrapped around desiring man's approval and winning the attention of man. This verse in Ezekiel brought about quite a stab of conviction:

"And so you were adorned with gold and silver. Your clothes were made of fine linen and were beautifully embroidered. You ate the finest foods—choice flour, honey, and olive oil—and became more beautiful than ever. You looked like a queen, and so you were! Your fame soon spread throughout the world because of your beauty. I dressed you in my splendor and perfected your beauty, says the Sovereign Lord. 'But you thought your fame and beauty were your own. So you gave yourself as a prostitute to every man who came along. Your beauty was theirs for the asking'" (Ezekiel 16:13-15).

In addition to cleansing me from the past, the Lord was also working preventive measures within me for my future. During this year of consecration, the Lord made me beautiful inwardly. I believe I will have success in all that the Lord has done in my life. He has made me His own and I am His. This beauty is for His glory and not for anyone else. I wanted to make a covenant with the Lord just as Abraham did. You know how the story goes—the sign of the contract between Abraham, the Patriarch of Israel and God was the rite of circumcision, a type of branding.

"You [God was speaking to Abraham] must cut off the flesh of your foreskin as a sign of the covenant between me and you" (Genesis 17:11).

"Circumcision was a sign that Abraham already had faith and that God had already accepted him and declared him to be righteous—even before he was circumcised. So Abraham is the spiritual father of those who have faith but have not been circumcised. They are counted as righteous because of their faith" (Romans 4:11).

Even though I did not literally have an actual mark like a tattoo, and thankfully I didn't have to be circumcised, I still had to undergo the circumcision of the heart; and that is what counts to God. "It doesn't matter whether we have been circumcised or not. What counts is whether we have been transformed into a new creation" (Galatians 6:15). (Also Philippians 3:3 and Galatians 5:6.)

114

Chapter Six: The Beauty Treatments

The faith that I had in what the Lord had done in my heart as well as in what He was continuing to do in me expressed itself in outward ways too. Because He loved me and I felt His love, I wanted to outwardly show my love to the Lord, just as I had outwardly shown my affection to men in the past. During my year of consecration, I did not wear any makeup. I put my hair in a ponytail while in public to let the world know that I was unavailable. I did not dress up nor wear jewelry. I gave no attention to my outward appearance at all. I focused solely on what the Lord was doing within me. I exchanged outward adornment for an unfading and priceless inward beauty, a prize of great value.

"Don't be concerned about the outward beauty of fancy hairstyles, expensive jewelry, or beautiful clothes. You should clothe yourselves instead with the beauty that comes from within, the unfading beauty of a gentle and quiet spirit, which is so precious to God. This is how the holy women of old made themselves beautiful. They trusted God and accepted the authority of their husbands" (1 Peter 3:3-5).

God's circumcision, His branding made me completely aware of who I used to be and who I was in Christ. It reminded me of where I came from, so that I might not forget the circumcision I have in Christ.

When hardship and suffering comes—because it comes to everyone regardless of who you are—we sometimes allow the hardship to harden our hearts. When this occurs, the refining process actually takes longer than it should because a hardened heart needs to go through more havoc in order to make it soft and pliable and easier to work with.

I think of the story when the Israelites were freed from the slavery of the Egyptians. We were also freed from the slavery of sin. However, they still needed to journey through the desert (wilderness living is hard!) in order to get to the Promised Land, the land of identification for every believer. The Bible says that it was an eleven-day journey, but it took them forty years! We can allow the cross to do its work in us and crucify all our fleshly desires in a shorter time as well. In studying the example of the Israelites, we learn that it took them a lot longer because they complained all the way there. Because of their complaining and grumbling, many of them never could enter the rest of His promises. One reason they did this was that they failed to identify themselves as children of the Almighty. They had their minds stuck on slavery, and what it was like before they were freed. They refused to be healed in their minds from the branding of the Egyptians. The Israelites were God's chosen people, and yet they still felt like slaves.

I have a very dear friend who is very precious to me. We have shared much in life together and grown through many experiences, both wonderful and tragic. We have loved and laughed, fought and forgiven, bewildered one another and yet always believed in each other too. She is someone in whom I have always managed to see the face of God, even though, I must admit, at times I had to strain my eyes pretty hard to see Him there. She is the kind of friend it would be easy to lay your life down for, and one whom I wish I could have sheltered from many storms in life, even though I failed to do so when given the opportunity. I always saw her as valuable; however, she failed to see it herself because she had been lied to about her identity for so long. She was a teenager who gave herself away too soon, and she became pregnant. When she told her dad about her pregnancy, he called her a whore and agreed with the father of the child that abortion would be the best thing. He had no hope for his daughter. How could he when he himself had violated her as a child? As a nine-year old child, her dad saw her as a goddess, in part because of the drugs that he was using. He caressed her body, and rubbed himself against her. For two long years, this girl remained quiet as her father continued to sexually abuse her, leaving the mark that sex was what she was made for. That was her only way of making her dad happy; therefore as she grew older, she gave herself away to any boy that paid her any attention. She gave herself over to many abusive relationships, and then she became pregnant with a man who wanted nothing to do with the child.

Personally, I had high hopes for the child in her womb. I knew that there was greatness in her womb because there was such an intense struggle to destroy this child. Just as the enemy tried to destroy the seed that would birth the Messiah, so too the enemy was trying to destroy the child that was inside this mother. She really had the potential of being a good mother, and even though I knew that her road would be hard, I knew that she could learn to trust the Lord through it. However, as many women do, she decided to believe the lies her earthly dad told her, and she went through with the abortion. To this day, that decision still weighs heavy upon her heart. She refuses to hear the truth that God says about her, and her identity is still branded by the past. God wants us to live in the present, not in the past.

When we become new creations and old things pass away, that does not include hardships. Hardships will not pass away. I am not sugarcoating this at all. We still have to go through the desert. We still have to endure the sufferings. As Christians, we need to understand and believe that what we perceive as suffering is not always a bad thing. Paul even said "for to me to live is Christ, and to die is gain" (Philippians 1:21 NKJV).

One day my ex-husband decided, after a two-year affair, that he was leaving me and our three children for the other woman. We were left homeless because I was going to school full time and doing a work study program; there was simply not enough money to support us. I had already gone through so many hardships by this point in my life that I knew it was now time to put all that "trust in the Lord" talk into action. I decided I would not complain at all as I had in the past. I made up my mind that I was going to rejoice in everything that came my way. And I was put to the test. After getting evicted, a dear lady from my church who had also adopted three others, adopted my family as well and allowed us to move into her home. All of our belongings were placed in an empty warehouse belonging to another dear family in our church. The very next day, I was in a car accident which totaled our car. Things were not easy at this point, yet I kept rejoicing.

I decided I had done enough complaining in my life. After about three months of sharing a small room with my children, I knew I had to take some kind of action. This friend suggested that we ask the church to help us build onto the house and to our amazement, the church invited us to live in the mission home they provided for missionaries while home in the states instead. We were able to stay there until the government could help me with housing. Finally, the day came when I got the call about our new home. We were able to move into the government housing rent free for two years because we were homeless. The Lord was really taking care of us. I went to get all my belongings from the warehouse where they had been stored away for eight months, and lo and behold, my things had been destroyed by raccoons. Some may have cried and complained in that circumstance, but I did not. I chose instead to allow this hardship to shape me for the better.

People want something to believe in, whether it's family, a set of values, or some passion they can pursue. Your beauty treatment begins when you start taking a long, honest, and serious look into yourself—one that reveals the often hidden truths about your personality, your character, and the values that drive you.

The cross is what drove me to change; the cross was the branding of my heart and soul. It was at the cross where I first saw the light, the place where I found forgiveness of my sins. It was also the place where I found my identity. The cross is the branding for every believer and it identifies us as a new creation. When we come to realize that the cross is meant for us to bear, but not bear alone, we can then experience the wonder of resurrection. Suffering and hardship are good for us, whether we admit it or not.

Some people believe that Christ Himself bore that cross so that we would never have to, and that the cross we are to bear is something else entirely. It is true that He Himself bore the penalty for our sin, but it does not mean that we are not meant to walk the walk that He walked. Jesus Himself said to all: "If you do not carry your own cross and follow me, you cannot be my disciple" (Luke 14:27).

The cross is a place where the shaping of your heart takes place. Yet, for many people, it is also a place they struggle, or even refuse, to put their trust in. You cannot see it; how can you put your trust in something you cannot see or feel? This is why He tells His children that they must walk by faith and not by sight.

If you are a child of God, then you belong to God and you are chosen. He owns us and He places His mark, or His seal, on us as His very own treasured possession. "He has identified us as his own by placing the Holy Spirit in our hearts as the first installment that guarantees everything he has promised us" (2 Corinthians 1:22).

Treatment 3: Simplicity

Why do we need a beauty treatment of simplicity? Because our culture has made life so multifaceted that we need to slow down, rest, and trust the simplicity of our Maker. You have to admit that even the church has made the gospel of Jesus Christ seem complex. It was never intended to be as complex as religion as made it. Do this, and do that.

Don't get me wrong—we are to serve. Jesus came to serve, not to be served. But there is more on the topic of "rest" in the Bible than there is about serving the church. I have been involved in women's ministry, children's ministry, retreat ministry, evangelism, missions trips, greeting team, and even the janitorial team. However, none of those ministries are more important to God than us spending time in rest with Jesus. It is in these times of quiet intimacy with Christ that our spirits are refreshed and renewed—the fruit of this time is the gift we receive from God to share and minister unto others. For though it is imperative that we give unto others, how can we give if we have not first received ourselves? And how can we possibly receive if we don't value and honor the importance of sitting at the Master's feet and abiding in His presence? This principle is set forth wonderfully in Luke 10. Jesus had arrived as a guest at the home of some friends. Amid the flurry of activities going on, a woman named Martha was busy getting things in place to serve a feast. Martha had a plan, and she was determined to make it happen, no matter how many people she needed to help her.

119

One of those she had her eye on was her sister, Mary, and yet there Mary was, slacking off with the company while Martha did all the work. I am sure that Martha truly was anointed and given the unction to be an excellent host. The problem for her was that, at that moment, Mary was also anointed to simply rest at Jesus' feet and listen to Him a little. To Martha, that was not nearly as important as what she needed done. And that's the way it often is when someone's all fired up with the Holy Ghost and seeking to do great things for the glory of God. We tend to forget that there are always a lot of other equally important things going on as well. And if we "Marthas" had our way, there would literally be too many cooks in the kitchen. Jesus might end up all alone, talking to Himself! But Jesus, ever the lover of our souls, gently acknowledged Martha and all that she was so sincerely trying to do. However, He also made sure she understood that He was pleased with Mary and their time together, and that He would not let that be taken from her. May our hearts never fail to grasp the importance of this lesson.

The church, the bride of Christ, has become so concerned with how the church looks on the outside of the building that we have lost touch with what is better. Simplicity is having freedom from pretense or false show. The church is in need of simplicity now more than ever as our culture tries to force us to conform to the vanity of this world. It almost seems like we have to compete for who has the better building, or who works harder, because special acknowledgements only go to those people who are seen working or serving. And when all our time is focused on the outside, the inside is left to crumble. Families fall apart, leading to communities falling apart, and finally the nation falls. The ones who are living the life of simplicity are the ones that stay together.

Jesus went with Peter, James, and John to the olive grove called Gethsemane, and He said to them, "Sit here while I go over there to pray" (Matthew 26:36).

The best explanation I have ever read concerning rest was in a devotional compiled by Mrs. Charles Cowman:

"In the Garden of Gethsemane, eight of the eleven disciples were left in the garden to do absolutely nothing. Jesus went to

120

the front to pray; Peter, James and John went to the middle to watch; the rest sat down in the rear to wait. Methinks that party in the rear must have murmured. They were in the garden, but that was all; they had no share in the cultivation of its flowers. It was a time of crisis, a time of storm and stress; and yet they were not suffered to work."[28]

I knew that experience well, that disappointment of not being involved, especially during my sabbatical. There were a great many opportunities for Christian service, whether through my community, A.S.K. Ministries, in which I had heavily been involved, and even the ministries that were planned from my church, and I was not moved. However, some are sent to the frontlines, some sent to the middle, and some are made to lie down in the back. The author of the devotional continues to say:

"We do not see why we should be excluded from a part in the Christian life. It seems like an unjust thing that, seeing we have been allowed to enter the garden, no path should be assigned to us there.

"Be still, my soul, it is not as thou deemest! Thou art not excluded from a part of the Christian life. Thinkest thou that the garden of the Lord has only a place for those who walk and for those who stand! Nay, it has also a spot consecrated to those who are compelled to *sit*.

"There are three voices in a verb—active, passive and neuter. So, too, there are three voices in Christ's verb 'to live.' There are the active, watching souls, who go to the front, and struggle till the breaking of the day. There are the passive, watching souls, who stand in the middle, and report to others the progress of the fight. But there are also the neuter souls—those who can neither fight nor be spectators of the fight, but have simply to lie down.

---

28. Mrs. Charles E. Cowman, *Streams in the Desert* (Cowman Publications, Inc., 1925), 371, public domain.

"When that experience comes to us, remember, thou are not shunted [moved]. Remember it is *Christ* that says, 'Sit ye here.' *Thy* spot in the garden has also been consecrated. It has a special name. It is not "the place of wrestling," nor "the place of watching," but "the place of waiting." There are lives that come into this world neither to do great work nor to bear great burdens, but simply to be; they are the neuter verbs. They are the flowers of the garden which have had no active mission. They have wreathed no chaplet; they have graced no table; they have escaped the eye of Peter and James and John. But they have gladdened the sight of *Jesus*. By their mere perfume, by their mere beauty, they have brought Him joy; by the very preservation of their loveliness in the valley they have lifted the Master's heart. We need not murmur if we are one of those flowers!" [29]

For most of those in the enclosed garden of the King's palace, there will be seasons of change. There will be moments of action, moments of watching, and moments where you must be still. We don't just stay still though. I want to clarify this so that it is not thought that we always lie down and do nothing. For me, the Lord set aside a whole year for me to lie down and do nothing of seeming importance. I still took care of the needs of my family, but I rested in being united with Christ and believing who He said I was. The time would be sure to come when I would "Go into all the world and preach the Good News to everyone," (Mark 16:15) but for a time there were no outreaches, no ministering to the lost, no important missions trips or missions projects, just cleaning the toilets on Sunday mornings. Sitting still, lying down, doing nothing that looked important and resting in His promises has taught me the simplicity of who God says He is, and who God says I am. Like a fragrant flower that does absolutely nothing, yet radiates the beauty of its Maker, or a diamond that is fit for a King and yet cannot make itself shine, so did I discover that the greatest gift I had to offer God was to simply receive from Him the grace I needed to become who He had created me to be.

---

29. Mrs. Charles E. Cowman, *Streams in the Desert* (Cowman Publications, Inc., 1925), 371, public domain.

Simplicity is not striving to be, but resting in who God called you to be. Laziness is not the same as resting in simplicity. There is a job for each one of us. And the King desires that we do our jobs with excellence and in a diligent manner, leaving the outcome and results to Him.

The woman described in Proverbs 31 is the kind of believer that every woman should desire to be: she is a woman of action because she is clothed with (His) strength and dignity; she can laugh at the days to come because she rests in knowing He has her future in His hands. She is a woman that humbly fears the Lord. When we fear the Lord, we are simply resting in His sovereignty. We, as mothers and wives, should take care of the possible, or simple, things and trust God for the impossible, or the complex, things.

Simply put, my part is to love and express love in tangible ways. It is my responsibility to pray in faith without ceasing. It is in my power to enjoy being the mother that God called me to be. I am to provide a warm, happy home for them, and I am to minister to my children's physical and emotional needs as I am able. That is the beauty of simplicity. It is not our responsibility to take on the burden of the impossible. For example, it is impossible for us to create a hunger and thirst for righteousness, or to bring about the conviction of sin. We cannot convert our children. We cannot bring them to the place of total commitment. It is God's job to show us who we really are, and it is His job to continually fill us with His Holy Spirit for our sanctification and His service. There have been so many times when I have made a mountain out of a mole hill; in every case my perspective made everything more complex than it really was.

When we do not integrate rest into our life, we are in sin. We become exhausted. We begin to do things in our own strength. That is why God commanded us to rest. Rest is important as He prepares to move us to conquer the areas in our lives that don't please Him.

Prepare for rest and set aside time devoted to being still and quiet before the Lord. Prepare your family for it as well. Don't let the busyness of today take the simplicity out of your life. You have choices—make the best choice to determine that you will be simple. Rest needs to be prioritized if you want to gain God's simplicity in your life. If you have to schedule it in, then do it; and do it for your family too. What a blessing it will be to them.

There were many times in my search for inner beauty that I tried to be the person who I thought someone else wanted me to be. There were people who loved me so much that they hated to see me suffer as a single mom. They tried to persuade me to go out and get a job. They didn't like the fact that I decided to homeschool and be a stay-at-home mom. They felt I needed to do something "better" with my life and with my degree. I built up quite a portfolio as a computer programmer. And many times, I wondered if they were right. Many days in my journals were filled with the mundane. From the day-to-day of homeschooling my children, to the places we went, to the things we did—it all seemed so monotonous. However, reading back through my journals, I noticed that I was constantly reminding myself to be where Christ is, where my desires lined up with His, and this was where He was. His cloud rested upon my home.

My children were used by God in this season of simplicity to speak to me as well. For example, one day I was in a hurry—I am always in a hurry. I was in the car, and said, "Come on, Isaac, what is taking you so long?" Daniel calmly, and with authority from the Holy Spirit, said to me, "It's okay, Mom, be patient; just slow down." I knew that the Almighty God was speaking through him, and that gave me peace to just take my time the rest of that day. I cannot promise that I changed from that day, because I am still usually in a hurry even when I do not have a time frame, but the Lord is at work in me to still me and help me to pace my life in a way that brings Him glory.

During this time, Pastor Bill from Calvary Assembly of God spoke about who was the greatest in the kingdom:

"The disciple's question revealed a serious misconception about the kingdom of heaven. They assumed God's kingdom would be like any other kingdom on earth—one in which rank, status, power, and authority were the marks of greatness. However, Jesus corrected this error by asking them the question, 'Who is the greatest in the kingdom of heaven?'(Matthew 18:1-9) The fact that Jesus had been sharing with the disciples the truth about His coming suffering and death did not affect them. They were thinking only of themselves and what position they would have in His kingdom. So absorbed were the disciples in this matter that they actually argued with each other. The selfishness and disunity of God's people is a scandal to the Christian faith. What causes these problems? Pride—thinking ourselves more important than we really are. It was pride that led men into sin at the beginning. When Christians are living for themselves and not for others, there is bound to be conflict and division. The disciples waited breathlessly for Jesus to name the greatest man among them. But He bypassed them completely and called a little child into their midst. This child was the example of true greatness. Jesus' response to the disciples showed how selfish and foolish their question was. They were thinking childishly, but Jesus showed them that mature faith is the opposite. Mature faith is a childlike humility. The more mature a disciple's faith becomes, the more brotherly kindness and love it demonstrates. Jesus was not rejecting the positive aspects of adulthood, but the self-sufficiency, pride, sophisticated denial, and self-deception that are learned with years of practice in a sinful world. At the root of true maturity is simplicity, not sophistication."[30]

Simplicity is humble acceptance. It means avoiding two extremes: thinking less of yourself than you ought, or thinking more of yourself than you ought.

True humility means knowing yourself, accepting yourself, and being yourself—your best self to the glory of God. The truly humble person does not deny the gifts God has given him, but uses them to glorify God. An unspoiled child has the characteristics that make for simple humility: trust, dependence, the desire to make others happy, and an absence of boasting or selfish desire to be greater than others. The person who comes to Jesus in simple humility, recognizing Jesus' beauty and His own lowliness, is the most beautiful in God's kingdom.

True beauty is a matter of inward spirit and heart. Inner beauty is best seen in the person who expresses his or her love for Christ in sincere humility, in a desire to serve both God and man, and in a

30. Bill McGinnis; message was preached on 6-18-08.

willingness to be seen as the least important in God's kingdom. We must understand that to be beautiful and great is not found in position, office, leadership, power, influence, academic degrees, fame, ability, great accomplishments, or success. It is not so much what we do for God, as it is who we are in spirit before Him. True beauty requires that we become beautiful in the right areas. We need to learn His beauty in faith, humility, godly character, wisdom, self-control, patience and love. It is to have the beauty of Christ, who loved righteousness and hated wickedness. True beauty is a matter of heartfelt love for, and commitment to, God. It requires being consecrated and faithful wherever God chooses to place us. Consecration will improve your results in God's work, but only in that area in which God has placed you and in the context of the gifts He has given you.

There was a struggle within me as I knew that, with my credentials and experience in the computer industry, I could easily find a job, and become self-sufficient; I could care for the needs of my household, and work my way up the career ladder, and become successful in the eyes of the world. However, through my time with the Lord, He has revealed to me a greater and more beautiful plan for my life. He has called me to be a servant who knows simplicity. He will be the One who cares for me and my children as we serve in whatever capacity He desires. As a simple servant, we become like children who are depending on our Daddy to provide all our needs. It is as simple as that. It is time we get back to simplicity in life. That is truly beautiful.

Treatment 4: Silence

This is the beauty treatment that touches our mouth and our ears. Forget the lipstick and the gloss that brings shine to the lips, because it doesn't matter how much gloss we wear if our breath stinks. Instead, get out the mouthwash and the floss to get rid of the ugly plaque of bacteria that has been building up over the years.

Chapter Six: The Beauty Treatments

It was my desire to cultivate the same character in my heart that Esther had in being able to restrain herself, to contain the fire within her bones. This was definitely an area that needed a change in me. In fact, this may be an ongoing process in the Lord for me. I have such a hard time controlling the excitement that I feel in my bones.

There were many times in that year, and even now as I write this, that God the Holy Spirit has given me a word in due season, but not the permission to share that word with anyone else. I had to learn the hard way that when God spoke a word to me, He didn't necessarily want me to repeat it to anyone else. I've discovered the wisdom of keeping a thing hidden until He decides whether or not to reveal it. I say the hard way because I am just not one to keep silent, and that sometimes is not a good thing. There is a natural excitement that runs through my bones when I receive revelation from God. It's like a fire that is hard to contain. I want to shout it out, almost immediately after I have learned something. In fact, there were many in my circle of friends that have heard this book in pieces long before it was printed.

Recently, a friend of mine called me after six months of no communication and said she had seen me in a dream. In the dream, I was on a train, or some kind of vehicle, and persuading everyone to jump on with me. I was so excited and focused on getting everyone on the train with me, that I lost focus on my destination and crashed. She prayed for an interpretation, and said, "Jodie, honey, you are so zealous, and have more excitement than I have ever seen in anyone, but your zeal can sometimes be without knowledge." She was used by the Holy Spirit to teach me that knowing the right time to reveal what God has shown me will keep me and the people I lead safe from crashing—not literally of course. I found out that when I released the word I felt was from God before the proper time, I was not completely prepared for the backlash. My words were misunderstood and twisted. This caused division, and where there is division, there is no power. The word that was spoken to me lost the power that it would have had, had it been contained and prayed over, and prepared through time. It was like the bad breath you have in the morning when you turn and say good morning before brushing your teeth; no one likes that. And so I have learned. Mordecai must have learned that too as he was taken into exile and saw firsthand what happens when we speak too quickly; he instructed Hadassah from his own experience.

Esther revealed her identity as a Jewish girl at the right time. As Mordecai instructed her, she kept her nationality a secret until the time came for her to save herself and her people. If she had revealed her identity before she was chosen to be queen, the story may not have been written. The glorious anointing of her words—spoken at the proper time—kept the queen and her people safe. When it came time for her to reveal her identity, she was prepared to do so. She and her people fasted for three days, and the Lord built courage in her to reveal the truth—the truth that set her people free.

It was the same for me. God exchanged His beauty of silent restraint for my overzealous state. With that bit in my mouth, I am able to live freely within His limits. Esther lived within limits and showed amazing verbal restraint as an example to us of the character God desires in each of us so that we can be His effective mouthpieces at the right time.

Early in my journey, my excitement was intense and hard for me to contain. I wanted to tell the world all the Lord was sharing with me. I learned a lesson from this.

A friend rebuked me (gave me some mouthwash) and told me that I should not be sharing my treasures from the Lord with everyone so quickly. I spoke too rashly, she said. If you were married, your husband would want to know that he could trust you if he shared his heart with you, she continued. He would want to know that whatever he told you would not also be shared with all your closest friends. He would want to have full confidence in you. Only then would He reveal the hidden things of his heart with you. So it is with our heavenly King, or Husband; if He shares a word with us, He wants to be able to trust us with that word. Our King might allow us to reveal it in His time, or He may want to keep it hidden. Can He trust us with His word?

She was right, and I thanked her for being an example of one who kept the hidden mysteries of God. God would reveal the hidden things in His time for everything that is hidden comes to the light. But sometimes the hidden things are hidden because we are not ready for those mysteries yet.

The Lord gave me the analogy of an eagle—the eagle digests its food quite slowly. It chews, and it chews and then, after digesting the food, it regurgitates the food and feeds it to its young. The Lord showed me that this was an area in which I needed Him to work on. He wanted me to be silent and hold on to His treasure, His knowledge for the whole year, to really meditate on it myself. A misconception I had was that, in order to get it into my spirit, I needed to tell everyone. But that wasn't true because the more I spoke the word prematurely, the more I lost in the process. The Lord was feeding me and I was digesting some; but before letting it sit in my spirit, I would tell the world and the birds of the air (the enemy) would come and take it from my memory. Much of the time that I thought I had written a great deal about what the Lord was teaching me, I really hadn't. Going through my journals, I couldn't help noticing all the times the pages were bereft of real food. This might be why I wasn't able to complete the book in one year as I had anticipated. Nevertheless, His timing is perfect. Now that I have truly digested the words He fed into my soul, I can regurgitate them and feed them to others.

Gingivitis is an inflammation of the gums. When I think of gingivitis in the spiritual sense, I think of gossip. When someone gossips, they are inflamed with a desire to spread the germs, or spread the news. Gingivitis is an infection that destroys the tissues that support the teeth. Likewise, gossip is an infection that destroys the support system that you have. It ruins and separates close friendships. The cure is a deep cleansing of God's Word. God, in His beauty, is completely trustworthy; He wants to exchange the spirit of gossip for His trustworthiness so we can be like Him.

My poor spiritual oral hygiene was exposed once when a friend approached me about breaking a confidence. I call it the tartar of mistrust. My heart was exposed; I realized that this was an area in which I needed a deep cleaning. Through the years I have been a gossip, and I have not been trustworthy to hold what others told me in confidence. My mouth has been a source of trouble for me. Thankfully, I did not lose this friend for breaking trust. She was a friend that I could trust, and she has been used by God more than once to expose areas in my life that needed Him. She was a vessel used by God to speak His truth into me, and so I learned from her to not break a confidence with someone, and be respectful of boundaries.

We need to avoid a man who has bad breath, or talks too much, because a gossiper always betrays a confidence (Proverbs 11:13). And I have talked too much. Learning silence was the medicine I needed. My friend encouraged me to go on a talking fast. I laughed, and so did a few others that I told. I thought fasting from talking was impossible for me. But the Lord never gives us impossible tasks. In fact, if He wanted me to go on a fast from talking, He would help me do it. And He did! He wanted to give me the unfading beauty of a gentle and quiet spirit.

When the Lord convicted me of the bad breath of gossip again, it was different because it was with my best friend. I just felt like I could tell her everything. I knew that she wouldn't tell anyone else; she was a safe person to confide in. But the Lord showed me that speaking about others to her caused my best friend to distance herself from the one I was speaking about. It also caused my heart to be puffed up, as if I were better than they were. The sin of this practice made my heart heavy; I needed God to touch my mouth with His cleansing coal. Dear Lord, exchange the gossip in me for the quiet spirit that is in You!

Everything was going well until I opened my big mouth. My mouth was always breaking confidences. I knew then that I was nothing like Esther. I had not shown verbal restraint through instance after instance and I felt ugly about it. I was caught up in a disaster that only God could get me out of. I wished I would have read Proverbs 25 before I had done it—it might have prevented me from opening my mouth.

"Just because you've seen something, don't be in a hurry to go to court. For what will you do in the end if your neighbor deals you a shameful defeat? When arguing with your neighbor, don't betray another person's secret. Others may accuse you of gossip, and you will never regain your good reputation" (Proverbs 25:7b-10).

If ever there was a day that I regretted the words I had spoken, it was when I broke a confidence that my daughter had entrusted to me. I was so ashamed. I fell to my knees in repentance and prayed, "Please forgive me, Lord! Cleanse my mouth; help me keep it shut. Make me mute. Keep my tongue from evil. Rebuke me, Lord; I am listening!" When that coal touches our lips, we are receiving a beauty treatment for our tongues. That coal turns filth into pure gold.

I am sure that many of you will share my pain when we talk about going to the dentist. I absolutely hate going to the dentist, even though I know it is in my best interest to get that darn cavity out of my mouth. This cavity had been screaming at me to be removed, and I endured the pain until it was filled. I thought of the Holy Spirit filling me up to be able to speak with His anointing. How could I not?

If we have to shout, we are not anointed. I can be loud and vocal; this was exposed during an exercise we did as our small group was preparing to minister to others. The object of the exercise was to make people guess what character trait we were exhibiting based on how we acted in the group. We were given a small piece of paper with random traits to act out. I handpicked the one that, of course, would describe me. It was an eye opener to see how self-centered I was in my heart; it was like a cavity screaming to be removed. This is what I read:

LOUD and VOCAL: You take lots of time pulling attention to yourself and take lots of time in the group. You are convinced that your answers are the right ones, and once you are done giving an answer there is no need to talk about anything else because you've said it all. You interrupt other people. You use phrases like "...and another thing"; "That reminds me of the time that I..."; etc.

The handheld instrument called an explorer that the dentists use spotted that decay of selfishness instantly. But the hidden cavities of pride needed the x-ray vision of the Holy Spirit to be detected. That was me in real life. In my life, the decay was spreading, making me centered on myself. Once the hidden cavity of pride was brought to the light, I made it a point to remove it from my life. I confessed it as pride and selfishness, and then the Lord gave me a dose of His beauty that drilled right into the root, removing the decay and brightening up my smile with His radiance. He makes me whiter than snow.

Flossing out the filthy language was another beauty treatment I needed. When I first gave my life to the Lord over twenty years ago, He began to deal with my filthy language. I was accustomed to talking like a sailor or a truck driver. Cussing just seemed so normal. My parents cussed, my friends cussed, and so naturally I cussed too. I remember when I was little and had cussed. My mom said she was going to wash my mouth out with soap. I learned right away that it was not pleasing to the Lord—one of my first beauty treatments as an early believer. Now when I hear foul language, it does not stick to me like plaque; instead, it is quickly forgotten.

With pride and haughtiness comes a lot of trash talk, and that needed to be removed if I was to be a virtuous woman whose speech was humble and gracious. It was time for me to grow up into that woman. This verse came to mind "When I was a child, I spoke and thought and reasoned as a child. But when I grew up, I put away childish things" (1 Corinthians 13:11). Another word for this prideful talk is godless chatter, and we are instructed to turn away from it and avoid it because those who indulge in it will become more and more ungodly (2 Timothy 2:16). The Bible is the best mouthwash out there. It cleanses your mouth as you read it. We need a Spirit-filled cleansing mouthwash for any unwholesome, foul, or abusive talk that comes out of our mouths.

The beauty comes when we turn from trash talk and become discreet and chaste in our speech. That, my friend, is better than lip gloss. It has been my prayer that when I open my mouth, I only do so to let my speech be filled with humility and wisdom, in kindness, and for edification only! Oh, how attractive it must be for a queen to have speech that is sweet and gentle. This encourages me that I could be the crown to my future husband, and precious in the sight of God. There is beauty in speaking to one another with psalms, hymns, and spiritual songs (Colossians 3:16), or in other words, being your friends or your spouse's cheerleader.

The treatment needed for our ears goes deeper than the pretty little dangling earrings hanging from them. It goes inside the ears and cleans out the earwax.

"To one who listens, valid criticism is like a gold earring or other gold jewelry" (Proverbs 25:12).

Listening requires getting out the cotton-tipped swabs and removing earwax. We may have preconceived opinions that clog up how we hear. It has taken many beauty treatments for me to learn that my opinion is not really what is important—it is God's opinion that matters. Listening is beautiful and valuable.

Every day I asked the Lord, "What kind of character do You want to cultivate in me today?" On one day in particular He whispered, "The ability to listen to others."

I knew that this was from the Lord because just that morning my daughter had said to me, "I'm never talking to you again because you never pay attention or listen to me!" Ouch! It was true though. I could not afford to be insensitive, to not discern the feelings and needs of others.

"When Queen Esther's maids and eunuchs came and told her about Mordecai, she was deeply distressed. She sent clothing to him to replace the burlap, but he refused it. Then Esther sent for Hathach, one of the king's eunuchs who had been appointed as her attendant. She ordered him to go to Mordecai and find out what was troubling him and why he was in mourning" (Esther 4:4-5).

Esther had to discern what was being said and know how to act on it. She was a good listener. The Lord cultivated in her the ability to listen carefully to others, and it was my prayer that He would do the same with me. Having earwax in your ear is like having prejudice in your mind. I learned that I must not be subjective when listening to others. As I listened, I needed to lay aside my prejudices. When I talked with others, I had to be careful not to force my diagnosis upon them. Sometimes people simply need a listening ear.

Because my mind tended to wander when others were talking, the Lord gently reminded me about the beauty treatment of silence. It was a time to restrain my mouth from speaking and discipline my focus on the one I was attending, the one who needed a listening ear. I knew myself. I knew that it would be easy for me to be thinking of something else entirely (having earwax) while someone was pouring their heart out to me. I am not alone in this. It is very difficult for all of us to discipline our mind and our tongue. When we are very active in our minds, we need the Lord's beauty treatments for our mouths and ears to discipline our minds in order to be steady and calm in our thoughts. If He can calm the storm, He can definitely calm our thoughts. We must learn to actively enter into the feelings of others.

Before we can listen quietly and understand what others are saying, we must be in perfect stillness, void of our own thoughts or our own subjective opinions and feelings—void of earwax.

It does not mean we have to agree with the person we are listening to, but we must discern as we listen. We must discern whether God is speaking in the earthquake or the whisper. For example, a friend called to tell me that she thinks that our other friend should give her baby up for adoption. I listened to her and her reasoning behind her conclusion, but I didn't agree with the way she was pressing her opinion on our friend—it was not necessarily an eternal opinion.

We learn in Proverbs 11:12 that a man of understanding holds his tongue. (Cross references: Proverbs 11:12; Proverbs 14:21; Proverbs 11:12; Job 6:24).

After David felt betrayed, he was in no mood to listen; nevertheless he stopped to hear what Abigail had to say. "She fell at his feet and said: 'I accept all blame in this matter, my lord. Please listen to what I have to say'" (1 Samuel 25:24).

No matter how right we think we are, we must always be careful to stop and listen to others. Sometimes we require a hearing aid to be able to hear God whisper. A hearing aid is something that helps you to hear if your senses are failing. Sometimes this means we have to wait on God in silence so He can speak. God is more than willing to pour out His heart and make known His thoughts to us, but we must be willing to listen since He is often speaking in a gentle whisper. The busyness of life prevented me from stopping to hear His whispers, so I needed to make time for silence. When I was a kid, I always had a hard time going to sleep because I was afraid that I would miss out on something. That is the same way I felt about not hearing God's whispers in my everyday busy life; I felt like I was missing out on something and it took away my sleep. But once I used my hearing aid—a silent place in my bathtub—I heard His whispers and went to bed in peace knowing that I wasn't missing a thing.

The Lord told Elijah to go out and stand on the mountain, for He was about to pass by. He was not in the wind, He was not in the earthquake, and He was not in the fire. But then came a gentle whisper and it was He (1 Kings 19:11-13).

"Then he [Jesus] said, 'Anyone with ears to hear should listen and understand'" (Mark 4:9). We hear with our ears, but there is a deeper kind of listening with our mind and heart that is necessary in order to gain spiritual understanding from Jesus' words. The Holy Spirit is also my hearing aid. Sometimes we need to turn up the volume on our hearing aids, so we are able to listen carefully and be ready to carry out His instructions. Paying careful attention is hard work, especially for me. It involves focusing our mind, body, and senses. It requires restraint.

"Understand this, my dear brothers and sisters: You must all be quick to listen, slow to speak, and slow to get angry" (James 1:19). Talking in itself is not wrong; on the contrary, there is a time to speak and a time to be quiet. During the quiet and still times, I heard the Lord more clearly. If I am doing all the talking then I am not listening. Listening is just as important in any conversation as talking.

We have the power to either tear down or build up with our tongues. It is true what our parents told us, "If you don't have anything nice to say, don't say anything at all." In other words, shut the mouth, and open the ears. Let's start building God's beautiful kingdom as we genuinely listen and speak life to each other.

Now that is the beautiful breath of God!

Treatment 5: Contouring

Do you ever get the feeling like someone is jealous of you? I do. Sometimes I feel like there are people that are jealous of what God has done in me. Maybe you feel jealous of someone who you think looks better, talks better, and lives better than you? What if God so shaped our beliefs that we were content in who God made us to be?

Do you ever feel like you are so beautiful on the inside that anything you put on the outside is just for fun? I feel incredibly beautiful without makeup, without doing my hair, without doing my nails. I do not spend a lot of time in front of the mirror. I spend probably twenty minutes a day in front of the mirror, and I feel confident in the beauty that I already have. I just think it is fun. I have fun dressing up, and doing my hair, nails, and face. I think that there were times in the past that I looked in the mirror and needed to put on makeup because I needed to cover up the ugliness inside, but that is not how I feel now. I feel like I radiate the Son of God. But if my beauty and outward appearance causes my sister to stumble because of jealousy, or my brother to stumble because of lust, then I choose not to have fun with it. It does not matter to me what other people think because I am accepted just as I am. I believe wholeheartedly that I am wonderfully and fearfully made. When I look at myself, I see no flaws in the way the Creator made me. I am made in the image of God and I am not ashamed to say that I am beautiful! I love attention, yes, but the attention that I have received from God is enough for me, and everything else is an extra benefit.

Exactly six months into my consecration time, my daughter and I went shopping for makeup. I do not use makeup all of the time, but I think it is nice to enhance my natural beauty once in a while. Some makeup leaves my face oily and makes me break out, so I use it sparingly. However, just a little bit of contouring can shape your face and make it shine. God gave me a spiritual application of this to apply to my heart.

Contouring is an ancient concept that has to do with shadow and light, and shaping the structure of your face and/or body. When I thought of contouring in the spiritual sense, I was drawn to the sanctuary where God dwells. He said in Hebrews that the sanctuary in which He dwells is a copy and a shadow of what is in heaven. He says that we are His temple, and that He dwells in us. As He dwells in us, and we in Him, then we rest in the shadow of the Almighty God (Psalm 91:1). I think of the Bible as the tool that contours our spiritual bodies.

Contouring shapes our beliefs and brings light to the truth of who we are. When contouring is applied to our lives, we are content with what we have and who we are.

Spiritual contouring is the remedy for coveting. One of the Ten Commandments tells us not to covet. God's commands were only given for our benefit. He wants us to know that every good and perfect gift comes from Him; when we receive those gifts with a smile on our face, we have contoured our spirit.

Society, as a whole, encourages us to contour our bodies to look like someone else's. Some undergo breast enlargement and various kinds of plastic surgery as a means to contour their bodies. However, our frame was designed by God in our mother's womb after a pattern that was a copy and shadow of what is in heaven. When we don't allow God to shape our beliefs according to His Word, our beliefs are distorted.

However, when we do trust God at His Word, then it shapes the very nature within us to be content with who God created us to be. Contentment is the state of being grateful, peaceful, and satisfied. It is satisfaction with possessions, status, or situation. It is freedom from the care of discomfort. It is freedom from coveting what others have. It is knowing that despite the positive or negative circumstances around you, the cloud of the Holy Spirit is hovering over it all.

In the year 2008, when God called me to this consecration, I faced many hardships that loomed like heavy shadows over my life. My van broke down on New Year's Day so I gave it away; then my car broke down too. I got another car, and that broke down as well. Not being mechanically inclined is a hardship in itself. Next, my heart was crushed in a relationship that I deeply desired. This was very difficult for me to go through, but the Lord had made me more than an overcomer. He has given me the healing that comes from the balm of Gilead. That same year, my son Isaac was beat up twice by neighborhood kids. He had a better attitude than I did. This mother bear was out for blood (an exaggeration, but I was very upset). Then, I got fired from my job as a computer programmer—which actually was a blessing. But being fired is always an ego issue, not to mention a loss of financial security. After one month of journaling my time with the Lord, my laptop was stolen. It turned out that the neighborhood kids I fed and took care of were the ones who informed the thief I had a laptop and became the lookout (which was disheartening). I was also engaged in a constant battle with my daughter regarding her past decisions. And in the midst of all that, I had to pick the boys up from their dad's in Tennessee prematurely because his girlfriend had tried to commit suicide while my children were there.

As a mother who was raising children with little or no help from their father, it was heartbreaking to see them struggling to understand why things were the way they were. The stress of adding a third adult, with all of their own problems, into that situation can often make things much more difficult than they already were. My son, Daniel, in particular, had to work his way through some nasty aggression. We were also living on a very limited income: $250 dollars a month. During the year, I was separated from my closest friends and lonely times became another hardship. I even had some sister rivalry, and her decision to leave me out of her life was yet another shadow in my own. To top off the year, I was thrown in jail overnight because of an exaggerated accusation.

I list these trials and mishaps as the things that would drive most people to some type of comfort. I found my comfort in the shadow of the Almighty. One might even assume that, because of these problems, God's favor was gone and His cloud had moved elsewhere. After all, that is how the church is conditioned to think now. A very common misconception is that if you have a lot and everything is going smoothly, then you are favored by God. Likewise, the prejudice remains that those who are without material possessions and are going through a rough time have incurred God's displeasure. But James 1 nurtures both hope and humility in the church by explaining how those who have very little are wealthy because they possess the richness of fellowship with Christ Jesus, while those who have great possessions are to remain mindful that their greatest treasure is still that same closeness and union with our Lord. Therefore, whether abounding or abased, we all rejoice and celebrate with one heart the love of God our Father, who has promised the same crown of life to us all.

Through all the circumstances I have just mentioned, I found myself completely at peace and in the shelter of my God's strong arms. He has held me and sustained me. He has been my provision in every way, and I have lacked no good thing.

God is great and worthy to be praised, and I give Him all the glory. Just as God's Word instructs me, I do not get overawed when a man I know grows rich. It has never really been in my nature to be impressed with big houses and many possessions. I am not a materialistic woman.

In the garden of Eden, Adam and Eve were content until the serpent told them they were missing out on something. Isn't that where we go wrong too? We start looking to what we don't have instead of appreciating what we do have. To be honest, I have been contoured by the Lord and given an inner harmony which makes me as fulfilled as, and perhaps more at peace than, the richest person in the world. "Yet true godliness with contentment is itself great wealth" (1 Timothy 6:6).

Those who know the name of Jesus trust in Him because we know that He has never forsaken those who seek Him (Psalm 9:10). Trust is automatically established at birth by our Creator. He brought us safely from our mother's womb and led us to trust Him at our mother's breast. We are born with the ability to trust. Somewhere along the way as we grow, we stop trusting that He will always take care of us and provide for us.

I lacked faith in trusting God as my Provider, especially with our limited income. I have learned to trust the Lord and not try to find my own way out of a hole. I have determined in my heart to trust Him like a little child. I don't have to worry about all the bills that are overdue because the Lord knows our needs before we even ask. He is really good at taking care of us. He watches over His children with a wrathful, possessive protection. He sees when we are running low on groceries, and because He sees, we are confident that He will provide. Even if it is in the eleventh hour, we can trust that the Lord will provide—He always has and He is not going to stop now. When you're in the thick of it, it helps to look back to see how the Lord has come through for you in the past. He will come through for you now too. We must completely trust and know that God will supply all our needs according to His riches in glory (Philippians 4:19).

While I was trusting the Lord for provision, there was someone who anonymously dropped off $200 at my church with my name on it. I felt like it was a reward from the Lord for serving him. It is the Lord who sees and rewards those who diligently seek Him. I am grateful to know that, because I have obeyed the prompting of the Holy Spirit and stayed home to raise my children, God responded to my obedience and provided for all our needs.

Ultimately, my dependence did not rely on food stamps or people inviting us over for dinner. My dependence was on Him alone and I wanted to do things differently. I did not want to be known for begging for bread, because I am a righteous one—I am His. I wanted to completely, wholeheartedly trust that He would provide in whatever means possible. He has often provided for us through my church. The Love in Action program at our church has helped us for years with groceries for which we are thankful. His help can come in many ways, and I have not been too proud to receive it from wherever it comes.

During this financial hardship, I felt like God was saying to me to give everything away. I literally felt like I had given all my money away and I was back to square one, as my dad would say. I often woke up discouraged because even though I had put all my faith and trust in God and His provisions and was not lacking in anything, I felt my immediate and vital need for a van was not met, even though I had asked God for one. I reasoned with God, but I did not want my eyes to be on material things and I wanted to realign my focus on heaven. I realized that my kingdom perspective needed cosmetic surgery. I realized that giving all my money and things away was of God and He would bless me for doing it if it truly was His will. I asked the Lord, "But should I be giving everything away?" I guess if I looked at it with a heavenly perspective, then it shouldn't have mattered to me because they were all material things that would burn up when Jesus came back anyway. I just wanted to be wise with what I had, and to me, giving everything away seemed kind of foolish. This is not God's will for everyone, but it was His word to me in this season of my life. The Lord was teaching me that I needed to trust Him, follow Him, and believe that He would give back.

Jesus reminded His disciples in Luke 22:35 that He always provides: "Then Jesus asked them, 'When I sent you out to preach the Good News and you did not have money, a traveler's bag, or an extra pair of sandals, did you need anything?' 'No,' they replied." We constantly need those reminders: when the Lord sends us out, we will lack nothing.

God loves a cheerful giver, so why was I feeling like I wasn't being a good steward of the money He gave me? I didn't get much to begin with, so the idea of giving it all away really made me pause and wonder. I asked Kevin, a good friend of mine who I believe has made wise investments in the kingdom, and he encouraged me with these words: "Your return on your investment in this world may not be immediate, but the Lord is faithful." He also told me that it may not return in a monetary form. My investment is into the kingdom of God. This world has nothing for me. The Scriptures that I read in God's Word bear witness to what my friend spoke to me.

"Blessed are those who are generous, because they feed the poor" (Proverbs 22:9). After I saw that verse, my attention was drawn to this next verse, which opened my eyes to this beauty of trust: "Whoever gives to the poor will lack nothing, but those who close their eyes to poverty will be cursed" (Proverbs 28:27). I lived in a very poor community. People called it "the Projects" because it was government-owned housing, given to the poor for shelter. The people that lived there were all in great need. I felt that, even though I was in need, I had more than most people there did. I decided to invest in that community with whatever I did have. I felt compelled to act upon the literal interpretation of this verse, and so I did. "Sell your possessions and give to those in need. This will store up treasure for you in heaven! And the purses of heaven never get old or develop holes. Your treasure will be safe; no thief can steal it and no moth can destroy it" (Luke 12:33).

If I did not let the contouring of the Lord touch this part of my heart, then I could very well have ended up with a "woe is me" complex because I was in need as well. But the Lord reminded me of all the times that He had not let me down nor forsaken me before. I knew He was faithful to provide for me, and that it was His will for me to give freely, and that I should not be tightfisted with any amount that I have, even if it was my last dollar.

Don't be hardhearted toward your poor brother who needs your help. Be openhanded, lend to him without wondering whether he will ever pay you back. A loan in the kingdom of God is a gift with no strings. If you don't lend freely, your brother will have the Lord on His side. Let the Lord be on your side, too. He will bless you in ways you can never foresee, for He Himself is openhanded.

I had to come to a place in my life where I was seeking Him only and not merely His gifts, even as Esther had chosen to make no special requests, even though she had the opportunity to ask for anything and it would have been given to her. She wanted only to do as the eunuch suggested. He was close to the king; he knew that the king desired her to seek his face and not his kingdom.

The Lord used this time of hardship to give me a beauty treatment and contour contentment in me. After the treatment, He was faithful to provide my needs according to His riches in glory. Let me tell you what happened once the year was up and I was ready to go out and minister wherever He led me. There came a day when I received a call from a church that offered car help to single women with children. I was in New Orleans on a mission trip helping to rebuild the ruins from Hurricane Katrina when I got the call. The church had me come in for an interview to receive a vehicle. The man interviewing me said, after a two hour interview, that I did not meet the qualifications needed to obtain a car from them, but he loved my philosophy of kingdom living and so he gave me the car. I literally felt like that gold van fell from heaven. I still have it and it is still a royal gift from the Lord. He is and was and will always be faithful!

Contouring touches not only the lack of trust in God for our finances, it also touches our trust in God for our future plans or mates. Sometimes this particular lack of trust caused me to lose sleep because my imagination kept drifting off, planning something in my future, dreaming of a warm body lying next to me. There is nothing wrong with this desire; however, I knew that it was not my time. I needed to be content in my singleness. Aware of the possibility that it might not be God's will for me to ever marry again, my time alone with my King needed to be sufficient. I thought to myself, "Heck, I really should be enjoying every minute that I am alone." So often we rush into relationships, thinking that after we have the warm body next to us, we will be secure and happy. However, that is a lie. The truth that set me free was His promises.

During those sleepless nights, my heart cried out like David's did when he was in the desert: "O God, you are my God; I earnestly search for you. My soul thirsts for you; my whole body longs for you in this parched and weary land where there is no water. I have seen you in your sanctuary and gazed upon your power and glory. Your unfailing love is better than life itself; how I praise you! I will praise you as long as I live, lifting up my hands to you in prayer. You satisfy me more than the richest feast. I will praise you with songs of joy. I lie awake thinking of you, meditating on you through the night. Because you are my helper, I sing for joy in the shadow of your wings. I cling to you; your strong right hand holds me securely" (Psalm 63:1-8).

The last thing I want to touch on is being content with the person God made you to be. Most people associate beauty with the outer appearance. Our flaws in the mirror are ever present and who we look at in the mirror does not compare to the model we see on television. We are faced with the reality that we have imperfections that everyone can see, and we are always looking for ways to look better. Who said that we would look better without the moles on our faces? If we were born with any deformity at all, the world around us would be sure to point something wrong with us. Before the world set out to try and deceive us into believing we were inadequate in some way, we were content as His children.

We see this in our children more than ever. My daughter has been told all her life what a beautiful creation she is, and how much she is loved for being who she is, just the way she is. Okay, maybe there were moments when her being her was not working at all with me being me, but even then my opposition towards her attitude was intended to help her achieve her very best in life. I believe that having that foundation of acceptance, self-worth, and godly expectation enabled her to approach life with confidence and stability. When the day came when it was time to send her out into the world, she found herself in a school filled with other kids who had each been raised in their own environments and on their own foundations. None of these children were bad people, but, tragically, many had been taught to view themselves and others through the world's eyes, and not through God's. They had been raised to see themselves as flawed, by families who had also been deceived into seeing themselves as flawed too.

Once the world has convinced someone that their value is limited because of all their flaws, they are also convinced that the only way they can feel better about themselves is to tear others down and undermine their self-image as well. They do this by seeking to expose any weaknesses they see, and by attempting to make others believe that they will never be accepted nor valued if they don't fit perfectly into a particular mold, shaped by popular falsehoods and impossible expectations. Some of them attacked my daughter. They tried to convince her that she should see herself as lacking perfection, that she was not all that valuable, that she should feel bad about herself, too. She was so crushed and devastated that she questioned her identity. She learned to fear being rejected. She saw herself as flawed for being who she was and the way she was. But each one of us is completely different from the other—no two are the same. We are all born with different qualities that set us apart from each other. We are perfectly created by our Maker—some with freckles, some with moles, some with birthmarks, and some with _____ (insert your own personal beauty mark here).

God created us in our mother's womb and He knew how He would form us. We are shaped differently, but we all make up the body of Christ. The feet will not look like the hands and so on. When we are content in who God made us to be, we actually fit into the puzzle to make us one. If we remain determined to change the way God created us, then we go against His plan. He formed each one of us with a unique purpose in mind. See for yourself in the following verses, and be content with who God created you to be. He is the Potter and we are the clay (Isaiah 64:8; Romans 9:20-21; Jeremiah 18:4-6).

"'What sorrow awaits those who argue with their Creator. Does a clay pot argue with its maker? Does the clay dispute with the one who shapes it, saying, "Stop, you're doing it wrong!" Does the pot exclaim, "How clumsy can you be?" How terrible it would be if a newborn baby said to its father, "Why was I born?" or if it said to its mother, "Why did you make me this way?"' This is what the Lord says—the Holy One of Israel and your Creator: 'Do you question what I do for my children? Do you give me orders about the work of my hands? I am the one who made the earth and created people to live on it. With my hands I stretched out the heavens. All the stars are at my command'" (Isaiah 45:9-12).

The Lord has contoured me as He shaped me and caused His face to shine on me. I'm completely content in where God has me and at total peace with where I am in the Lord. I am content with what I have and who I am. I can relate to Paul in that I know what it is like to live on almost nothing and also having learned the secret of living in every situation, whether it was with a full stomach or empty, with plenty or little (Philippians 4:12). That has not always been the case, of course. Contentment is a character that needs to be shaped, cultivated, and established. It does not become a part of your life until the soil of your heart is ready for it. It is in our nature to covet and want what everyone else has. Somehow or some way, we end up wanting something more, something bigger, better, and more up-to-date. Media has made it hard for one to be content—advertisements always leave you feeling like you can't live without something.

Do you find yourself wanting what others have? Can you find satisfaction in what you have or do you always want more? Is it difficult for you to value your present station in life or are you focused on the life that someone else is living? Maybe your neighbor appears to have the happy life that you want? Do you think that your life would be much easier if you had what she had? What about the gifts God has given you? Are you trying to be like Jane the Prophet, or can you be content in the gift God has given you to serve, even if it serving as a janitor? Being content frees us to be who God wants us to be. If we can be content in who God made us to be, we can truly smile with confidence, and smiling contours our faces. It makes them shine. May the Lord shine His face on you and shape your future to shine brighter each day.

Treatment 6: Detoxing

*N*atural health practitioners believe that our polluted environment has left us toxic, and our bodies need a little help. People are turning to detox diets to have healthier lifestyles and weight loss. Detoxing your spiritual body has application here as well. Sin is poisonous, and though people may pick different types of poison (sin), the effect is all the same.

The detox is the antidote for removing the poisons that we have indulged in. As we give in to the cravings of the flesh, we find ourselves wrapped in addiction. The poison releases strong toxins into our systems, and the detoxing of our soul requires intense treatment. Sometimes that treatment is immediate, but there are other times that those toxins remain and require an antidote to completely detox from your life. The antidote is in the vessel of praise!

At the age of thirteen, I started meddling with drugs. This was about the time that my mom came back into my life; she'd been gone for six years in and out of a mental hospital. She was also traveling around the United States with truck drivers. I left my dad's to begin a relationship with my mom. She had addictions of her own. After being gone so long, she didn't know how to be a mother. Instead she tried really hard to be my friend. She knew I had dabbled with marijuana with my friends from school, and so she said, "I would rather you smoke weed with me, safe at home, than out on the streets with strangers." Her intention was to keep me off the streets, but she didn't have the sense to know that you shouldn't get high with your kids. She smoked weed at breakfast, lunch, and dinner and so, yep you guessed it, so did I. In fact, we stayed high; this was a gateway for me to get into other drugs that were more addictive, like cocaine. Once I started using cocaine, I really got involved with the wrong crowd. I was pressured into selling the cocaine in my middle school. I was caught and put into a rehabilitation center, but that didn't stop me from using.

Once I had a taste of something that could numb me from my problems, I had to find a way to get more. And I did. And it numbed me so much that I honestly can't even recall much of my teenage years. This poison was in my system my entire teenage life, until I turned 20. Then, one day after being evicted out of my apartment for not paying rent, the gang that I was involved with decided to help me move out. We destroyed the place with graffiti and stole the landlord's freezer. I felt like I was hitting rock bottom. I moved in with a girl that had connections to the gang as well, but my intentions were only to stay with her temporarily. My boyfriend at the time was the head gang member of the Southwest Detroit Cobras, and he had gone to New York to jump parole. I was going to sell everything I had and run to New York to be with him.

One day, as I was sitting on the porch selling all that I had—from my little girl's toys to the freezer that I'd stolen—a missionary stopped to visit. He was actually there to pick up Cuba, who was also in the gang, for church. He had met him the night before in a laundromat. As he waited for Cuba to come out, he invited me to church too. I was not too enthused and I refused, but Cuba came out and told me that he didn't want to go alone, so grudgingly, I tagged along. When we got to the church, I remember hearing songs that were peaceful. Something in my heart was stirring. I can't remember what the pastor talked about, maybe something about stealing. All I know is that during his sermon, I felt a tug on my heart, pulling me up to the altar. I ran to the front in the middle of his message. Something was happening inside my heart; it was pounding intensely as I knelt down to ask God for forgiveness. I didn't know the right things to say because I had never really prayed before. All I knew in that moment was that I was wrong and I wanted to make things right. I was tired of the life in which I was living and raising my child. As I prayed and asked Jesus to come into my heart and clean me up, I heard the words in my head, "Thou shall not steal." At that moment, I asked the missionary to help me to take the freezer back to the landlord from whom I had stolen it.

My life began to change. Getting saved stopped me from going to New York, but I still continued to get high for several weeks after that first night at the church. However, while I was getting high, I was also reading my Bible. In fact, my friends were with me and I was pointing at the words in the Bible and told them that the words were speaking to me. I was saying, "Dude, this book is alive." They all said, "She has done lost it," as they twirled their fingers next to their ears meaningfully. But it really was alive and it was cleansing my mind. It was detoxing my soul. It was transforming my life.

The next morning, I woke up with the feeling that what my friend was doing was wrong. I told the girl I was living with that I did not want to watch her children any longer while she "worked" (stripped). She kicked me out. I had never had a problem with it before, I had even gone to watch on occasion, but something was happening in my mind and heart. I packed up my belongings and began to pray in the only way I knew how.

Someone from church had handed me a number. I called and told the lady my story and asked her if there was a place where my daughter and I could go; after a long pause, she said, "You and your daughter can come and live with us." Her home was surrounded with Scriptures, and the sounds of Christian music could always be heard. I could feel the poison of drugs leave my body as we rested in her home. I never picked up another joint or snorted another line of cocaine. I never returned to that lifestyle. My life changed completely as I surrounded myself along with people who sang His praises—people who gave God all the glory. It is praise that breaks every yoke. Today, I marvel at how God strategically set it up to rescue me from that utter darkness. I was like one walking in darkness who saw a Great Light (Isaiah 9:2; Leviticus 26:13). He brought me out of darkness so I was not held back by the shameful yoke of slavery. I am now able to walk with my head held high.

Throughout the years of my journey with the Lord, there have been many other things that I needed to be delivered from as well. Drugs and alcohol are a pretty obvious poison in a person's life, but there are other poisons that are less easily detected, yet just as deadly. Sin is poisonous. Sin has costly repercussions. It is toxic and pollutes your soul and it will put a heavy yoke of slavery on you. Stay away from toxic addictions!

Although we have yet to banish it entirely, the vast majority of the world now cringes at the thought of slavery. The very idea of slavery makes most people angry. But if we are really paying attention and being honest with ourselves, we are all slaves to something or someone, whether we like it or not.

Some are slaves to drugs, food, riches, and even technology. Some are enslaved by unhealthy or abusive relationships. Some are even slaves to religion and following a law that keeps them in chains, for a man is a slave to whatever controls him (2 Peter 2:19).

God's detoxing of sin is a deep cleansing from His Word. Singing His Word, praying and speaking His Word, loving and living His Word, and believing His Word are the ingredients to this antidote that removes the toxins from our lives. As we detox from the passions of the world, we are cleansed and transformed by our minds being renewed (Romans 12:2). The will of God is your sanctification: you should abstain from sexual immorality (1 Thessalonians 4:3).

Anything that is shaped to the pattern of this world has the capacity to become an idol in our lives and become a poisonous toxin to our soul. "I am making this covenant with you so that no one among you—no man, woman, clan, or tribe—will turn away from the Lord our God to worship these gods of other nations, and so that no root among you bears bitter and poisonous fruit" (Deuteronomy 29:18).

We were created by God to worship Him, but more often than not we worship idols. Let's get real and a little personal here. He created within each one of us the desire to worship. Since creation began, the desire to be our own god has enticed us with its poison. We want our own way, we want to do our own thing, and deep inside we all want to be worshipped. There are also tangible poisons that we like to taste "just once." Unfortunately, that one time of pleasure turns into a lifetime of regret. I am referring to sexual immorality. Our culture spreads the poison that we have to have sexual fulfillment now.

For some reason, we feel like God is holding out on us, like we are missing out on something. But Paul saw how this poison was rampant in his day, and he warned us to, "Run from sexual sin! No other sin so clearly affects the body as this one does. For sexual immorality is a sin against your own body. Don't you realize that your body is the temple of the Holy Spirit, who lives in you and was given to you by God? You do not belong to yourself, for God bought you with a high price. So you must honor God with your body" (1 Corinthians 6:18-20). Sexual immorality is a poison that destroys your body, home, and soul.

Premarital sex has become the norm, while the divorce rate is even higher than that of those getting married. We have to ask ourselves why. There are countless women that I have counseled to not give in to premarital sex; it ruins the relationship before it even starts. Having sex before marriage is poisonous to both people, and should be avoided. Run from it. Unfortunately, I did not run from it; it ensnared me. I am not proud to admit to the sexual immorality of my past. Having sex before marriage poisoned my identity and my future. After I was saved, my mind had to be renewed because I kept allowing it to go where it should not go. Sexual thoughts attacked me; the only way to combat this problem was to apply the beauty treatment for purity. My love language is touch; I love to be touched more than you can imagine. God's detoxing was a time when the Lord gave me His touch, but first He opened my eyes to see where the poison of immorality had crept into my life and defiled my heart, even after I had been saved.

"Then Oholah lusted after other lovers instead of me, and she gave her love to the Assyrian officers. They were all attractive young men, captains and commanders dressed in handsome blue, charioteers driving their horses. And so she prostituted herself with the most desirable men of Assyria, worshiping their idols and defiling herself. For when she left Egypt, she did not leave her spirit of prostitution behind. She was still as lewd as in her youth, when the Egyptians slept with her, fondled her breasts, and used her as a prostitute" (Ezekiel 23:5-8).

"You sisters sent messengers to distant lands to get men. Then when they arrived, you bathed yourselves, painted your eyelids, and put on your finest jewels for them" (Ezekiel 23:40).

The name *Ohalah* means "her own tent." It's an example of an idolatrous sanctuary.

But God had a plan to rescue me from my own tent and, as those toxins were cleansed, He put a stop to the lewdness and prostitution that I brought out of my Egypt (Ezekiel 23:27). Then I received His detox to clean up my mind with His Word. He transformed me and I was consecrated to my God.

As He put a stop to the lewdness in my heart, I began to feel enclosed. I began to feel like I was a sealed fountain. The enclosed garden is a place of intimacy with the Lord. He gave me the verses in Ezekiel 36:34-36: "The fields that used to lie empty and desolate in plain view of everyone will again be farmed. And when I bring you back, people will say, 'This former wasteland is now like the garden of Eden! The abandoned and ruined cities now have strong walls and are filled with people!' Then the surrounding nations that survive will know that I, the Lord, have rebuilt the ruins and replanted the wasteland. For I, the Lord, have spoken, and I will do what I say." That, my friend, is a toxic-cleansing verse.

It is God who cleans us up. He is the gardener. He cleans the toxins that have laid waste to our hearts; then, as the gardener, He turns our desolate and ruined lives into a beautiful garden of life that springs up in a cleansing flow.

Our God is romantic. This is how He spoke to me through His Word to cleanse my heart of the poison of lewdness: "You are my private garden, my treasure, my bride, a secluded spring, a hidden fountain....You are a garden fountain, a well of fresh water streaming down from Lebanon's mountains. Awake, north wind! Rise up, south wind! Blow on my garden and spread its fragrance all around. Come into your garden, my love; taste its finest fruits. I have entered my garden, my treasure, my bride! I gather myrrh with my spices and eat honeycomb with my honey. I drink wine with my milk" (Song of Solomon 4:12, 15-16; 5:1) Awe, isn't He sweet? I drink deeply of His love for me.

Tell me the Lord is not romantic. He pursued me with His love and His presence and caused me to be a garden full of beauty. He changed me. He did it so He could come into the garden of my heart and taste the choice fruit of the Spirit.

Isaiah 51:3 reassures me that the Lord does not stop at only looking on my ruins with pity and compassion, but He made my desert blossom like Eden, and my barren wilderness like the garden of the Lord where there was no shame. I believe it was in these moments with the Lord that I became a virgin again. And you wonder why joy and gladness has been found in me. Thanksgiving and the sound of singing are ever in my heart and life because of how the Lord cleaned up this garden. I can rest in His plan. It is the best. He is transforming my thinking so that it lines up with His perfect will. I don't want second best. His plan is perfect and there is no flaw in it. The world settles for second best because they don't look intently into His perfect law that gives freedom. If we truly trust in His plan and purpose for our lives, we can release ungodly thought patterns and dwell only on His law that gives us true freedom. I have had it stuck in my mind that things should happen a certain way, with a certain someone; however, the Lord has taught me that my ways are not His ways. His ways are always prosperous. All the ways of the Lord are loving and faithful for those who keep the demands of His covenant. The Lord is righteous in all His ways and loving toward all He has made. His righteousness will be like a garden in early spring with plants springing up everywhere (Isaiah 61:11).

We always need a constant reminder of where He found us—where we began—because we tend to forget our progress when things are not going so good. We quickly forget what He has done. We end up taking matters into our own hands, not waiting for the counsel of the Lord. And in our wilderness, our desires run wild as we test God's patience in our dry wasteland. So He gives us what we ask for, but He sends a plague along with it (Psalm 106:12-15).

We should not be so concerned about our physical satisfaction that we lack spiritual satisfaction. Let's not be like the Israelites; they did not want what was best for them. They refused to trust God's care and provision. If I complain enough, God may give me what I ask for—even if it is not best for me. God knows what is in my best interest and I need to trust Him and trust in His care and provision. God will protect us from the cravings of the flesh as we wait on Him for His sustaining truthful counsel. Wait patiently for the Lord and be brave and courageous as you are waiting (Psalm 27:14). Exchange the cravings of the flesh for a craving for more of Him. Become addicted to Jesus. When we are cleansed of those filthy toxins and become vessels of praise, Jesus commissions us with a promise. He tells us that miraculous signs will accompany us as we go preach the good news to everyone. If we drink anything poisonous, it will not hurt us (Mark 16:15-18). Spiritually speaking, the poison of this world can no longer bring us any harm when we receive God's detoxing.

Since God created us to worship, let us worship the Lord with our whole hearts, minds, and souls. When we worship the Creator who gave us life, we find freedom from the slavery of addictions.

What is your passion? To what are you addicted? What do you worship: drugs, alcohol, media, electronics, men, etc.? Worshipping the Lord detoxes the soul. Worshiping and spending time with God renews the mind, and transforms you. It exchanges the unhealthy addictions for the Spirit-led addiction—addiction to Jesus.

Treatment 7: Exposure

What is the first thing you think of when you look in the mirror and see a pimple? I know my first thought is how can I cover that up? I reach for the cover-up and rub away, hoping to cover it up but usually to no avail. A facial mask is used to cover the face in its entirety. As the facial mask is removed, so are the impurities. A mask is a cover for the face used for a disguise or protection. It is something that conceals. It hides the imperfections, or the dirt.

Are you hiding behind a mask of some sort? The beauty treatment of exposure is truth in the inner parts.

When my heart is smothered in His truth then He will grant me the desires of my heart because my desires will line up with His truth and not my own imaginations. The mask has slowly made its way off my face as the truth exposed who I really was, who I am now, and who I will become in the future.

Freckles are predominantly found on the face, although they may appear on any skin exposed to the sun. Upon exposure to the sun, freckles will reappear even if they have been altered with creams or lasers and not protected from the sun.[31] Yep, you guessed it; I am turning this into a spiritual application.

The opposite of truth is deception. The freckles of deception have a pretty and colorful mask that easily conceals the truth. The only way we see the freckles of deception are when they are exposed by the Son. One way that deception becomes colorful is through our own desires. Our heart, the Bible says, is deceitful above all things and beyond cure. Who can understand it? (Jeremiah 17:9). Oh, we can follow our hearts alright—and what joy it brings temporarily when we pursue the poisonous pleasures of the heart—but we must know that wherever our hearts lead us, we will be accountable to God for every choice we make.

Our hearts literally ponder how life would all play out. I imagined certain men and how they would propose to me. I created a desire in my heart and mentally perceived it happening. I knew this was deception. All I was doing was setting myself up for disappointment. I was contaminating the truth. I had the beauty treatment of truth poured into my inner parts that only God knew my future. I needed to let this beauty treatment soak into my heart for all of my days here on earth. I need to

31. Wikipedia contributors, "Freckle," Wikipedia, The Free Encyclopedia, http://en.wikipedia.org/w/index.php?title=Freckle&oldid=549852531 (accessed April 23, 2013).

live in the here and now. I didn't even know who it was that God had for me, or whose helpmate I would become. I believe that is why God tells us not to pride ourselves on the things of the future, because we really do not have any idea of what tomorrow will bring (James 4:14).

There have been many times that I thought I had heard from God as well. I would actually think that God was telling me what was going to happen with people or situations in the near future. I would justify in my mind that I felt God was preparing my heart for this or that. However, that is deception also. Sometimes I had an inclination that something had taken place. For example, when a teenager confided in me that she was pregnant, I felt God had already prepared my heart for that and told me that she was, but I had no idea how it would all play out. I didn't see the bigger picture. Only God sees the whole thing, so He has the proper perspective for what we need.

Exposure uncovers the freckles of falseness. Sometimes we really need to be careful when others who call themselves prophets want to speak into our lives. One day I was among friends, and one of our friends was dating someone who called himself a prophet. He was telling everyone what the future held for them. He started flowing with prophecy, but it sounded a little bit like sorcery because he was revealing personal information about our futures. Although it was great to hear what he had said to me, I wanted to be careful what I received because, even though I was excited because my flesh wanted to know, I also knew that God may not want me to know what my future holds. He alone knows who it is that He has as a husband for me.

As it says in God's Word, our eyes, ears, and minds cannot even fathom what is prepared for us by God (1 Corinthians 2:9). The Bible also says that we are to weigh carefully what is said by prophets, whether it is from God or from their own thoughts (1 Corinthians 14:29). This man told me that as soon as he saw me, he saw marriage. He said, "That girl is going to get married." He said the man I would marry would meet my needs before I even asked for them. I said that sounded like how Jesus did things for me now. He said that my husband would be very handsome and very wealthy. He said he saw me working and being very successful. I told him that I was writing a book and he shook his head, yes, and said it would be prosperous.

All this talk sounded good: I did believe that I was to be married, and I did believe that I would be successful because I was putting the Lord first, and that He was preparing me to be a virtuous woman for the man He had in mind for me. But really, only God knows, and we can be easily deceived when we look to the knowledge of others. We need to place our futures in the hands of a God that truly knows what our next step will be, and not put our trust in any man that can only see in part. I laid it at the cross because I did not want to play on any self-deception in my emotions. I told Daddy that I only wanted who He chose for me.

I myself have been a false witness who poured out lies. There have been opportunities to share my faith, and I exaggerated my testimony to say I shot up houses while in the gang. The truth is that I have never held a gun in my life. The Holy Spirit exposed me; then I started to realize that I have actually freckled the truth a lot. I have made my story out to be more dramatic than it was to make myself look tougher. I thought that if I lied to others who were wrapped up in worse stuff than I was, then they could believe that they would be set free too. Because of my fear of man, this is an area in my life in which I have always struggled. I have always hated confrontation; I have always been one to strive for peace, and sometimes it caused me to revert to lying or deceiving to try to achieve it. Expose this, kill it, hang it, crucify it! No flesh can glory in His presence.

My personal disclaimer to exposing this area is that everything I have written in this book has been tried and tested by the Holy Spirit: it is the truth. "People with integrity will walk safely, but those who follow crooked paths will slip and fall" (Proverbs 10:9).

We have the power to deceive ourselves. We do that when we are not living in the present, and instead allow our imaginations to live in the future. This is why we are told to capture our thoughts and subjugate them, or bring them under, the submission of Christ. We do this by asking ourselves if these thoughts in any way rise up against the true knowledge of God, and if they do, we cast them down (2 Corinthians

10:5). For example, there have been times when my children have had a bad case of negative speaking. They would tell themselves that they had no talent and no purpose. They would declare that they were failures at life, and throw phrases like "I can't do it" and "everybody would be better off without me" into the picture. Those are some of the thoughts that need to be cast down and replaced with God's truth. Even though His truth was written a long time ago, it still has power for the present day. We know that those thoughts rise up against our King because they are in direct opposition to His truth. He attacks those deadly thoughts with the truth that He has a purpose and a plan for everyone; and that through Him, we can do all things. The truth will set us free!

The beauty treatment of exposure deals with the huge pimple of pride. When you pick at that pimple enough, it becomes a scar of self-righteousness. By nature, all of us are rebels who want to be celebrities instead of servants. It takes many of God's beauty treatments for us to exchange this pimple of pride for His spotless humility. This may be one that we will need for the rest of our lives until He calls us to come home. The most important thing is to always be aware of that ugly pimple of pride. It pops up when you least expect it, and it must be immediately removed. Otherwise, it will get worse and blind you from seeing the truth. Others will see it, but unless you look intently into the mirror, the perfect law that gives freedom, that pride will remain on your face and you will not even realize it.

"In your great pride you claim, 'I am a god! I sit on a divine throne in the heart of the sea.' But you are only a man and not a god, though you boast that you are a god" (Ezekiel 28:2). At this point in my life, the Lord exposed my heart. Though I would not actually say that I was a god and should sit on a throne, I acted it out in my foolishness. I asked the Lord to take me off the throne of my heart and allow Him to rule and govern there because I was not wise. He is, was, and will always be the Wise One. You can be sure that when our hearts become arrogant and hard from pride, God will depose us from our royal throne and strip our glory from us, just as he has done to any king that set themselves above Him (Daniel 5:20).

Chapter Six: The Beauty Treatments

It was said that Moses was more humble than anyone else on the face of the earth (Number 12:3). If Moses was humble, then I want to be humble like him because he got to see God's glory. He was chosen to be the leader, not because of his eloquence or education. He was chosen simply because he was humble. So what was it that made Moses so humble? Why was he able to ascend the mountain of God and come away with a radiant face? If I want the radiant face Moses had, I need to get rid of pimples of pride. Humility comes in different forms. If someone was correcting me, then in humility, I received the correction, knowing that I do not know everything and I could learn a lot from others.

It was also humbling to do kind things for others and not let anyone else know; I was careful to not take the credit. One day it was pressed on my heart to give a large amount of money to someone that needed it more than I did. It was tempting to tell my friends that I had helped out in this way. However, I could tell the Holy Spirit was exposing my heart—I wanted my friends to think more highly of me and recognize what a good person I was. With that conviction, I stopped myself from telling anyone. I may not have received any credit in man's eyes, but I know in my heart that the Lord witnessed what I did and was pleased. With humility, all the glory goes to God. God is humble, and He wants to give us His humility in exchange for our pride and arrogance.

In my heart, I've always wanted to be praised and lifted up by men. I wanted to get to the point where I would simply say, "Why praise me? I am only human." I wanted to have freedom and rest from my secret desire of praise for myself. For example, when people in my neighborhood would say, "Miss Jodie is a warrior," I loved it. I loved being the center of attention. I desired the praise that was due to my King. He deserves all the glory, all the honor, and all the praise, for He is the one who created me in His image.

Next, the beauty treatment of exposure uncovered the blackhead of bitterness. There were many times that I got angry and frustrated with my children; I would yell and yell until my head felt like it was going to explode. Looking back now, I haven't yelled in a long time. The root of my yelling was control. I wanted control, and if I felt like I had none, then I yelled to, hopefully, scare my kids into obedience. That is what my dad did. He yelled at me so loudly, it scared the daylights out of me. I attempted to follow in his example.

There are times when I need a continual beauty treatment on certain areas in my heart. I would reach the point where I would think that I had exchanged all my bitterness for His tenderness, and then boom, I got bitter again. For a while there was need for daily beauty treatments—a daily exchanging of my bitterness for my ex-husband for the tenderness of my beautifully kind King. I didn't feel vengeful, I just hated hearing from him. My insides would get all tangled up, and it would push some ugliness from my heart to my mouth.

I had reason to be upset. He would slander my ability as a mother, even though he had no room to talk. He fathered from a distance— from another state. He never gave me child support and I felt as if he had no right to tell me anything. Satan used my ex-husband to steal my joy, and most often when my guard was down.

Then I would realize that if I was still speaking to him with bitterness and resentment, I obviously needed another beauty treatment. If I shared all the hurtful things that happened, you would probably be disgusted with my ex-husband too. I clearly had good reason to be angry with him after all he had done to me and his own children. But this book is not about him. It is about the beauty that God wanted to bring out of that circumstance. It is about what God wanted to do in me. He wanted to heal my heart of the bitterness and resentment so that it would not hinder my walk with the Lord. Staying bitter and angry at my husband only darkened my outlook on life, and my face did not shine.

When I first read how enraged Haman was at the sight of Mordecai, it was easy to side with Mordecai and think about how evil it was for Haman to even think about destroying the Jewish people (Esther 3:5-6). However, the Lord always wants to show us our own heart in the matter. Far too often we point the finger and fail to acknowledge the sin in our own heart. We end up comparing ourselves, and then we feel justified when others do worse than us. So when I asked the Lord to examine and expose my heart to see if there was any wicked way in me, He uncovered that blackhead of bitterness.

A friend had approached me about the way I was raising my child. I felt almost as if I were being judged. I realized that the enemy was trying to drive a wedge between us, and I was allowing it. If I was not careful, I would basically destroy my relationship with a good friend because of stupid and immature reasons that weren't even worth mentioning. I could see how pride and bitterness could creep up to destroy God-given friendships. It's very easy for hurt to creep into your soul. By the time you realize it, resentment has left a residue that stinks. I was ready to put an end to the friendship, making it a point that I would never call, text, or email again. Later, I learned that my offense was just a miscommunication. I realized that it was I who was being unteachable and selfish, and I was looking out for my own interests. I was offended; I took things personally, and I became unfriendly. Wherever you have any kind of selfish ambition, you will find disorder and every evil practice (James 3:16). The reason you find disorder is because this is not how our Creator has designed us to be.

This is how you are to treat that blackhead of bitterness: If you harbor bitter envy in your hearts, do not boast about it or deny the truth (James 3:14). Admit that you have been wrong; make things right with God first, and then with the person with whom you were bitter. I did, and that person is one of my best friends to this day. Instead of leaning toward selfish gain, I turned my heart toward His statutes, and that blackhead of bitterness was removed.

Thank You, Lord, for the changes You have made, are making, and will make in my life. I know that You will not be done with me until it is time for You to take me into Your palace in heaven. Until then, I will gladly receive all the beauty treatments You want to give me to make me a more blameless and spotless bride.

Church, we need to be completely available for a dose of His beauty. Even just a smudge of His beauty is better than what this life has to offer. You are so beautiful, Lord! The more that we gaze upon His beauty, the more His beauty reflects upon our own faces. I prayed that God would change me into the beautiful image of His Son, and though perhaps not yet completely in my heart, I humbly accepted whatever lot was given to me because the Lord knows what is best. My prayer was that God would create in me the beauty of gentleness and tenderness, and take out the ugly bitter root that was in my heart.

Are there areas in your life that need to be exposed in order to remove the impurities? Everything hidden will eventually come to the light. Are you hiding behind a mask of hypocrisy? Are you trying to cover up that pimple of pride, or the blackhead of bitterness? Or maybe the wrinkles of wrath and oh, wait, that huge zit of gossip is just about ready to pop. Those scars of sin and spots of self-righteousness are even harder to cover, but as we take off our masks, we will be removing those impurities. When we confess our sins to one another, we will be healed. There is so much freedom in being open and vulnerable. As those impurities are removed from our life, we begin to radiate from the inside out.

Treatment 8: Solitude

Solitude touches your eyes. It gives you spiritual vision.

At a young age, I had rather poor eyesight and was forced to wear glasses in order to see. My sight was so bad that when I woke up in the morning I had to feel around the nightstand for my glasses. I couldn't see them even though they were right at my fingertips. I learned early on that corrective lenses were beneficial to my vision. However, I hated the look of glasses on my face, so I went on to contact lenses. When I took the contact lenses out, I still had terrible vision. I wanted something a little more permanent, so I tried laser surgery in hope of never having to wear glasses again. But here I am ten years later with myopic vision.

Myopia is a condition of the eye in which the light that comes in does not directly focus on the retina, but in front of it. This causes the image that one sees when looking at a distant object to be out of focus, while a close object is in focus.[32] It's often referred to as nearsightedness.

Sometimes we just need to get up close and personal with God to get things back into focus. Spiritual myopia is looking at everything at a distance and having no real clarity of vision.

Myopic vision blurred the way I viewed my circumstance. I knew that there were countless others on the same journey, but in my bed I was all alone. I wanted to be held and I wanted to hold. I hated being a single parent and making the decisions of the home. I was tired of it. I wanted to be cared and provided for. I wanted a husband who would stand by me—one who was faithful and wise—one who would pursue me and love me like Christ loved the church.

In this time of solitude, God gave me permission to be weak, to be vulnerable, and to grieve over the loss in my life, so I could move on. This was not where He wanted me to stay. He wanted me to enter into His chambers of intimacy—in this chamber there was no wailing over the circumstances of life. In this place, confidence rose inside my heart that my King would come to the rescue.

Mordecai needed to learn this lesson as well. As soon as he learned about all that had been done against his people, "he tore his clothes, put on burlap and ashes, and went out into the city, crying with a loud and bitter wail. He went as far as the gate of the palace, for no one was allowed to enter the palace gate while wearing clothes of mourning. And as news of the king's decree reached all the provinces, there was great mourning among the Jews. They fasted, wept, and wailed, and many people lay in burlap and ashes" (Esther 4:1-3).

Mordecai could only go as far as the gate of the palace, and why was that? Because no one was allowed to enter the palace while wearing clothes of mourning, or sackcloth. Mordecai was nearsighted—he could not see past his circumstances. This verse also spoke to me about not being able to go past the gates because of my "crybaby" mentality. The

32. Wikipedia contributors, "Myopia," Wikipedia, The Free Encyclopedia, http://en.wikipedia.org/w/index.php?title=Myopia&oldid=551594230 (accessed April 23, 2013).

door was not going to open to me—because I was whining. The Jews only saw their circumstances at large, and they wailed loudly.

There have been many times that I was incredibly lonely and felt like wailing because of my solitude. I prayed that God would go to that place within me where it hurt so bad, and touch that pain and heal me of that need. It was in this solitude that I found all my needs met by God. Now, if a man ever came into my life, it would be an added blessing. Isaiah 54:2-3 is a constant reminder to me of my turning point. The morning I cried out in self-pity to God regarding this matter, He opened my eyes to see that the tent I was surrounding myself with was too small.

From that very same verse in Esther, the Lord showed me that when the news of the king's decree reached all the provinces, there was great mourning among the Jews. They fasted, wept, and wailed, and many people lay in burlap and ashes. Our vision can be blurred by grief and our eyes can be blinded by our tears (Psalm 6:7; 31:9; 88:9).

Dear friends, turn the television off. The news today is discouraging; it will make you nearsighted and place you in a whirlwind of worry. I call it "devil vision," because the media is clouding our spiritual vision which is full of hope and encouragement. "Turn my eyes from worthless things, and give me life through your word" (Psalm 119:37).

Our eyes are the gateway to our souls; that is why it is said in His Word that we should put no vile thing before our eyes (Psalm 101:3). In my opinion, it is only getting worse as time goes on. We are listening to the media, to our coworkers, and to our families who are also blind. The mainstream is definitely not without their opinions on directions for your life. Other people think they can see more clearly for your life than you can, and they offer their advice with good intentions. But the only One who really knows the best plan and how your life will unfold is the One who created you. It is only when we get alone in the quiet place with Him that we can get a better picture.

Chapter Six: The Beauty Treatments

Jesus said, "So ignore them. They are blind guides leading the blind, and if one blind person guides another, they will both fall into a ditch" (Matthew 15:14).

There are other vision problems in the body of Christ. Diplopia, commonly known as double vision, is the simultaneous perception of two images of a single object that may be displaced horizontally, vertically, or diagonally in relation to each other. It is usually the result of impaired function of the extra ocular muscles, where both eyes are still functional but they cannot converge to target the desired object. The brain naturally guards against double vision. In an attempt to avoid double vision, the brain can sometimes ignore the image from one eye, a process known as suppression. [33]

Spiritual diplopia is when our vision is on our past. David could relate with this. He says in the Psalms, "My heart is breaking as I remember how it used to be: I walked among the crowds of worshipers, leading a great procession to the house of God, singing for joy and giving thanks amid the sound of a great celebration! Why am I discouraged? Why is my heart so sad? I will put my hope in God! I will praise Him again—my Savior and my God! Now I am deeply discouraged, but I will remember you" (Psalm 42:4-6a). David had to suppress the thought of the past as he asked himself why he was discouraged.

Jeremiah needed to suppress his emotions to be able to converge and target the desired object in his life too. He wrote, "The thought of my suffering and homelessness is bitter beyond words. I will never forget this awful time, as I grieve over my loss. Yet I still dare to hope when I remember this: The faithful love of the Lord never ends! His mercies never cease. Great is his faithfulness; his mercies begin afresh each morning. I say to myself, 'The Lord is my inheritance; therefore, I will hope in him!' The Lord is good to those who depend on him, to those who search for him. So it is good to wait quietly for salvation from the Lord. And it is good for people to submit at an early age to the

---

33. Wikipedia contributors, "Diplopia," Wikipedia, The Free Encyclopedia, http://en.wikipedia.org/w/index.php?title=Diplopia&oldid=548199731 (accessed April 23, 2013).

yoke of his discipline: Let them sit alone in silence beneath the Lord's demands. Let them lie face down in the dust, for there may be hope at last" (Lamentations 3:19-29).

Another example of spiritual diplopic vision is the church in Laodicea. They were a church who saw things one way; yet God saw it in another way entirely. They said "I am rich. I have everything I want. I don't need a thing!" But they did not realize that they were wretched and miserable and poor and blind and naked. So God advised them to come and get ointment for their eyes so they would be able to see (Revelation 3:14-20).

I needed ointment on my eyes too. My double vision was an inner conflict about who I imagined my prince charming was going to be. I knew that God said that I was to remain unavailable for any dating relationships, and that during this whole year I would not be pursued by anyone. But there were brothers on my mind, and one in particular that I had a hard time letting go of and getting off my mind. Would I ever get to the place where I was completely content with not being with a man? The Lord needed to do a work in my vision so that my eyes could guard against this double vision. I had to accept that this man was not the one and I was not available. I had to stop standing at a closed door, hoping it would open. I had to walk away with Jesus on my mind.

During that time, God even sent him out of the country so that I could get heaven on my mind. Sometimes the Lord has to take away those distractions so that we can focus. If you are praying that God gets you out of an unhealthy relationship that is not honoring Him (and by that I mean not married), then you better get prepared because God will move them out of your way. The biggest mistake I have made, and one I have seen so many women make, is that after God moves them out of the way, we go back to them. We go crying to them, as if we owe them something for causing them to leave. We don't owe any man anything. We owe God our lives, and our lives are in His hands. So when He moves that man or woman out of your life, no matter how strong the tie was between you and that person, you must allow them to leave.

Chapter Six: The Beauty Treatments

We can also be blinded by our emotional needs; we don't even see what is right in front of our face. "We grope like the blind along a wall, feeling our way like people without eyes. Even at brightest noontime, we stumble as though it were dark. Among the living, we are like the dead" (Isaiah 59:10).

Many of us are accustomed to being with people; sometimes we are actively looking for company to entertain us. The feeling of being alone is often hard to endure. When you're alone, it is easy to spend your time dwelling on where you went wrong with your life. Your pain can blind your perspective of the future completely. Solitude seems to be an unfamiliar path for most of us, but it is an opportunity for the Lord to lead us down a new avenue of trust. This way is the Lord's way. He will brighten the darkness before us and smooth out the road ahead of us. He always goes before us.

One day I took my son to the park. As I sat on the bench watching my son play, I started a conversation with a girl who sat next to me. I smiled at her and she started to open her heart to me. She said she had no one to talk to; I assured her that she did now. As I listened intently to her, I realized that this dear woman was so mired in despair and defeat, she was almost on the verge of taking her own life. She felt that everything she did was a failure. She had lost everyone who was close to her. She was in the park because she wanted to remember what she once had as a child. She had to grow up and experience the pain of suffering, the agony of being alone. She talked to me for about an hour before I intervened. I let her know that I had been in a similar situation. We all have. We have all felt alone with absolutely no one to talk to. In that place, we feel so invisible to the world around us that, even if we were surrounded by people, we would still feel alone. In our solitude, we need to take hold of the inner person we are and allow God to reveal to us what our worth is, without needing people and possessions to make us feel like we are special. After we talked, my new friend and I embraced and she walked away with both a fresh perspective and a smile on her face.

Mary Magdalene was too blind to realize that Jesus was right in front of her. She couldn't recognize Him because her whole focus was

167

on her loss, what had been taken from her. When the Lord gave her sight, she could declare, "I have seen the Lord!" (John 20:12-18).

Thank You, Jesus, for opening the eyes of the blind. The beauty treatment for 20/20 vision is found in John 20:20: "As he [Jesus] spoke, he showed them the wounds in his hands and his side. They were filled with joy when they saw the Lord!"

Are you as excited about that verse as I am? When we can see the Lord, we have spiritual 20/20 vision. Of course, I am not talking about our natural eyes. To see the Lord is to see His character, His beauty, His plan, His way; then we see His purpose more clearly. One day, when the Lord takes us to be with Him, we will see Him face-to-face; until then, we can see Him in part. To see any part of the Lord is truly beautiful. Every time someone in the Bible sees the Lord, it occurs when they are alone, in solitude. When Moses was on the mountain alone for forty days, he saw the Lord (Exodus 24:18); when Jacob was left alone to wrestle with God, he saw Him face to face (Genesis 32:24, 30).

David said about Him: "I know the Lord is always with me. I will not be shaken, for he is right beside me" (Psalm 16:8; see also Acts 2:25).

Even a wicked man named Balaam had 20/20 vision in His presence. Balaam went to God to put a curse on God's children, but in that place of solitude in seeking God's hand, his vision was touched by God to see the blessing that God had put on His people. After his encounter with God, Balaam said "This is the message of Balaam son of Beor, the message of the man whose eyes see clearly, the message of one who hears the words of God, who has knowledge from the Most High, who sees a vision from the Almighty, who bows down with eyes wide open: I see him, but not here and now. I perceive him, but far in the distant future. A star will rise from Jacob; a scepter will emerge from Israel" (Numbers 24:15-17).

God ministered in this way to a very sad and lonely woman named Hagar in Genesis 21:14-19. After Abraham sent Hagar and their son Ishmael away, she had no place to go. She wandered in the wilderness with her son, feeling all alone because she had no way to take care of him. They were dying. All the water they had was gone. She literally left her child under a bush, feeling hopeless for the life of her son. But he lifted up his voice and cried out, and God heard the boy's cry. An angel was sent to that lonely place where nobody else could see. The angel asked Hagar what was wrong. The angel told her in her anguish not to fear, for God had heard the boy. He told her to get up and take the boy, for God would make him into a great nation. At this point, the beauty treatment of solitude had touched Hagar's eyes, and God gave her vision to see a well of water nearby. She went and filled up with God and then she was able to give a drink to the boy.

It is in solitude, our time alone with Jesus, that we get clear-cut distinctions of the direction He is leading us. No shades of gray. He said this is the way, walk ye in it. In this time, our vision is not blurred with rationalization.

In my own personal solitude, the Lord gave me the Spirit of wisdom and revelation. He exposed my fears and anxiety so He could teach me to rest. He taught me how to be still with Him. He taught me how to live in Him, and not be subject to the things around me. He showed me what He is really like, and I learned how to see God in everything: from the sunrise, to the sunset; from the quality time with my children, to my solitude in the bathtub. It was in this solitude that I connected with God. This was a season in which I learned the walk of faith, knowing that God would never leave me. I have learned how to access the presence of God, as Esther found access to the king. Access to His presence is in solitude. No one else can go there with you: not your imaginings, not your dreams or expectations, not your thoughts about how you think things should be. This is a place where the King gives His verdict. This is the place where He tells you His thoughts about you and gives you peace. It is a quiet place. This is an intimate place where you can hear His heartbeat and know His heart. God touched my eyes and gave me 20/20 vision in the time that I spent alone with Him.

"Open my eyes to see the wonderful truths in your instructions" (Psalm 119:18).

When our vision is clouded, blurred, or obscured in any way, we fail to see the small God-given gifts that are right in front of our face. We tend to overlook the comforting Scripture, the encouraging note from a friend, the unexpected income, the provision of groceries that just suddenly appears on our doorstep, and the like. His small packages of love are unnoticed because we can only see the huge mountain of bills that seem impossible to pay. If we lift our eyes off the problems and onto the Maker of heaven and earth, the mountain doesn't appear so large—it's no more than a molehill.

If you're single, this beauty treatment can be your best friend. Hope can be your companion as you journey through this solitude. No matter how long it may take for God to match you up with someone whose vision is purposeful, soak up as much solitude as you possibly can. Lie down in your bed, and cover your eyes to the possibilities that have the potential to make you nearsighted. I know what I am talking about because when I dwell on what could have or should have been, then I am left with myopic vision as to God's brilliant and magnificent plans for me. Enter into the rest of God, looking away from all that will distract you; look unto Jesus who is the author and the finisher of our faith (Hebrews 12:2).

If you're married, you might be wondering how you can find solitude. It has to be a deliberate choice to be alone with God. It might require some sacrifices to wake up an hour early or some creative thinking to arrange an hour to take a long bath; but any time alone with the Lord will help to refocus your spiritual vision. And if you're married, yet feeling alone, make it a priority to spend time apart with God; it will not only bring you closer to the King of Kings, it will also bring back intimacy between you and your earthly king.

A friend called me on the day I was learning this. She was telling me that she felt she married her husband out of insecurity. She now regretted marrying him because he did not meet her needs. She wanted him to be playful and wild, yet he was reserved. She was hoping that he would open up and talk to her, but he didn't express himself in the way she wanted. She basically wanted him to conform to her image of the perfect husband. Her husband is a good man; he is a faithful and God-fearing Christian, but He is not God. God alone is our source, the One who can fulfill our expectations, and most often He exceeds them.

Esther was married, but there was a time when she had not seen her husband in thirty days. Even though Esther had all those beauty treatments to prepare her to be without a physical companion, she found hope in the Lord instead. As she poured her heart out to God first, her intimacy with her husband was given back to her. That relationship was renewed.

Having the practice of solitude in your life enables you to keep a proper perspective on your wants and needs before you enter into relationships with others. We, as humans, cannot completely fulfill each other's needs. We might be able to do it temporarily, but the divorce rate is proof that any marriage that is not built upon the foundation and inclusion of Christ doesn't last long. There are countless marriages that suffer because both partners struggle with loneliness and a sense of isolation. They are looking for someone to fill them up and meet all their needs. They fail to understand that only God can complete us and enable us to be all that our partners need. Therefore, they find themselves entangled in despair and without hope.

The beauty treatment of solitude is all about restoring your spirit, soul, and mind in an oasis of hope. An *oasis* is "a fertile or green spot in a waste or desert, especially a sandy desert."[34] It is literally a place of spiritual solitude and refreshing. Our King desires us; He wants to spend time alone with each of us. He is that source that fills every void. If we do not allow Him to fill every void, we try to fill those voids with other relationships. Those relationships will turn out to be dissatisfying because no one can fill the void in our hearts like the King who knows us best.

I once was blind, but now I see clearly—transforming and beautiful vision at its finest!

---

34. *Webster's Collegiate Dictionary*, s.v., "oasis."

Treatment 9: Stretching

*Y*ou build your spiritual muscles in the same way that you build your physical muscles. Building your muscles requires repetition and persistence. The bigger your muscles are, the more weight you are able to lift. In the same way, the more you build your spiritual muscles, the more weight that you are able to bear. If the burdens of life are getting bigger and you don't seem to be able to bear much more that is coming your way, then it is time to start building your spiritual muscles. When you do not build up your spiritual muscles, you have what I call flabby faith.

Those of us who suffer from flabby faith are those who are not making spiritual fitness a priority. Our spiritual fitness is just as important to the health of our whole being as physical fitness. First, starting off with our daily bread is essential to having a healthy spiritual body. Secondly, building up our spiritual muscles by praying in the Holy Spirit in faith will make us strong in the mighty power of the Lord (Jude 1:20). Thirdly, the spiritual muscles need to be stretched out to bear with the failings of the weak. Instead of just building ourselves up, we are to build up our brothers and sisters for their spiritual good (Romans 15:1-2). We help build their spiritual muscles by cheering them on and encouraging them with the promise that they can do all things through Christ who strengthens them (1 Thessalonians 5:11; Philippians 4:13). As we build others up with the Word of His grace, we are not only being made stronger, but we are also becoming a healthier vessel for God to use in His works of service to build up His church (1 Corinthians 14:12). "Now these are the gifts Christ gave to the church: the apostles, the prophets, the evangelists, and the pastors and teachers. Their responsibility is to equip God's people to do His work and build up the church, the body of Christ" (Ephesians 4:11-12).

The purpose of stretching is to reach to the whole measure of the fullness of Christ.

Chapter Six: The Beauty Treatments

We are going to start with our spiritual diet. When an athlete is training or exercising and building muscles, they eat lots of protein; meat is usually the preferred source. You know where I am going, don't you? In order to build up our spiritual muscles, we need to eat the meat of God's Word. The Bible says that we need to leave the milk, or the elementary truths, at the foundation and build on that foundation with meat. We do that by chewing on the tasty Word of God, and slowly digesting them so they go down deep. Milk is swallowed quickly, leaving no time for reflection on the taste. Milk is good for the baby Christian, but once we have our foundation, it is time to grow and build on our faith in Christ. Milk is full of fat. The fat becomes the security most of us fall back on, because it sure is easy to get fat on God's Word, but it is not as easy to build the spiritual muscles that produce a strong foundation.

When God told Moses to tell the people that every day they should go out and collect their daily bread, there was always enough. Anything that was left over turned into maggots. It's not about how much we take in of God's Word; it is how much of it builds our faith and stretches us to trust beyond our own understanding that matters. That is why we are told not to lean on our own understanding. Our understanding will only produce weak theology. If we are spiritual beings, our food must be spiritual. To be honest with you, I am tired of the soulish talk I hear. I want to be dead to the world and alive in Christ, talking only about Christ and how He fits into the picture. But not everyone is there yet. I want the Lord to lead me to the people who know their identity in Christ so that we can discuss this delicious topic. The meat at this banquet is for the royal officials. This meat is not for those who desire only milk.

Recorded in my journal of the special foods Jesus gave me during this time of consecration, there was a day that I woke up with the feeling that I had allowed the yeast of the Pharisees to seep into my spiritual walk. In Mathew 16, Jesus used the picture of yeast to describe the teachings of the Pharisees. He used yeast because of its ability to grow invisibly within the lump of dough, just as the poisoned teaching of hypocrites could grow in the hearts of the disciples without their awareness. I felt like I needed to cleanse myself of any yeast, or any sin, that might be hindering me from entering into His presence.

Two of my friends, Jodi and Billy, noticed that there was something not right with me. Billy said that my joy was being depleted, and Jodi agreed. Both of them saying that gave me reason for concern. I knew that it was the little foxes that spoil the whole vine (Song of Solomon 2:15), and that the little bit of yeast worked its way through the whole batch of dough. The Lord showed me that the joy that I had was dependent upon my circumstances. Because I felt myself growing impatient and considered my circumstances to be unfavorable, I took my eyes off Jesus and started to pull the strings myself. I tried to manipulate another person to pursue me by my outward appearance, wearing clothing that made me look more appealing. The year was almost up. I had lost a lot of weight while fasting every other day for the entire year. It was hypocrisy in me exposed; that little bit of yeast had a way of permeating the whole batch of dough. After Jodi rebuked me for it, she stretched out the dough of the Pharisee. She encouraged me and built me up in the Word of grace that cleanses us from the yeast of the Pharisees. Jesus' special food of truth was exchanged for the yeast of deception in me.

While learning firsthand about stretching out the dough to remove the yeast of the Pharisee, I went to the gym with a friend that I hadn't seen in a while. She and I got on our treadmills and we began to talk about our lives. I began to feel that what she was saying was not right. I felt I had to speak truth to her to realign her focus. I needed to help her remove the yeast. She had been living with a man who was not her husband. Although I had spoken to her about it many times, she had refused to listen. She had wanted to leave that relationship for quite some time, but she had become so dependent on him that she felt if she asked him to leave, she might find herself being unable to afford her mortgage alone and therefore end up homeless. It was a stretch for her to believe that God would provide for her needs. I told her that she was not being fair to the man, pretending to be his love so that he could pay the bills. As we were running on the treadmills, she began to get a cramp in her leg and I asked her what she thought cramping meant in the spiritual sense, and she said, "It is getting your attention." I laughed and thought how true that was. God was getting her attention. She needed to release that man and stop using him to get ahead. My friend received the beauty treatment of stretching that day as she was stretched in her faith to trust that God would provide for her and her children.

Spiritually speaking, when the Lord gets your attention by way of the conviction cramp, one finds relief in the confession of the sin which is causing us to cramp up spiritually. My son tells on himself every time he does something wrong. He cannot stand to have anything on his conscience. He knows that once he confesses what He has done, he immediately feels better. The beauty treatment of stretching alleviates the pain of holding onto guilt.

This is the beauty treatment that deals with our tendency to reach back into our own treasure of security. This is where we need to stop trying to pull the tendon strings for ourselves as we manipulate people and situations. We need to be quiet and be convinced, absolutely convinced that God is at work amid the gallows of our life. We can see the gallows in the dawn of the morning sunrise, but in the beauty of trust, we know that God is at work! We cannot change the events, but we can know that He is still in the midst of them and He can still the storm to a whisper (Psalm 107:29).

Working out is not easy. In fact, when we workout we tear our muscle fibers. Have you had just about all you can take? Do you feel like you are going to crumble? Ultimately, it is God who formed you. You may have more control in how you build the physical body, but the cool thing about our spiritual body is that God is the One who forms and shapes and builds you into the beautiful fullness of Him. He is the Potter and we are the clay. He is in total control; He allows everything that comes our way to build us and prepare us for His coming. Whether you have lost loved ones; been without a job or income; raised your royal children as a single parent; dealt with rebellious teenagers; lived in darkness, shame, guilt and depression; held onto the past; feared the future; or endured any affliction that tore at your heart; it is all used to

175

make you a more beautiful bride of Christ. So let Him stretch you to capacity—you will benefit from the results.

When we are lifting heavy weights, a chemical called lactic acid is released that causes pain and tells the body to stop. Most often, when the pain of life pops its ugly head, we immediately want to stop building. This is when we quit as believers too; we just give up trying because it is too painful to continue. I have been in that position more than once. I relate in the physical sense. When I try to lose the extra weight that is making my body weak, I give up all too quickly when my body becomes sore from working out. It is like a roller coaster—losing weight, gaining weight—it never ends. It is the same for the roller coaster Christians in the wilderness: we are up, and then we are down. We gain strength, and then we get weak.

When I think of the tendons of our body, for some reason my mind thinks of the story of *Pinocchio* by Carlo Collodi. In the book, Pinocchio was a puppet that was controlled by his kindly maker; he only moved in the direction that the master puppeteer would maneuver him. However, when Pinocchio turned into a boy by way of magic, he ran from his maker, getting into all kinds of mischief.[35] This silly analogy caused me to think about what controls me. Even though the Holy Spirit does not control us like a puppet, if we stay connected to Him and allow Him to move us in the direction He is leading us, we avoid the path of mischief. No one really likes the thought of being controlled by something, but in reality we all are. We are either controlled by the flesh or we are controlled by the Spirit. Each one will lead us down a path that could benefit or bother us, bless us or curse us. We will ultimately pay the consequences for the choices we make and the road we follow. If we allow the Lord to pull the strings, we will not lose. The battle belongs to the Lord and He fights our battles for us. This gives us stability and a better stance in Him. He knows how to hold us, build us, keep us, move us, stretch us, and use us for His glory.

---

35. Carlo Collodi, *Pinocchio, The Adventures of a Marionette,* (Boston: Ginn and Company, 1904).

Chapter Six: The Beauty Treatments

Stretching your faith is like trusting the Lord for the unknown. When I try to wrap my mind around trust, the best way I can describe it is when I was first asked to go on a "God's Unfailing Love" retreat some time ago. Before attending this retreat, the guests were not allowed to know what the weekend would hold. At first, this was hard for me, because I like to have it all mapped out for me. I wanted to know what the schedule of events was, and at what time everything would happen. But the beauty of this retreat was that we were to place our trust in the person who invited us to come, and believe that we were in good hands. That was a bit of a stretch for me. The structure and nature of these retreats were to reveal God's unfailing love for us in tangible ways; the team members had put a lot of work into creating an environment that held many surprises for the guests that attended. If I had gone on this retreat with foreknowledge of all that was to take place, I would have been robbed of the wonderful surprises that were planned on my behalf. I put my trust in my friend Jodi instead. She knew the plan, and she kept it hidden so that it would not hinder my ability to walk into the unknown. This was only one weekend, but it built in me the ability to trust God for a lifetime of uncertainty. God knows the plan, and we can trust that He has many surprises planned for each one of us.

The beauty treatment of stretching is simply walking out what you believe, moving upon the principles in His Word, and stretching your faith to do good works. Stretching is more beneficial to those who do it regularly, making it a daily practice. Stretching actually increases the blood flow and releases a fluid that lubricates the joints that surround our muscles. Oh, the blood of Jesus! How precious is His flow—to cover over our sins and make us whole. One of the spiritual conditions that affects the hands and feet of Christ when we are not being stretched is the arthritis of apathy, or laziness. Stretching your sore muscles is like stretching your faith: going over and beyond what you think you can do, and doing the impossible through Christ. However, some of us don't want to believe God in regard to the impossible—we want to stay right where we are as lethargic, lukewarm Christians whom Jesus will not use. We complain that He requires of us more than we are capable, and punishes us for things we cannot help. Ultimately, we just dislike the process necessary for us to develop the character that the Lord is trying to cultivate. We close our hearts to receiving the Lord's beauty in this area. The slothful servant's choice is to be deprived of his talent. This could apply to the blessings of the natural life, but it has a greater application to the means of grace. It is a guarantee that those of us who think like that are not spiritually fit for His kingdom. God said in His Word that it is impossible to please Him without faith (Hebrews 11:6). If we are to run this race with perseverance, we are to be diligent and follow through with strengthening our faith.

> "And now, just as you accepted Christ Jesus as your Lord, you must continue to follow him. Let your roots grow down into him, and let your lives be built on him. Then your faith will grow strong in the truth you were taught, and you will overflow with thankfulness" (Colossians 2:6-7).

The reason we have to apply this beauty treatment to our lives consistently is because physical laziness and sloth can be one of the greatest enemies to the Christian life. Nothing steals our devotion quicker than boredom. If the devil can't get us to sin morally, he usually succeeds through apathy and inertia. I believe that's what's happening in the church today. He says in your conscience: "You cannot possibly get up this morning to pray. You can't get up this morning. You worked hard all week. God doesn't expect this of you. God doesn't expect you to fast. He knows that that's beyond your ability. That's for others."

Christ keeps no servants to be unused: we have received everything from Him, and have nothing we can call our own except sin. Our spiritual fitness from Christ is given to equip us for working for Him and through Him. The manifestation of the Spirit is given to every man to profit everyone else. The day of the Lord will soon come when we must all consider the good that has been accomplished by God within our own souls, and what we have done unto others. The improving of natural fitness can not entitle a man to divine grace. Stretching is the real Christian's liberty and privilege to be connected as part of His body in promoting His glory and the good of His people: the love of Christ restricts him to live no longer to himself, but live instead for Him that died for him, and rose again. We are to be connected to His heart and follow Him.

Laziness, when indulged, grows upon people so that they have no heart to do the most needful things for themselves. The sluggard will not even bring the Word to his own mouth to feed himself. He expects that the meat of the Word should drop into his mouth (Proverbs 19:24). A slothful or lazy character trait is the biggest weakness in today's culture. Slothful people are not looking for things to do, therefore, only diligent people can be useful. Diligence is stretching with perseverance and consistency. With that quality built in your life, you will not become spiritually dull and apathetic. Instead, you will follow the example of those who are going to inherit God's promises because of their faith and endurance (Hebrews 6:12). "Give your complete attention to these matters. Throw yourself into your tasks so that everyone will see your progress" (1 Timothy 4:15).

"Preach the word of God. Be prepared, whether the time is favorable or not. Patiently correct, rebuke, and encourage your people with good teaching" (2 Timothy 4:2). Paul was diligent in serving the Lord and so must I be. He called on me to write this book with full authority, and so I must be diligent and purposeful in it. I learned I must not simply write about the details of my day, but rather I must write about the truth. I can only accomplish that by being diligent in seeking the Lord and searching for ways to cultivate character that is useful to God. God reveals truth to people who act on it and who make it visible in their lives.

There's a wonderful story in Matthew 25 of how some men stretched the measure of what was given to them. It was about a man who went on a journey and he entrusted all his belongings to his trusted servants. Before he left, he gave each one of them an advance in pay according to their abilities. The man who had received the five talents went at once and put his money to work and gained five more. So also, the one with the two talents gained two more. But the man who had received the one talent went off, dug a hole in the ground, and hid his master's money. When the master returned to see how they had each invested the advance they received, he was quite pleased with the ones who had a better return on their investment. He allowed them to share in his happiness and gave them a greater reward. However, with the man who did nothing with what he was given, even what he had was taken from him and given to the one who had the most. He was then thrown outside, into the darkness (Matthew 25:14-30). That poor man needed the beauty treatment of knowing how to stretch what was given to him.

In the areas of diligence, I needed His grace more than ever, for I had fallen short of that calling. I often found myself thinking that I always had something to do, or that I was always looking for stuff to do, but was I looking for something to do for the Lord? I wanted to be sure that it was God's will for me to stay home and not look for work. I didn't want to appear lazy or slothful. I just wanted to receive all that God wanted in me first. I found that the days that I failed to be diligent in writing in my journals were days that were ineffective and unproductive, to say the least. This is when I asked the Lord to exchange my slothfulness with His diligence, and to stamp it in to my character. I needed a U-turn to get me off the dead end road my laziness was leading me down.

Any turnaround always begins with a stretching step. Esther stepped through, Haman stepped off, Xerxes stepped in, and Mordecai stepped up. A step in the right direction is the stretching step I always strive to take.

The tendons connect the muscles to the bones, and the ligament is a fibrous tissue that connects the bones to other bones. Since I think of the Holy Spirit as the ligament, I picture Him connecting us to each other.

The king's party shows that he wanted to be a part of the people's lives. He could have remained in his cozy little palace, barking out orders and never meeting the people he governed, but he demonstrated relationship with the people. I love to be with friends. Building relationships and connecting with one another is something about which I feel most purposeful. After spending so much time in the book of Esther, I got the feeling that King Xerxes loved his company as well. Yes, it was for the purpose of getting their vote because he was running a campaign to attack Greece, but let's take this deeper—to his belief system and what possible spiritual application it may hold. I think that Xerxes knew that there was power in the battle when there was unity among friends. The enemy of our soul is always at work and wants to injure us by keeping us divided. He seeks to destroy the connective tissue that binds us together. Relationships are what our Creator created us for.

In relationships, I have learned the importance of connection. I am a party planner. I plan birthday parties, holiday parties, and many different kinds of social gatherings. The reason I love to plan those events is simply because I feel that God has anointed my hands and feet to connect the body of Christ. I see the importance of breaking bread together, praying together, laughing together, playing, and just enjoying life together. As we connect with the body of Christ we become one, even as God the Father is One with God the Son, Jesus Christ, our Head. As we become one as a body, we radiate the reflection of our Maker, and the Lord wants to show us off as His bride. We become His splendor. We become the warriors and the conquerors in His kingdom. He wants to reveal to the world who He is in us. It is time to start flexing our muscles to show the world where our strength comes from. When we do things on our own, we get weak and exhausted. But when we allow the Holy Spirit to be the fuel in our body, then we have pure performance for our spiritual life fitness.

Stretching may also come as discipline. God will stretch out His hand to strike us because He loves us; He wants to break our stubborn wills so we can be secure in His leading. I heard an analogy once of a little lamb that kept going astray. In order to keep that little lamb from leaving the flock, the Shepherd had to break its leg. He then put the little lamb over His shoulders with the lamb's head hanging near the Shepherd's heart.

It is not worth fighting with God; but if you do, you may end up like Jacob—with a socket out of place for struggling with Him (Genesis 32:25). Or you may end up like David as he cried out in the Psalms, "O Lord, don't rebuke me in your anger or discipline me in your rage! Your arrows have struck deep, and your blows are crushing me. Because of your anger, my whole body is sick; my health is broken because of my sins. My guilt overwhelms me—it is a burden too heavy to bear. My wounds fester and stink because of my foolish sins. I am bent over and racked with pain. All day long I walk around filled with grief. A raging fever burns within me, and my health is broken. I am exhausted and completely crushed. My groans come from an anguished heart.... I am on the verge of collapse, facing constant pain. But I confess my sins; I am deeply sorry for what I have done" (Psalm 38:1-8, 17-18).

Stretching can be hazardous when performed incorrectly, even to the point of causing permanent damage to the tendons, ligaments, and muscle fiber. When I refer to the spiritual health of the body in this way, I am alluding to stretching out your fist to harm others; stretching out your finger to blame someone else for your problems; stretching an accusing finger; stretching out your lovely legs to trip another, causing a brother to stumble; or stretching your foot across a line you should not cross with someone else.

If done properly, stretching can prevent injury, relax the muscles, increase the range of motion and flexibility, and better one's performance, especially when it comes to athletics. Likewise, the Christian who properly receives the beauty treatment of stretching can relax in the Scriptures that are hidden within their heart. Their range of motion can reach to the ends of the world. They are flexible in schedule and can move about as the Lord directs (Proverbs 22:1). They are able to perform the works that Christ has called them to do in excellence.

"He makes the whole body fit together perfectly. As each part does its own special work, it helps the other parts grow, so that the whole body is healthy and growing and full of love" (Ephesians 4:16). With that in mind, my friend, "Stretch out your hand with healing power; may miraculous signs and wonders be done through the name of your holy servant Jesus" (Acts 4:30). God wants to be the church's personal trainer, preparing each of His children for a heavenly race of Olympic proportions.

Treatment 10: UV Protection

*O*ur God is in control—there's no need to worry, no need to fear. He is our "Universal Protection" through every small and overwhelming circumstance. Everything has a purpose. God doesn't make mistakes.

As small and seemingly unimportant as the nails seem to be, this beauty treatment is for the spiritual fingernails. Where am I going with this? We can agree that we as the bride of Christ make up a body. There are many parts to our body, and we make up the whole body. Every organ has some kind of covering or protection over it. Even the nails of the body have a function and purpose.

Did you know that a person's nails can tell you what is happening inside of the body? Your nails reveal clues to your overall health. Healthy nails are smooth and uniform color. Greenish nails may indicate infection. A yellowing tint may point to internal disorders. Spots or textures problems like ridges indicate vitamin or mineral deficiencies. Dry and brittle nails may be an indication that the body is low on calcium. Similarly, you can tell a lot about a person's spiritual condition by what comes out of their mouths, for out of the abundance of the heart the mouth speaks (Matthew 12:34). Infectious infirmities may be lying dormant inside a soul until one opens their mouth to complain; then, unfortunately, it spreads.

Here is the spiritual application. Are you a nervous wreck? Do you worry over just about everything? Are you walking in fear? The nails protect the nerve endings in your fingertips, just as the Lord protects you. It is time to get out our cuticle stick (the remembrance of the cross) and get rid of the fungus of fear and those worry warts. This will be a time of letting go and letting God heal those nervous nail biters. The nail itself is dead cells. Likewise, without Christ, we can do nothing. Our hands and feet must go and touch as He directs if we are to touch the world.

The beauty treatment for the fungus of fear is faith and courage. Courage is a protective coating on our hearts. The Manicurist is holding your hand—you're not alone.

Mordecai would not kneel down or pay Haman any honor. In the same way, I chose not to bow down to the fear of what I should do or shouldn't do. I made up my mind to trust in the Lord as He promised in His Word, "There is no one like the God of Israel. He rides across the heavens to help you, across the skies in majestic splendor. The eternal God is your refuge, and his everlasting arms are under you. He drives out the enemy before you; he cries out, 'Destroy them!' So Israel will live in safety, prosperous Jacob in security, in a land of grain and new wine, while the heavens drop down dew. How blessed you are, O Israel! Who else is like you, a people saved by the Lord? He is your protecting shield and your triumphant sword! Your enemies will cringe before you, and you will stomp on their backs!" (Deuteronomy 33:26-29). God, whom shall I fear? You are my refuge, my only true security. You are always holding out Your arms to catch me when the shaky supports that I trust in collapse and I fall.

The knock on the door was more like a bang. It was a United States Marshal and they came to arrest me. There was a warrant out for my arrest because, three months prior to that day, my daughter and I had a physical struggle, and I hit her. I was at a loss as to what I should do. I called the police for intervention; instead, they put out the warrant for my arrest. It did not make sense that the ones who I looked to for help would do this. When I arrived at the station, they booked me and treated me like a criminal. It was an incredible frightening time for me. The minute they put me into a holding cell, I got on my face and stayed there for the three hours as I waited to be moved into an actual jail cell. It was truly the scariest place I have ever been, and in that moment, I needed to trust that the Lord had a plan and a purpose in this. Otherwise, He would not have allowed it. He was going to protect me and I needed to hide in Him. This is how I did that. Every opportunity the Lord gave me to talk about Him, I did not keep silent. I did not fear how others would respond. I did keep silent when religious debates broke out. There was

184

a religious spirit among many of the women there as they claimed to know God better than the rest. One girl even said that she was the second coming. They used foul language, as if they were trying to impress the other inmates by how corrupt there were. They interrupted me and the Lord instructed me to walk away. The Lord told me to look for the broken ones, the frail ones, the ones all alone—the ones needing the beauty treatment of a covering. I found a few and I reached my hand out to them in their fearful moments. I let them know that they were not alone and that the Lord was with us. Later that evening, all the ladies were escorted to a gym for some exercise.

As I walked around that gym, I sang praises to the Lord and I felt His presence there with me. Someone who had been sitting against the wall stopped me to tell me, "You know something, lady, as you were walking you looked like a bright light walking up a mountain." I was so grateful to hear that because I knew that the Lord was right there by my side, covering me in that time. It gave me the courage that I needed to get through the night. We went back to the cell and I read my Bible for more courage, and then I heard my name called because a pastor was there to see me. It was Pastor Bill. My heart leaped for joy as he let me know that the church was a hundred percent behind me with support in prayer; that gave me yet more courage to face the night. It was a long night indeed, but I sang myself to sleep thinking that the cells might just burst open like they did for Paul and Silas.

The next morning, we were taken to court with handcuffs and shackles and put into another holding cell as we waited to appear before the judge. As I was waiting, a public defender came and asked me if I had my own lawyer or if I needed a public defender. I told him that I did not think I needed one since I was not guilty. He looked at my paperwork and said, "Ma'am, you could be facing up to six months in jail. I think it would be best and wise for you to have a public defender." He had given me the worst possible news; it frightened me to think that God would keep me here for six months. Did God think this was the best way to totally separate me from the world? Tears rushed from my eyes; all the other ladies saw me on my face in prayer. They all asked for prayer as well. Finally, it was my turn to face the judge. When I came out and saw my daughter, Victoria, and my best friend, Jodi, I was strengthened in heart. I watched my daughter break into tears as she saw her mommy in shackles like a prisoner; it was an awful feeling, to say the least. Victoria's defender spoke on behalf of Victoria, saying that she did not feel endangered at all. She said we had a rough night; she admitted having blowing it out of proportion, and that she just wanted her mommy home. I was so happy that the judge released me and thought to myself, *thank You, Lord, for the protection that gave me courage when the fungus of fear was tiptoeing its way into my heart.*

Interestingly, the timing of that incident was right before the presidential election of 2008. How appropriate, I thought to myself. I sensed that the fungus of fear was tiptoeing its way into our nation. The nervous nail biters sat glued to the television to see who our next president would be. I heard much prophecy that America would elect its most ungodly president ever. Ultimately, it will depend on the Christians and those who stand up for what they believe. Those in the church who believed in the values taught through God's protective covering would be those who would protect our nation. This election would define the future of millions of unborn children, not to mention the millions of women who must experience the agonizing pain and the regret of post-abortion trauma. I was one of them. I know that agonizing pain. When I was seventeen, I had an abortion; to this day, I regret that decision. I know that there was truly life inside of my womb; I determined the fate of a child who could have been used mightily by God. I will never know. It grieved my heart to know that the first thing this new president would do when elected would be to pass the Freedom of Choice Act, which would be an act that would effectively remove every abortion restriction that had been passed since Roe vs. Wade. Now, as I am revisiting this chapter to edit the book four years later, we have just reelected the same president, thereby possibly subjecting our country to four more years of ungodly rule.

I do not pay much attention to the political campaigns out there because of the ungodly speech that comes out of each candidate as they push for votes. However, I have heard this president speak about how he thinks that gay marriages should be allowed. He was basically speaking what the itching ears wanted to hear. But God says that anyone who practices these indecent acts will not inherit the kingdom of heaven (1 Corinthians 6:9; Leviticus 20:13). The fungus of fear has caused us to put our fingers in our ears to not hear the truth of God's Word that protects our nation. "Your ancestors refused to listen to this message. They stubbornly turned away and put their fingers in their ears to keep from hearing" (Zechariah 7:11).

Listen, bride of Christ, we cannot put our fingers in our ears. We are in an Esther age in the divided states of America, and since God intervened at the cry of Esther's voice, He will hear ours too. A house divided will not stand. It is time we stopped biting our nails and got a better grip on God's Word to prepare our hearts for His return. We, as children of God, have nothing to fear because we cling to the Word of God and worship Him in the beauty of holiness. "For the law was not intended for people who do what is right. It is for people who are lawless and rebellious, who are ungodly and sinful, who consider nothing sacred and defile what is holy, who kill their father or mother or commit other murders. The law is for people who are sexually immoral, or who practice homosexuality, or are slave traders, liars, promise breakers, or who do anything else that contradicts the wholesome teaching that comes from the glorious Good News entrusted to me by our blessed God" (1 Timothy 1:9-11).

Nails protect the tips of the fingers. Fingers are essential for manipulating and grasping objects, as well as for contact with other individuals. Likewise, the covering of God's Word serves to protect us and give us a better grip of reality. The Lord promises to come to our rescue. I encouraged myself with many Scriptures that gave me courage as I faced the fungus of fear in my own life as the elections came. "The Lord replies, 'I have seen violence done to the helpless, and I have heard the groans of the poor. Now I will rise up to rescue them, as they have longed for me to do" (Psalm 12:5). He is our hiding place and He will protect us from trouble and surround us with songs of deliverance (Psalm 32:7). His love and His truth always protect. He promises in His

Word to protect us from wicked men who set traps for our feet (Psalm 140:4). He will protect by the power of His Name (John 17:11). The Lord Jesus even prays for us that God would protect us from the evil one while we are still in this world (John 17:15). The Lord is faithful to strengthen us and protect us while we wait for His return. Proverbs says that His wisdom will protect you, and we are instructed to love wisdom and wisdom will watch over us (Proverbs 4:6). If we are wise, our lips protect us, not like the foolish whose ruin comes from their corrupt speech (Proverbs 14:3). And since the beginning of wisdom is to fear the Lord, let us rather have that healthy fear that keeps our hearts from sinning, instead of letting the fungi of fear keep us from trusting, thereby infecting our whole being. "For the angel of the Lord is a guard; he surrounds and defends all who fear him" (Psalm 34:7).

In regard to the dedication of the priests, they were to be consecrated; they had to perform many rituals to be set apart as holy. One act in particular that the priests were commanded to do was the slaughter of a ram. They took some of its blood, and put it on the lobes of the right ears of Aaron and his sons, on the thumbs of their right hands, and on the big toes of their right feet (Exodus 29:20). The significance of putting it upon the tips of their ears, thumbs, and toes was intended to signify that the priest should dedicate all his body parts and powers to the service of God: his ear to the hearing and study of the Law, his hands to diligence in the sanctified ministry and all acts of obedience, and his feet to walking in the way of God's precepts. The ear is the symbol of obedience, the hand of action, and the foot of the path or conduct in life. Faith without works is dead (James 2:20).

Paul goes on to instruct us in the book of Romans to not allow any part of our bodies to become instruments of evil to serve sin, and that includes our nails. We should use our whole body as instruments to do what is right for the glory of our God (Romans 6:13).

When I go to the nail salon, it is usually to get a filing because my nails tend to be brittle and they tear off easily; real manicures require more upkeep than the fake ones do. There are many women who embrace the idea of covering their real nails with fake ones.

Chapter Six: The Beauty Treatments

Fake nails offer many advantages that make life easier: they provide immediate gratification, they don't require as much attention, they can easily be replaced whenever keeping them would otherwise require a lot of personal effort. The reasons are endless, but the fact remains: they are fake. They may look just like the real thing, but they're not. And while a real nail is actually a living, growing, active part of a healthy body, these counterfeits are just a small, dead, thin slab of who really knows what. Many people also seek out a god who offers these same benefits, and for the same reasons. And what they end up with is a sad, empty collection of false hopes and false gratification—totally false to the core. Some of the things people find falsity in are horoscopes, tarot cards, palm readings, and reading of the stars. I will be the first to tell you how fake all these practices are. I practiced them. I used to study the horoscope like I now study the Word of God. I was diligent to find the source of power within, and answers to all my questions. It led to more deception in playing with a Ouija board, later demonic power took hold of my life with its grip of fear. It was an ungodly fear. Scary movies only fed that fear. I became a walking fungus of fear.

The Holy Spirit is the only filling that is capable of fulfilling our destinies. He is the Universal Power behind every single step we take. It is He who trains my hands for war and gives my fingers skill for battle (Psalm 144:1). The Holy Spirit fills me supernaturally, bringing nourishing minerals to the health of my whole body.

As I went in the nail salon to get my nails done, one of the things that blessed me was that the lady doing my nails held my hand in such a way that somehow felt as though I was not alone. Likewise, I love the fact that God is never far away. He is always near. He is holding us and sustaining us. He never leaves us alone.

I first received the beauty treatment of protection on a morning when my mind wandered into the wasteland of worries. To be honest, my troubles seemed overwhelming. I needed Him to come to my rescue and cause my mind to rest in the pastures of His Word. The following Scriptures brought me comfort and replaced my worry warts with His beauty as I waited on His protective covering.

Jesus told us not to worry about how our daily needs would be met. Isn't life more than food? Aren't our bodies more than the clothes on our backs? He taught us to see things in His creation as promises of His constant care. Doesn't He feed the wild birds, and aren't we worth much more than they are? Doesn't He clothe the ordinary grass with gorgeous wildflowers? And even Solomon's royal robes could never compare with them! Why do we have so little faith? All the worrying in the world won't help. Unbelievers worry about these things, and Jesus said we shouldn't be like them. We are God's children. He knows what we need. We must seek His kingdom, and while we are busy with His kingdom, He will take care of everything else. He added these words, "Today's trouble is enough for today" (Matthew 6:25-34).

I am not the worrying type, and I had no reason to worry. I had a consistent income. Although it wasn't that much, I'd been able to provide for my needs without having to ask anyone for help. But my unemployment was about to end and I wasn't sure how it was all going to work after that. I wondered and worried how I would get money to support my children. I didn't trust the Lord to provide. I needed His beauty treatment of protection. I didn't want anything to interfere with the time I had consecrated to God for this season. As the worries disappeared in my life, I found it much easier to listen. The worries became a distant issue because I found myself trusting and releasing control to the Lord. There was nothing I could do about my present situation of myself. I cannot do anything apart from Christ. That is the beauty of God protecting us from ourselves.

God will protect us just as long as we obey Him and submit to His rule and sovereign authority. Even though most of the Christian church is against what the president stands for, we must understand that God is the One who allowed him to be put there (Romans 13:1-5). I know some of you want to squirm in your seat at the thought of that, but it is true. We are to submit to the governing authorities because we are His children, and following Him means submitting to the authority that He has placed over us. This will be a beauty treatment that protects us from walking outside His covering. This is like what David experienced as he saw thousands fall by his side and yet no harm came to him (Psalm 91:7). We as believers can live upright and be protected in an ungodly environment. Do what is right and the ungodly will notice, and you may be able to grasp those fingernails around the loved ones who need to be pulled from the fires of hell. If we do what is wrong and walk away from our God-given principles, we will lose the covering that protects our own souls. If we leave our protective covering, we will fall under a curse. It is not a curse when we willfully obey our authority; it actually brings us much life and joy when we are walking under the covering of the leadership of Christ.

Men are to be the head of the household. Rebellion can, and usually does, take place if the woman does not have a God-ordained relationship with her husband. This really does become a curse. However, it does not have to be this way. As a woman takes on the responsibility to be submissive and obedient to her husband, he will love her for it. The relationship becomes intimate and satisfying. The woman should ultimately seek to please not only her husband, but also her King. It pleases the King to have an honorable queen.

Okay, I know this might be easy for me to say because, at the present time of writing this, I am not married to anyone. However, the desire was implanted in me to be submissive to my husband, when and if, the Lord should bring him into my life. This was part of the year's preparation. He was giving me His beauty treatment of protection. I desired this because I knew that it would keep me safe in Him. There would be no need to be ashamed and hide from God because I would be walking in His perfect light and order. He has established the husband as the head of the woman because He knows that the woman is easily deceived and sin is the result (1 Timothy 2:14).

From the beginning of time, when God placed Adam over Eve, He did so to protect her from the curse. However, God said to the man, "Since you listened to your wife and ate from the tree whose fruit I commanded you not to eat, the ground is cursed because of you. All your life you will struggle to scratch a living from it" (Genesis 3:17).

King Xerxes did not listen to his wife; he listened to the wise men of that time. He was the ruler of his household and, in my opinion, finding a wife that would suit him (a helpmate) would actually prove to be the best option. Esther made a great queen, and whether she loved him or not, she respected him and he loved her for it. She gained much favor. I see a lesson to be learned for women in this. I do not agree with many commentaries that the decision the king made was a bad one. Many women I have encountered get upset because their husbands will not be the leader of the household. These same women pick up the towel, take on the role of the leader, and then cry about it. We are not made to handle the whole thing. I can say as a single mom that God has definitely given me the strength to handle more than I am supposed to, but I also see where I would be better off having someone to trust as a decision maker in the home. I believe I make a better helpmate than I do a leader. I became exhausted by leading my family. I would rather have a husband to lead whom I could follow and support in that role.

Man was made to lead, provide, and protect; woman was made to respond, nurture, and provide the moral influence of society. Our modern view has changed drastically, but the built-in needs have never changed. This remains evident in the way Christ leads the church, provides for the church, and protects the church. The church, being His bride, is to respond, to nurture the relationship, and to influence society as a spotless bride.

Just as God made Eve to be Adam's helper, He also has a desire for the church to help Him build His kingdom. The female side of God is His church! We must submit to and obey His authority because He protects us, leads us, and can be trusted to provide for us. Jesus refers to the Holy Spirit as His Helper. Leadership was not intended to be domineering though. God doesn't dominate us or smother us. He gives us His protection as He gives us an identity of our own, as well as the ability to follow the lead of our King. Can you grasp how deep and how wide this universal protection is?

Treatment 11: Exfoliation

*A*re there people in your life that rub you the wrong way? Are there circumstances that place those people in your path consistently? Exfoliation in the Spirit reveals to us one of two possibilities: Either it is time for us to leave the dead friendships behind and begin to moisturize our lives with healthy ones, or else it is simply God's way of using salty people, those seasoned in the Word, to have an exfoliating effect on us. Either way, it is often a message our flesh has no desire to hear.

The definition for exfoliate is: "to separate or split off in scales."[36] In a physical sense, this is referring to when the body is scrubbed with some kind of abrasive to remove the oldest dead skin cells that cling to the skin's outermost surface. Examples of exfoliation include a salt glow, a body scrub that might use sugar or coffee grounds, or skin brushing. When done correctly, exfoliation leaves the skin smoother, softer, and fresher looking. It also makes penetration easier for products like serums and lotions that nourish the skin. "The lips of the righteous feed many, but fools die for lack of wisdom" (Proverbs 10:21 NKJV). As people rub us the wrong way, so to speak, or as they tell us things we would rather not hear, it represents those dead skin cells being removed by exfoliation on our heart's surface. After the dead skin cells, or the dead ways, are removed, it makes way for the penetration of the serum of God's Word; hence, the lips of the righteous that moisturize our soul.

I am pretty sure that you know by now how much I like to spiritualize everything, so I will give you some examples of exfoliation. The first part touches on how the salt of your spirit can push others away or make them fertile. Then I will bring to light the body scrubs that are sweet (sugar) or bitter (coffee). Finally, I'll touch upon skin brushing in the spirit. This is how I see this beauty treatment come into play.

One day, someone I knew fairly well said something to me that really wasn't appropriate. I let it go, but another friend that had also heard the conversation came to me later privately to make sure I was ok and to voice her objection to what had been said to me. Not really

---

36. Webster's Collegiate Dictionary, s.v., "exfoliate."

even thinking about it, I said, "It's okay. She just gave me the beauty treatment of exfoliation." It was then that I felt like the Lord wanted me to add this one to the book. Exfoliation can happen when someone rubs you the wrong way. The people who you think don't quite fit into your realm of influence are actually the people who God uses the most to remove those scales off your eyes, and the dead skin cells off your spirit.

Dead Sea salt body scrubs are well known for their beautifying and therapeutic results when applied to the skin. Because they are loaded with the same minerals which are naturally present in our skin, they are able to help restore and replenish skin that suffers from mineral deficiency due to unfavorable environmental conditions, as well as from unhealthy lifestyle choices. Many people even travel to the shore of the Dead Sea to take full advantage of the healing salts, but you can also touch that healing power through the power of the Holy Spirit, who is called to be the Salt of the Earth.

The purpose of exfoliating is for us to all become one, even as Jesus is one with the Father. He wants us to stand together in unity. Where there is unity, there is beauty refined. Just as iron sharpens iron; so it is that one man sharpens another (Proverbs 27:17). We are created for each other, no matter what nationality we come from. We are to love everyone.

Shed the prejudice with a sweet body abrasive. Although most Christians would be embarrassed to admit it, the sin of prejudice is an enemy most of us have failed to overcome. In fact, the church can be the most segregated organization around. We discriminate rich from poor, black from white, heathen from holy, Jews from Gentiles, etc. However, just a little bit of love can be the abrasive that we need to shed the walls of hostility. We can learn a great deal from each other if we take the time to look at things from another's perspective.

I grew up with prejudice all around me, as I am sure most of you have too. When I was forced to live in the projects of Toledo, I decided I had better get to know the people I lived with. I knew I would rather have friends than enemies in there. I discovered that my neighbors were very precious people who were really not much different than me. The story I like to share most is about the day I approached Slim. Slim was a huge, black man that stood like Goliath. I am only five feet tall, so next to me he appeared even larger. Slim was someone that everyone in the neighborhood knew; no one ever messed with him. The neighborhood itself was known to be pretty rough, too. My children witnessed a shooting, as well as many drug transactions that took place just outside of our home. Every time I saw Slim, I would smile. He always just grumbled at me and gave me the "birdie" (meaning he would flip up his middle finger). I could tell that he did not like me one bit, and he was not my favorite person either. On the day I was learning about shedding prejudice with the abrasive of love, I went on a prayer walk in my neighborhood. On that walk, I saw Slim. In order to keep on the prayer path I was determined to walk on, I had to walk right through Slim and his buddies. I decided to stop right in front of him, and as I did, I smiled and look up into his eyes. At this point, Slim was curious as to what I was doing so he just stood there looking at me, almost dumbfounded. I felt the courage that David felt as he approached Goliath. I lifted my hand and reached out to him, placing my hand on his heart. The Lord touched him through me in a mighty way; I saw the hostility melt away and tears filled his eyes. In that moment, as I prayed with Slim, the wall of hostility was removed and the prejudice that we had for one another was smoothed out. Slim asked Jesus to be the Savior of his life soon after. The body of Christ is moisturized when different races come together. We all bleed the same blood under the colors of our skin.

Our King has come to bring us life, and life more abundantly, so we need to shed the dead stuff. There is a lot of dead stuff to be removed. Here are a few things that the Lord dealt with me about so that I could experience the fullness of this moisturized life.

Let's start with dead friendships. The Bible says that bad company corrupts good morals (1 Corinthians 15:33). If you are trying to live a life that is pleasing to God, it is a time to shed the people who lead you astray. I want to make myself clear before we go any further. I am not talking to married couples here. What God has joined, let no man separate. I am, however, talking to you if you are living in sin. I know you were hoping I would not say that, but this is the beauty treatment of exfoliation, isn't it? Therefore, if you are a new creation and old things have passed away, that means old things really do pass away. Old friends that want to party, must pass away; old buddies that you used to sleep with, that passes away; old colleagues that used to sit around talking about everyone else, that passes away. "All things become new" means exactly what it says. You must find new friends that will moisturize your life.

Exfoliate the friendships that make you dry and lifeless. For the first few weeks after I was saved, I continued to get high on drugs with my old friends. However, "all things become new" became the foundation of my born-again journey, and I wanted the new badly. I wanted my friends to come too, but they chose to not pursue Christ, so I had to walk away. I knew in my heart that if I chose to stick around, I would most assuredly continue using drugs. Once I walked away and found new friendships that were healthy, my life began to change and I never went back to that lifestyle again. And I don't regret it, nor do I miss those friendships that once held me in bondage. Dead friendships have a way of sucking the life right out of you. Although you have begun the process of allowing the Holy Spirit to wean your soul from worldliness, you should not be eager to return to your former environment to try to help someone else. Based upon my own experience, it is more likely that the person still firmly rooted in the world will pull you in their direction than that you will carry them in yours. In order for the Word of God to penetrate into your very being, you need to throw off everything and everyone that hinders you from abiding in this new way of life to which you have been called.

I also needed to shed worldly theology that did not moisturize my life. Many people, including members of my own family, tried to help me by encouraging me to develop a relentless desire to get ahead by any means. They believed that success and prosperity were defined by having power. But God desired me to pursue success by being strong and courageous in the strength of the Lord. Knowing the path I walked might be difficult, and that the world would never judge me successful by its standards, I possessed the assurance that the eyes of my King were ever upon me, and that He was pleased with me. What could possibly define success better than that? I have seen Jesus do amazing and miraculous things in my life and in the lives of others. On a daily basis, He has been there for me. I had no reason to doubt that He would take care of me. I had no reason to believe that He would ever abandon me. Still, I felt Him working in the deepest parts of my soul to shed all my self-sufficiency, and enable me to trust Him even more to provide for all my needs.

Many people, including my own daughter, could not understand the peace I was walking in, even though I was unemployed. Nor did they support my decision to not be actively seeking any job to provide for myself. Victoria wanted me to have a job so I could get us out of the place where we lived. Others tried to convince me that God had allowed my laptop to be stolen as a sign that He wanted me to move out too. But I was not worried. So why was everyone else so concerned? It was because it is only in losing sight of all our own sufficiency, and allowing all our needs to be provided for in Christ, that we come to see the world as Christ Himself sees it. When one who believes in Jesus views life through the eyes of Christ, the fruit of that vision is always peace, hope, and assurance which the world will never understand.

Shed the dead habits that could have an effect on others. When our earthly lover does come knocking, it would be wise if we were not a liability to him. It would be a good idea to have all our debts paid before we enter into a relationship, so as not to bring any extra burdens. Shed the idea that you need someone to take care of you. Your God will supply all your needs, and He will never leave you stranded. He will also provide means of help. One thing I have learned is that going into debt by borrowing is a bad habit, and such habits are definitely dead cells that need to be removed from our lives.

The dead cells of selfishness can do some serious damage to the skin of our heart, as well as the hearts of others. It is important to exfoliate them completely because once your attitudes have scarred another person's heart, it can be very difficult to ever remove the damage. A friend of mine shared with me that she wanted to get a divorce because she felt that her husband only thought of himself. She said that she felt like he treated her as if she wasn't even in the room. He never helped her around the house, he never picked up after himself, the list went on and on about how selfish he was. But she knew me enough to know that I was not going to tell her what she wanted to hear. I was going to scrape some of those dead selfish cells off of her own heart. I began to ask her questions that made her squirm in her seat. She wanted this exfoliation because even though she did not see clearly at first, her heart needed to be moisturized. Otherwise, she would have just gone to someone who would have tickled her ears and stood in agreement with her emotions, someone who would have said this guy was a loser and should be dumped. Not me. If you come and tell me your problems, then you should expect exfoliation. I will probably rub you the wrong way, but I speak from experience and will say only what I believe is in your best interest. I will turn the finger that is pointed at someone else back at you. If you are married, divorce is not an option because of selfishness. Yes, it can harm the relationship, but it can be exfoliated and smoothed out. The Scripture for exfoliating selfishness is found in Philippians 2:1-4, which instructs us to aim to look to the interests of others. When we heed this advice, we become like-minded with Christ, having the same love, and being one in spirit and purpose.

If we seriously allow this beauty treatment to penetrate and touch our hearts, then God will bring healing. I love the following verse; it has a wonderful exfoliating effect:

"One day the leaders of the town of Jericho visited Elisha. 'We have a problem, my lord,' they told him. 'This town is located in pleasant surroundings, as you can see. But the water is bad, and the land is unproductive.' Elisha said, 'Bring me a new bowl with salt in it.' So they brought it to him. Then he went out to the spring that supplied the town with water and threw the salt into it. And he said, 'This is what the Lord says: I have purified this water. It will no longer cause death or infertility.'

And the water has remained pure ever since, just as Elisha said" (2 Kings 2:19-22).

As the word, "bath salts" implies, the main ingredient in the exfoliating scrub is sea salt. The obvious work the salt does on our skin is the removal of dead skin cells. Salt also has an antiseptic effect on inflamed areas. It will help you with the dry, irritated patches, and aid the healing of scratches.

Let's talk a little bit about those dry, irritated patches of our hearts. When everything is annoying you, from the slow cars on the side streets to the weather, what you are experiencing is the power of spiritual salts, scrubbing those patches of your heart that most need attention.

More often than not, the people who are brushing you are the ones who are the closest to you. They are the ones who see the real you. The reason they seem to irritate you the most is that, in seeing how they respond to you, you are looking at the shadow of your own reflection. They are the ones who are reflecting the things that you hate most about yourself. My daughter was the one who brushed against me the most, and it never failed to expose the rough patches each of us had that were inflamed and in need of some serious healing. And she can say the same about me, too. We really are very alike; and when I saw things in her that I didn't particularly like, I got angry and irritated with her.

She rubbed me the wrong way throughout her childhood and adolescence; she knew how to push my buttons. If I went one way, she would be determined to go the opposite way. If I said the sky was blue, she said it was gray. She argued with me constantly, relentless in her efforts to win every argument. It was wearisome, to say the least. She was rebellious, and became the thorn in my flesh that kept me on my knees. It got to the point that I had to ask my family for help; my sister volunteered to take my daughter for a while. She went through the school year and then came back home. Just two months prior to her coming home, the Lord had called me to this time of consecration. Although I was only two months into my personal beauty treatments, I was already cleansed enough to understand our relationship from God's healing point of view, and not only from my own wounded perspective. I saw how God used my daughter to shed some of the dead stuff in my life that had made my life so dry and irritated. God has brought about a lot of healing in our relationship. My daughter has her own take on it:

"From my experiences with my mom, I can truly say that she has changed drastically. We never really got along when I was growing up. I resented her, and it got so bad at one point that I actually went to live with my aunt across the country. When I finally returned a year later, my mom had changed completely. She told me that the Lord was doing a work inside her and it started to become very evident. I was even surprised that my mom did not react the same as she did in the past to negative situations. She was calm and understanding, which caused a very big change in our relationship. She made sure that I didn't feel that she was ever judging me, and she started to accept me and love me for who I was. I watched firsthand the dedication that she had in her life. She became a wonderful example to me. I started to trust her and make her a part of my life once again. I would call her just to talk or to ask her advice about my relationship issues—this was a big change in our relationship. I'm so proud of her and now look up to her.

I can now see that my mom is truly a wise woman. After so many years of providing her with more teachable moments than any author could possibly desire, I am thrilled to have been asked to now join my mom in sharing our lives with you in the hope that it blesses you and brings you healing as well. One thing is for sure: my mom wasn't just talking for years about writing a book; she was walking this one out. Her experience and her knowledge of God's Word will surely be a blessing to anyone who reads this book. I thank the Lord that I have a mom like her! She has so much love and she loves sharing it. Today she cares so much for everything and everyone. I'm very lucky; I love her with all of my heart."

"Season all your grain offerings with salt to remind you of God's eternal covenant. Never forget to add salt to your grain offerings" (Leviticus 2:13).

Chapter Six: The Beauty Treatments

Just as every burnt offering was seasoned with salt, everyone who denies himself and takes up His cross, offers himself up as a living sacrifice to God. Those people shall be seasoned with grace which, like salt, will make them savory, and preserve them from destruction forever. As salt is good for preserving meats and making them savory, so it is good that we be seasoned with grace for the purifying of our hearts and lives, and for spreading the savor of our King's Word wherever we may go. Such salt is good indeed—highly beneficial to the world, and we are the salt of the earth. See to it that we retain our savor; and as a proof of it, have peace one with another, even as we let our speech, seasoned with salt, be always full of grace.

Another purpose for salt is to melt the ice off sidewalks so we have a clear and safe pathway in winter. Since we as the children of God are the salt of the earth, then we have what is needed to melt hard hearts and clear the path for the lost to find the refuge they have been hoping for. It is in our best interest, and to the benefit of others, to be careful not to grow weak in our profession of faith, nor to be afraid of the cross we are to bear; if only that we may be the good salt of the earth, to season those around us with the savor of Christ.

Salt, in small quantities, can help the land become extremely fertile, but too much of it destroys vegetation. People who are seasoned in the Word can potentially spread too much salt, which can be overkill. An unsaved person cannot understand the mind of Christ. Being the salt of the earth is simply living out the fertile land that Christ gives, and that creates a thirst for more of Him. I learned that firsthand with my own children. I had a tendency to shove the Word of God down their throats. I had a lot to learn about that, and I am always thanking God that I have learned it in time to benefit my youngest child. I consider myself to be seasoned in the Word, so much so that I tend to speak the Word without even realizing it. There is nothing wrong with that, but we need to be careful that we are not so heavenly minded that we are no earthly good.

We can actually cause harm to our children's fertile land by throwing too much salt on it. My children have been raised up in the Word. My daughter was two when I gave myself to the Lord, and as children, both my daughter and my middle-aged children loved Jesus with their whole hearts. They read God's Word and they believed it. They lived it and their land was fertile. However, when they started sowing seeds of mischief, my first reaction was to give them God's Word. In fact, I made my daughter write Scripture as punishment. I continued to feel this way was best, until the Lord spoke to my heart that only He could bring about the conviction of sin. I was to love, love, love; that would savor their life more than pouring salt on them would. All through their teenage years, they seemed to revert: nothing sprouted, and no vegetation grew on it—it almost seemed as though there had been nothing planted at all. Even though God gives each one of us free will and we all have to choose who we will serve, I still had the responsibility to be salt to my children. If they were not thirsty for more of God because of the way I lived my life, then I was either too salty or else not salty enough. It was my responsibility to be well balanced for their benefit as well as my own. Now I am always careful to not rub my children in a way that could dry them out; instead I strive to season them with the spices of love, love, and more love, and trust the Holy Spirit to do the rest.

Every place in which much salt is found is barren and produces nothing. Sowing a place with salt was a custom in different nations to ensure permanent desolation.

"You are the salt of the earth. But what good is salt if it has lost its flavor? Can you make it salty again? It will be thrown out and trampled by men" (Matthew 5:13). This is pretty scary if you think about it. None of us are exempt. It could happen to any one of us. If we lose our faith and love, we are literally fit for nothing but to be utterly destroyed. Apart from Christ, we can do nothing. This reminds me of someone who knows God's Word, tastes and experiences His goodness, but returns to slavery. God gives them over to the lusts of their hearts. They are depraved, but yet very salty. In fact, many of the homeless people that I have come in contact with know the Word. They speak the Word of God as if they had memorized the whole Bible. They may even know more about the Bible than you and I. The difference is they have head knowledge, but not heart application. This causes pride and arrogance, and we easily forget who brought us out of slavery. Then, as we turn and look back, we become a pillar of salt. No one who looks back is fit for the kingdom of God. If we are not careful, having so much of the Word of God in our minds can make us quite proud, and then we end up making our own throne of salt to sit on. God will let us make that foolish choice; that's why it is crucial that we allow God's Word to season our hearts and not just our minds.

Salt makes you thirsty. When the Word of God seasons our hearts, we become thirsty for His righteousness and His ways. And His ways are fruitful and fertile. Here is a seasoned verse that I apply by using my own name instead of the pronoun given. Jodie is like a tree planted by streams of water, which yields its fruit in season and whose leaf does not wither. Whatever Jodie does, prospers (Psalm 1:3).

The beauty treatment for exfoliating the lifeless acts of every person is found in simply applying Ephesians 4 to the skin of our hearts. We are to shed or get rid of all bitterness, rage and anger, brawling and slander, along with every form of malice. And in its place be kind and compassionate to one another, forgiving each other, just as in Christ, God forgave you (Ephesians 4:29-32).

Treatment 12: Moisturizing

A good moisturizer will help skin preserve the water in your body, thereby reducing the fine lines of wrinkles caused by dry skin. At the same time, it gives the skin's complexion a healthy radiant glow. A good moisturizer will make the skin feel soft and pliable as well. Moisturizers also provide antioxidants that are needed for healthy skin. Organic plant oils are considered by many to be the best moisturizers on the market because they absorb easily and deeply. They are also packed with anti-inflammatory compounds that nourish, protect and rejuvenate dry skin.

This beauty treatment will apply moisturizer for the mind as an oil of joy to those who are mourning, and a garment of praise instead of the spirit of heaviness (Isaiah 61:3). Because the best moisturizers come from plants, and plants come from seeds, we will begin by examining the process of growth a seed goes through on its way toward maturity.

Spiritually speaking, the seed represents the Word of God that is first planted in our minds. As it is watered through faith and time spent studying and meditating upon it in prayer, it begins to take root and becomes established in our hearts. It is nurtured and matured into God's desired fullness as it is bathed in the life-giving presence of the Son. My pastor once spoke on the different soils that were described in the parable of the sower and, as I listened, I understood that much of this teaching applied to the events going on in my life at the time, as well as what the Lord was teaching me about how He uses His Word and the hearts of believers to moisturize the body of Christ, His church.

Listen then to what the parable of the sower means: Plant the seed; prepare the soil (Matthew 13:18). The heart is the place of decision, and so this is the place of preparation for the seeds. There are various conditions of soil mentioned. There is hard soil, shallow soil, distracted soil, and fruitful soil. Let's examine them a little more closely.

The hard soil is a rebellious heart or a hard heart. Even as Christians, we can have hearts that are hardened against the Word. This is what takes place when anyone hears the message about the kingdom but does not understand it—the evil one comes and snatches away what was sown in his heart. The seed never reaches the heart. This hard heart can be revealed in our attitude towards church life, or the subtle neglect of God's Word, or even in our failure to be doers of the Word as well as hearers. I confess that I have been rebellious at times and did not get into the Word when I knew that the Lord was speaking to me to do so. That is when the enemy keeps the Word from reaching and penetrating into our hearts. He is a thief, and he only comes to steal, kill, and destroy (John 10:10).

He is always looking for an opportunity to keep that Word from growing roots. In those days, I felt kind of empty and as though a huge void was in my heart because it was hardened against receiving the seeds. I recorded a day in my journal when I really felt the void of not spending time with the Lord, not to mention the fact that I had also knowingly been a little rebellious as well. I refused to feel better, and I was determined to spend a lot of time on the internet, interacting through social media, which I had previously committed to not go to because of its distracting tendencies. I could have been writing; instead I stayed on the internet and watched a lot of TV with the boys. To top it off, I ended my night with a huge bowl of ice cream. But the ice cream brought me no joy, the TV brought me no peace, and all my efforts to fill my mind with distractions did nothing at all to fill the void that could only be filled through fellowship with the Lord.

Do not harden your heart if you hear Him calling you. You will not grow and mature into the fullness God has prepared for you, nor will you be to the body of Christ that healing moisturizer He intends for you to be.

Some seeds also fell on the rocky places where what little soil there was, was shallow and therefore their root base was very weak. The seed that fell on rocky places represents the man who hears the Word and at once receives it with joy. But since his faith has no root, it lasts only a short time. When trouble or persecution comes because of the Word, he quickly falls away. This soil has no roots. It is a matter of the heart and not the mind. This is the soil where we receive the Word in our heads, but not in our hearts. When the message sounds good to us, we get excited; but when pressure comes, we dry up. It was true of me on more than one occasion. I got excited about what the Lord was telling me, but in reality it only gave me head knowledge. If I had truly allowed it to go into my heart, then I would have seen the fruit when the storms came my way. Instead, I gave into fear and anxiety, and started nagging and complaining. So if you are afraid, worried, or anxious, make sure that seed that was sown about Him being the One who protects and keeps you, remains in your heart so that you can grow and mature and become one of those who moisturize the body.

Other seed was sown among the thorns, but it could not grow because it became choked by distractions. I often found that the good seed that had been planted in me tended to become entangled in and choked by worldly concerns and distractions. I got distracted a lot, and I believe that it has been very unfruitful, even as God's Word has said, "The seed that fell among the thorns represents those who hear God's word, but all too quickly the message is crowded out by the worries of this life [friendships and finances for me]and the lure of wealth, so no fruit is produced" (Matthew 13:22). Or Luke 8:14 says it a little better: "The seed that fell among the thorns represent those who hear the message, but all too quickly the message is crowded out by the cares and riches and pleasures of this life [social media sites or other hidden motives to see friends]. And so they never grow into maturity."

Some distractions that were most prevalent in my life were in the form of internet surfing. I had also been distracted by constantly wondering who my earthly prince would be. I got off track and misdirected. I had weeds growing in the garden of my heart. When I realized that those nasty hornworms of distraction were eating all my beautiful plants, the Lord directed me to go back and read my entry for September 1, 2008 in my journal. It had not dawned on me until I went back and read it, that this had been the day that I purposed in my heart to consecrate myself to a deeper walk with God and to receive the mysteries of His Word and His kingdom.

Make sure that you are continuously evaluating what the garden of your heart looks like, so that you can identify the weeds and the worms and get rid of them quickly so that you grow and mature into that beautiful olive tree that releases the best moisturizer available. What are the worries of your life? Mine were being pursued by a loving man of God, staying home with my children, being a single parent, and financial security. These can be thorns to choke us out of our destiny, or they can be the thorns that keep us grounded in Him.

Still other seed fell on good soil, where I obviously would rather the seed fall in my heart. Just like the garden in my backyard, I planted the seed, watered it every day, and allowed the Son to shine and expose the nasty weeds and worms. I wanted to allow God's Word to penetrate into my very being so that it produced a harvest of thirty, sixty, or even a hundred times what was sown. Producing a harvest of plants that bring nourishment to the whole body of Christ is what the beauty treatment for moisturizing is all about. "The threshing floors will again be piled high with grain, and the presses will overflow with new wine and olive oil" (Joel 2:24).

Just as the olive tree starts out as a seed, then when fully grown, its fruit is pressed and squeezed into a moisturizer for the skin, the day will come when the seeds of God's Word in my heart will release a harvest that moisturizes the body of Christ. Until then, I must cooperate with the Holy Spirit to enable the seeds of God's Word to grow and mature.

Olive oil was not the only oil used for moisturizing the skin. There are many oils that come from plants: coconut oil, almond oil, and aloe. However, they all started out as a seed before they could grow and mature into the moisturizing plants that they are.

The oil of myrrh is not only something that I soaked in, it is also an oil that is valued for many other uses as well. During biblical times, myrrh was used in expensive perfumes. In liquid form, it was used as an anointing oil. Esther received a six-month long beauty treatment with oil of myrrh before she was brought in to King Xerxes (Esther 2:12). Myrrh was also used in the embalming and anointing of the dead. It came to represent mortality, suffering, and sorrow. The Israelites used perfumed myrrh in their funeral preparations to postpone the decay and alleviate the odor of the deceased. The balm of Gilead are leaves that have a strong aromatic odor when bruised; they are a part of a tree. He is the Vine, and we are the branches (John 15:1). When we are bruised we give off the fragrance of Christ, for we die in Him, and in Him we have the hands to heal the sick. We have the hearts to comfort the lost. We have the moisture of His Word to spread abroad.

The psalmist portrays Christ as a King on His wedding day being clothed in garments scented with myrrh, aloes, and cassia (Psalm 45:8). These perfumed garments represented the sweet-smelling character traits of Christ. Since we are God's chosen people, clothed by Him, covering our skin and our nakedness, we are to clothe ourselves with compassion, kindness, humility, gentleness and patience. These are the qualities that moisturize the whole body of Christ.

Are you spiritually dry? Do you feel like you are in a wilderness? Has stress caused a famine in your life? Are you depressed or oppressed by the enemy? Or maybe you feel like you're in a pit that you can't get out of. If you answered yes to any of these, you need moisturizing.

This beauty treatment will bring gladness back to your life. Floodgates of gladness, overflowing with joy, will burst wide open even if things are not looking so great on the outside. There were times when I woke up thinking, "What a mess things are, but God is so good," and that brought incredible joy to my life. God's children should be happy. So why are so many people in the church walking around with sour looks on their faces? The fact is, it is God's expressed desire that we know He loves us and that we trust Him. Once a person has received a real revelation of these facts, the things that used to trigger those emotions now simply awaken an even deeper need and desire for intimacy with Christ. For me, that is the beginning of all hope and joy.

If only we would allow ourselves to see God just as He reveals Himself to us through His Word—as a loving Father who knows His children and understands every thought that crosses their minds. He even understands the source of our thoughts. God understands why we struggle with depression, sadness, fear, and doubt. And as a loving Father, He longs for His children to come to Him with all their insecurities and share everything that is in their hearts with Him so that He can help us see things from His perspective, thereby overcoming all these things. But He has no desire to hear His children grumbling, complaining, whining, and expressing their selfish ingratitude. Every parent would say amen to that!

Do they not know that the same God who delivered the Israelites from Egypt can deliver them from the hand of their powerful and overwhelming enemy? For us to stay in a pit from which He clearly provided a way of escape would be like a slap in the face to the One who provided freedom. He wants us to live free from being moved by our emotions—unless our emotions are backed up by conviction and they lead us to His feet. It reminds me of the sinful woman who came to see Jesus at the house of a Pharisee. "Then he [Jesus] turned to the woman and said to Simon, 'Look at this woman kneeling here. When I entered your home, you didn't offer me water to wash the dust from my feet, but she has washed them with her tears and wiped them with her hair. You didn't greet me with a kiss, but from the time I first came in, she has not stopped kissing my feet. You neglected the courtesy of olive oil to anoint my head, but she has anointed my feet with rare perfume. I tell you, her sins—and they are many—have been forgiven, so she has shown me much love. But a person who is forgiven little shows only little love'" (Luke 7:44-47).

That woman, who had been a great sinner, showed her repentance and love of Christ by anointing His feet with the fragrant oil of myrrh and drying them with her hair. Jesus took this opportunity to point out that those who are forgiven much love their Redeemer more than those who are forgiven little.

This fit the description of yours truly. I was an incredibly sinful woman; it's no wonder I was depressed. I wasn't living the life I was intended to live. In fact, I was on the borderline of receiving the same title that was given to many others in my family. I cannot even count how many people in my family have been diagnosed as manic depressant, or bi-polar. In fact, there have been two suicides by my loved ones within my family. Depression has taken control of many of them, leaving them in a whirlwind of chaos and constant misfortune. I could easily have ended up that way too if I had kept running in the same direction. I even tried to end my own life on numerous occasions. Thankfully, I was protected from ending my life short of God's purpose and plan for me.

I know what depression feels like. I know how the feeling of utter hopelessness has a way of sucking every bit of life out of you, compelling you to believe that no one else can understand how intensely overwhelming your depression truly is. I've been through times when this pain was so real that it seemed as though the enemy was kicking me in my side to keep me down and in a fetal position. It is comparable to experiencing a mental, emotional, and physical short circuit, all at the same time. Everything makes you snap. Chronic pain begins to add to the weight of the world. There is nothing that motivates you to change because you have come to the conclusion that there's no use trying anymore. You feel like you gave life a shot and missed the target every time; and now you're done with it. I have been in those shoes, and I am living proof that once Jesus pulls you out and delivers you from the bondage of self-defeat, you can begin to walk in total freedom. That is right; your powerful self is what put you in that pit, and your powerful self has the power to keep you there.

There is so much talk in the Christian circles about that dirty dog Satan being the one to blame for so many people being in bondage to depression. That's because ultimately, it is easier to place the blame on someone else than it is to take responsibility for our own actions. In most cases, depression is our own fault, friends. It is something that comes from being spiritually dehydrated. Of course you're depressed; you're not connected to the Vine. You have to decrease in order for Him to increase. The devil is a liar and he will speak into your mind, lying to you, making you think that the thoughts that he puts into your head are your own thoughts. However, because you are a child of God, you don't have to allow the devil any power over you. He was defeated at the cross of Christ, and you have been given the power to overcome this adversity if you are attached to the Vine. If you are not attached to the Vine, you will experience a spiritual famine; it is inevitable.

Your physical body is made up of about sixty-five percent water (depending upon your body weight) and we are told to continually drink more water because our bodies need it to stay hydrated. Dehydration has many symptoms, including thirst and discomfort, dizziness, loss of appetite, and dry skin. Spiritual dehydration works the same way. We know that Jesus is the living water that sustains us—He says if you drink from Him you will never be thirsty again. The Word tells us that if we remain in Him, He will remain in us. We are grafted into a living tree that is planted near streams of living water, and that keeps us spiritually hydrated. However, when we do not remain in Him, we become thirsty and we experience a sense of spiritual discomfort. We become unsure of the things around us as spiritual dizziness kicks in. We lose our appetite for God's Word and our spiritual lives become very dry.

Being dry means nothing is flowing; it looks like a desert without an oasis of hope. Dryness in the physical sense causes your skin to become chaffed, rough, hard, and irritated. When I found that my skin had become rough and tough, I decided to soak in some anointing oils. I soaked in essential oils that rejuvenated my skin, and my skin became soft and more pliable.

What does this say to us in the Spirit? Hydrate your spirit by soaking in His Spirit. What do I mean by that? When I refer to soaking in His Spirit, I am basically talking about spending time alone with the Lord, almost as though we were immersing ourselves into a bathtub of Bible doctrine as His Spirit cleanses us from sin, releasing the things we cannot change into the hands of the Specialist.

Soaking in His Spirit also refers to just sitting still and listening to music that soothes your spirit. When I took my baths, I listened to many worship songs that had a heavenly sound to them; this moisturized not only my skin, but also my spirit. If I went into that bathtub full of depression, I came out full of joy. If I went into that bathtub of Bible verses full of my stinky self, I came out full of Him. If I went into that bathtub spiritually dry, then I would come out spiritually moisturized.

A sure way of becoming spiritually dehydrated is to open your mouth with complaining, arguing, or nagging. Picture a basin with a lot of holes in it; every time you fill it up, it is just as quick to pour out. Every time I complain, argue, or nag, then another little hole got poked in the vessel meant to hold the moisturizing oil for my soul.

During my consecrated year, I caught myself doing a lot of nagging toward my daughter, and I realized that I was actually the example she was following. I realized that if I was ever to be married, this area in my life could push a man to the corner of the roof if I didn't deal with it. So what is the beauty treatment for nagging? Exfoliate it, of course, but don't stop there. The next step is to pour in the oil of the Holy Spirit to keep your life moisturized.

Ultimately, your response to stress is what causes the problems that you have in your life. If I was to receive this beauty treatment of moisturizing from the Lord, then I would bathe His feet in my tears. He does not want me wailing to the world, because there is no one, not one single soul, who can moisturize my life more than He can.

With this beauty treatment, the Lord makes us into a people that anoint others, a people of His face and His feet: oil pourers and foot washers, humble lovers of Christ. This is what I imagined Esther bathed herself in—six months with oil of myrrh and six with perfumes and cosmetics. Moisturize with oils which provide spiritual hydration.

"That is why we never give up. Though our bodies are dying, our spirits are being renewed every day. For our present troubles are small and won't last very long. Yet they produce for us a glory that vastly outweighs them and will last forever! So we don't look at the troubles we can see now; rather, we fix our gaze on things that cannot be seen. For the things we see now will soon be gone, but the things we cannot see will last forever" (2 Corinthians 4:16-18).

Waking up to the Holy Spirit's sweet dreams of my future moisturized my Spirit. I knew that His mercies are new every morning. He gave me a conscious vision of the women's home I had desired to open one day, and what I would do as I received the women into that home. I envisioned washing their feet as they came into the home and looking into their eyes, telling them that they were loved and that they would experience real life change in this house of beauty. I realize this is part of the plan God has for me, so I will continue to pray over how the Lord will have me communicate to other women. I have definitely received more revelation because of the time I have dedicated to hearing from the Lord, as well as from making the decision to seek out the deeper things the Lord would have me discover in my heart.

Chapter Six: The Beauty Treatments

It is my opinion that this beauty treatment will moisturize our spirits unto wholeness and cause us to become radiant vessels. Every day we need to be saturated with His presence. We are heavenly creatures living in the earthly realm. Our spiritual body is more real than our physical one. Our physical body will perish and we will get a new heavenly one, but our spirit man is eternal. If we are not experiencing that deep well within, it may be clogged with earthly distractions. There is a safeguarding, discipline, and focus that keeps the well in your spirit flowing. We keep our well flowing by starting our day, every day, with praise and thanksgiving, communing with God in the Spirit. It starts with being Holy Spirit-sensitive and understanding the reality of having our spirit connected to the anointing of His presence. When you begin to develop the habit of opening your day with praise, you will experience a moisturizing flow from within. Live a life of thanksgiving, blessing, and encouragement, and displace complaining, criticism, and accusation. Complaining will keep you from entering into the Promised Land that is flowing. "Do everything without complaining and arguing, so that no one can criticize you. Live clean, innocent lives as children of God, shining like bright lights in a world full of crooked and perverse people" (Philippians 2:14-15). Thanksgiving opens the door to the healing and life-giving flow of the Spirit.

The bride of Christ cannot be dependent on the world's standard for happiness, fulfillment, or success. Joy will originate with Jesus, with His peace, and with His purposes being pursued. Life will be abundant for the church when we become the moisturized body.

As the Lord moisturizes my life, I have been given creative thoughts for my own edification. It is He who gave me the creative ability to write this book. It is He who moisturized my heart so I could put faith-filled action behind the concepts I was learning. I can do everything through Christ who gives me strength (Philippians 4:13). He is able, through His mighty power at work within us, to accomplish infinitely more than we could ever imagine (Ephesians 3:20).

When my son, Daniel, was four years old, he came to me quite depressed about something. Naturally, I hugged him and encouraged him. He felt much better after I told him about the worshipping little boy inside my belly. At that moment, I believe it penetrated his heart that he was special. I told him that, when he was in my womb, he would literally kick to the beat of the music. He questioned if he was special to God and I told him he was. Later, as he was playing, I heard him say to himself, "I am special." I thanked the Lord for the power and creativity of our words. Words possess the ability and the power to moisturize our lives and the lives of all those around us.

Every day I asked the Lord, "What is my beauty treatment tomorrow?" He has always been faithful to give me exactly what I needed. He exposed me, silenced me, detoxed me, stretched me, shaped me, simplified me, protected me, exfoliated me, and now He was moisturizing me. I thanked the Lord everyday for beautifying me and refining the jewel that He created me to be. The Lord always made me feel like a lady! He keeps the beauty treatments coming, and He will continue to do so until He returns for His spotless bride. We all have a lot of refining to go if we want to win the heart and favor of a king.

Esther's beauty and character won the heart of the king. Her form and features attracted the king, but it was her character that won his heart and favor. It was her character that made her more beautiful than the others. She had the beauty treatment of moisturizing applied to her life and she became queen. She then became the seed that grew and matured into a royal branch that produced much fruit. Let that be true in our hearts as well!

Chapter Seven: Meet Haman

To the Jews, Haman was an adversary and an enemy. Haman's ancestry has quite a history that leads all the way back to the birth of Esau. Esau was the twin brother to Jacob, and although they were brothers, they would later become enemies as well. The cycle continued throughout generations. Esau begot Eliphaz, Eliphaz begot Amalek, and from there you have a people called the Amalekites (Genesis 14:7). The Amalekites were known as deceiving and conniving people who were trying to establish their own kingdom—people who wanted to be their own god. They were described in Deuteronomy as a people who held no fear of God. Therefore this is what God says concerning the Amalekites:

> "Never forget what the Amalekites did to you as you came from Egypt. They attacked you when you were exhausted and weary, and they struck down those who were straggling behind. They had no fear of God. Therefore, when the Lord your God has given you rest from all your enemies in the land he is giving you as a special possession, you must destroy the Amalekites and erase their memory from under heaven. Never forget this!" (Deuteronomy 25:17-19).

The Amalekites were a merciless enemy that came against those who could not fight back. However, Joshua chose some men and went out to fight them; as a result, Joshua overwhelmed the army of Amalek. "After the victory, the Lord instructed Moses, 'Write this down on a scroll as a permanent reminder, and read it aloud to Joshua: I will erase the memory of Amalek from under heaven'" (Exodus 17:14). Later on, when King Saul was reigning, we read in 1 Samuel that the Lord Almighty says, "This is what the Lord of Heaven's Armies has declared:

I have decided to settle accounts with the nation of Amalek for opposing Israel when they came from Egypt. Now go and completely destroy the entire Amalekite nation—men, women, children, babies, cattle, sheep, goats, camels, and donkeys" (1 Samuel 15:2-3).

Saul did attack the Amalekites, and destroyed all their people with the sword. But he and his men spared Agag's life and kept the best of the sheep and goats, the cattle, the fat calves, and the lambs—everything, in fact, that appealed to them. They destroyed only what was worthless or of poor quality. Then the Lord was sorry that He ever made Saul king, because he refused to obey His command. Saul was more afraid of the people then he was of God, so he did what they demanded. As a result, Samuel ordered that King Agag be brought to him. When Agag appeared before Samuel, full of hope and thinking that the worst was over and that he would be spared, Samuel cut Agag to pieces before the Lord and finished the job that Saul failed to do (1 Samuel 15:5-33).

In the book of Esther, we see that Haman was a descendent of Agag. "Agag" was the usual title of the Amalekite kings, just as "Pharaoh" was the title for the Egyptian rulers. Are you kidding me? Here I thought that those pesky Amalekites were completely destroyed. However, they were still very much alive—hiding, pretending, mixing in, just waiting for the moment to rise to the top, take the throne, and hold the power to kill, steal, and destroy.

Haman reflects Satan, the fallen angel that is referred to in Ezekiel 28, Isaiah 14, and John 8. The story of how Haman plots to destroy the Jews is found in Esther 3. It is said that King Xerxes honored Haman, elevating him and giving him a seat of honor higher than that of all the other nobles. When Haman saw that Mordecai would not kneel down or pay him honor, he was enraged. Yet, having learned who Mordecai's people were, he scorned the idea of killing only Mordecai. Instead, Haman looked for a way to destroy all Mordecai's people, the Jews, throughout the whole kingdom of Xerxes (Esther 3:1-7). Sound familiar?

The devil has always been known as the accuser of the brethren. He is adept at using the Law to bring us under condemnation. The manipulative tactic Haman used when he approached the king is no surprise. He said, "There is a certain race of people scattered through all the provinces of your empire who keep themselves separate from everyone else. Their laws are different from those of any other people, and they refuse to obey the laws of the king. So it is not in the king's interest to let them live" (Esther 3:8). The enemy says it is not in the best interest of the king to tolerate those who do not obey the Law. Do you realize that it is virtually impossible for us to completely obey all of the rules and regulations that are laid out in the Bible? The enemy is always using the Law to bring condemnation upon the believer, but if you belong to Christ then there is no condemnation (Romans 8:1).

Haman even has the nerve to go on to say that, if it pleased the king, a decree should be put forth in order to destroy them all. Sounds just like that dirty dog Satan. Satan came to kill, steal, and destroy; and one way he tries to destroy us is through the battlefield in our mind. He doesn't like that we are different. We are very different because we have the mind of Christ. We are a peculiar people who do not always manage to follow all the rules, but we are a people who trust in the righteousness of Christ; His righteousness is all we need.

Satan wanted to kill off the entire race of the Jews because Jesus was a Jew. There are people among us that do not like us because we are Christians and followers of Christ. But Jesus said, "If the world hates you, remember that it hated me first" (John 15:18). We will not have everyone's approval. As Christians, we must be prepared to suffer temporary consequences rather than sin against our consciences. Mordecai was one who did not give into the man-made rule to bow down to Haman. He did not bow down to an idol, and that makes the enemy mad. Satan is always bringing accusations against the Lord's children. He will not stop either until the Lord comes back. That means we need to always be on our guard.

When Esther told the king that someone had planned to kill off all her people, King Xerxes asked Queen Esther, "'Who would do such a thing?' King Xerxes demanded. 'Who would be so presumptuous as to touch you?' Esther replied, 'This wicked Haman is our adversary and our enemy'" (Esther 7:5-6a).

Haman was not the only adversary in the Bible. The Bible is full of stories of good versus evil. Of the many enemies that our historic heroes have faced, the one who really makes the top of my list is Judas Iscariot. Think about it: He sat with Jesus, he walked with Jesus, he watched Jesus perform miracles, and yet it was Judas who agreed to betray our heavenly King for a measly thirty pieces of silver. Jesus, of course, knew who His betrayer would be. As he sat down to eat the Passover meal with His disciples, He handled His enemy by feeding him from the same bowl that He Himself had eaten from. He then makes this statement with the authority from above: "But how terrible it will be for the one who betrays him [Jesus]. It would be far better for that man if he had never been born!" (Matthew 26:24b) The enemy is always exposed and dealt with, and Good will always triumph over evil.

Haman in Me

Haman's pride and arrogance were brought to light every time he saw the face of Mordecai; similarly, when we see our sin, the Holy Spirit does not let us enjoy it. From this lesson, I asked the Lord to hang the Haman in me.

> "So Haman's wife, Zeresh, and all his friends suggested, 'Set up a sharpened pole that stands seventy-five feet tall, and in the morning ask the king to impale Mordecai on it. When this is done, you can go on your merry way to the banquet with the king.' This pleased Haman, and he ordered the pole set up" (Esther 5:14).

Have you ever experienced an uncomfortable disclosure that you feared would have negative repercussions? Haman was uncomfortable with the fact that Mordecai's face was ever before him. Zeresh didn't like to see her husband so discouraged, and her response was, whatever makes you happy, honey!

The woman of the house has much power of persuasion—both positive and negative. Many of my female friends did their best to persuade me to get a divorce so that I would be happy. And yes, I have indeed been happy, but the Holy Spirit was not allowing me to stay there. Let me explain.

It was Valentine's Day, and my mom had agreed to watch the kids so that I could treat myself to some special time alone with the Lord. I got to the motel about 12:30 in the afternoon, unpacked and got settled in. Putting my music on, I started to worship God. I was in high spirits and was happy to be in the presence of my one true love. I poured out my heart of love to the love of my life and asked Him in sincerity and truth to do in me as He pleased. I wanted Him to deal with my heart—no matter how painful having Him do so might be. I wanted the Lord to expose my Haman. I wanted the Lord to hang all that was standing in the way of me getting into the King's presence on His gallows. I poured out my frustrations on the home front, and I cried out a happy note to just be there with the Lord without any distractions. I wanted Him to reveal Himself and reveal where I was positioned in Him.

I opened up to my study on Esther, and this verse spoke deeply to me. At first, the application was not apparent, but after looking further, or digging deeper, I could see how it applied to me.

"Haman was a happy man as he left the banquet! But when he saw Mordecai..." (Esther 5:9).

Reworded as applied to my own heart, "Jodie was a happy woman as she left for her banquet of the Lord, but when she saw her heart of bitterness..." *Mordecai* means "bitter."[37]

The Lord revealed the truth of how bitter the mere thought of my ex-husband had made me; even the thought of God wanting to restore our marriage made me cringe. I tried to push it out of my head and think that it might not happen, that God would choose to bring someone else in my life. Whenever my ex-husband called, I hurried to pass the phone to one of the boys as to avoid talking to him. The day before I left to go to the motel, he called; I listened, refrained from respecting him, and just bragged about myself. Wow, how evident it became to me that the same evil spirit that had taken control over Haman way back then was now trying to take control over me as well. The Lord revealed where I faltered in my thinking. His purpose in calling me to that period of consecration

---

37. The Net Bible Study Dictionary Online, http://classic.net.bible.org/dictionary. php?word=TMordecai (accessed July 16,2013). Used by permission.

was that I would deny my selfishness, my ambition, or any damaged emotions the right to steal from me the far greater plans that He had for my life and the life of my children. Just as He restored the relationship that I lost with my mother, now I needed to be open to God's ability to restore the relationship I once had with my husband. As much as I wanted to fight the notion, it just didn't make sense to fight it any longer.

Anytime God calls us to die, His purpose is always to reveal a better life. The Lord revealed that the life I was living was flawed, to say the least. Beth Moore said it best, "Human character is never more flawed than when one person can reach his highest only when another is swept in the depths."[38] I could see that in my bragging to my ex-husband about everything God was doing in my life, while at the same time seeing the oppression that he was under because of sin, God was showing me that there was a need to cry out for his deliverance, appealing for God's mercy on him. My heart needed to be open for reconciliation. Regardless of whether or not God restored our marriage, my heart needed to be open to it. At this point in time, my husband had been living with another woman for three years; it was hard for me to even think about that. But the Lord keeps His covenant of love with His unfaithful people, and so must I (1 Kings 8:23).

Many people were advising me that divorcing my husband was the best thing to do; I had definite grounds because he had cheated on me so many times and defiled our marriage bed. However, the Lord was teaching me about my ungodly attitudes and how they could cheat me right out of my destiny. He was teaching me about death, and dying to myself so that His abundant life might be revealed in me.

My friends simply wanted me to be happy, hence their advice to divorce him. "Have him hanged" they were basically suggesting; and oh, how this pleased the sinful nature in me. But what neither they nor I could see at that moment was that, by indulging the sinful desires of my flesh to handle this in my own way, I was, in fact, ignoring God's ways by choosing instead to hang the spiritual nature of forgiveness that I had been called to abide in.

---

38. Beth Moore, *Esther: It's Tough Being a Woman* (Nashville, TN: Lifeway Press, 2005) 116. Used by permission.

Chapter Seven: Meet Haman

As I got real honest with myself, I saw the Haman in me. I wanted the control in our relationship. I had controlled my husband. I made him go to church. I made him tell me where he was at all times. I made him feel guilty when I didn't have my way. In a sense, I made him bow to my every wish. I knew full well that I screwed up. I constantly rubbed his sins in his face; as I continued to accuse him, I failed to see my own. I was just as guilty for the demise of our relationship as he was. I needed to stop pointing the finger at him, and make those same three fingers turn back on me. We are not anyone's judge. Everyone must learn their own way just as we have to learn our own way. But that wasn't as easy as it sounded. The challenge of hanging onto that bitterness confronted me yet again on a later date when I did not like what I heard.

After I had submitted to being open to the possibility of reconciliation with my ex-husband, disturbing news came. It came the very next day, shattering any hope of a restored marriage. My ex-husband told my daughter about some detestable things he had done, laughing about them with no remorse at all. This was in addition to the lie I had been told that he was in a Christian rehab, when all the while he was living it up with his girlfriend's insurance fund from her dead husband. Although we eventually divorced, I am by no means an advocate of divorce. Ultimately, a restored marriage would give God the greater glory. God wants you to practice setting your sights on reconciliation. That night I had cried out to the Lord with His own heartbeat; and He revealed that the plan He had was not to restore our marriage, but to restore our relationship. It was our relationship of hate and bitterness that God wanted to restore and heal. My ex-husband and I became friends. He still lives in some ungodly ways, but my heart towards him is nothing but love and compassion that only God could do. He has been released from the bitter hatred that I held towards him. I believe that one day he will have a testimony that will lead many to the Lord and will hopefully save marriages the heartache and contempt that we endured. We need to come boldly to the throne of grace to ask for help in time of need (Hebrews 4:16). He is the only One who can help us to forgive like that.

The Haman in me was hanged. The bitterness was turned into joy. The enemy was defeated.

But before we go and get too happy, those darn Amalekites will come again. "When the devil had finished tempting Jesus, he left him until the next opportunity came" (Luke 4:13). "And since you don't know when that time will come, be on guard! Stay alert!" (Mark 13:33).

Handling Haman

*S*tay alert! Watch out for your great enemy, the devil. He prowls around like a roaring lion, looking for someone to devour" (1 Peter 5:8). Be on your guard; do not sleep like the ones walking in the dark. We need to be just as alert as the enemy. He is always looking for a way to trip us up. He is always waiting for us to put our guard down and stop abiding in Christ. He is always trying to distract us from God's Word. When we start to get distracted, we lose sight of the eternal. We start focusing instead on the things that are temporary. When we have become distracted, our senses lose their alertness that they have if we were focused on God's eternal plan. I seem to hear Him quite often, telling me to get my mind on heaven. Nothing lasts here! The only thing that will endure here is His eternal Word, and it needs to penetrate my heart every day.

Mordecai was alert over the enemy. He waited, watched, and reported to the king at just the right time. Mordecai was sitting at the king's gate just minding his own business; and all of a sudden, he heard that the guards were plotting to kill the king. Once he heard this, he told the queen and she told the king and the enemies' plan turned on their own heads (Esther 2:21-23) We too need to be watching and listening; instead of taking matters into our own hands, we need to report to the King. The King is the only one who has the power to handle our enemy anyway.

About three months into my consecrated year, my house was broken into and my laptop was stolen. Everything I had written about these beauty treatments was gone. The enemy wanted to destroy the work of my hands. Just as Mordecai went to the king to report the plot, I reported to the Lord and asked that He would bring conviction upon the man that stole it, and that he would hang his sinful nature. I prayed that the thief would no longer be a thief. I really could have gone about this the wrong way. I could have retaliated like many others. I could have found a way to get back at this person because I knew who it was, but I could not prove it and do anything about it. Just as I was on the verge of crying about it, my friend, Kevin, called and encouraged me. He reminded me of the first time I was convicted, the first time I had a sudden feeling of knowing right from wrong. My very first conviction was, "Thou shalt not steal," and I returned a freezer I had stolen. I thought, "I bet that landlord prayed that I would return it." I laughed and somehow knew in my heart that God was going to have the glory! Even though the enemy thought he was getting away with this, the Lord was working behind the scenes to turn the gallows on him. These gallows would hang the enemy. The enemy was messing with the Lord's anointed one, and I had on my side an army of the living God!

Every time my mind wandered to the missing laptop, the Lord told me to stay out of it. It was in the Lord's hands; the Lord would take up my case and be my defender. It was not for me to avenge. The Lord knows how to handle our enemy, so we need to let Him. We need to trust the King to handle Haman or any other enemy that we might face. When handling the enemy, we are told to be alert, but we are also told to stand firm. We need to stand in God's mighty power. If we don't stand for something, we will fall for anything. That is why the Bible tells us that we need to take our stand against the enemy. Ephesians 6:10-18 is our blueprint for handling our enemy as we dress for battle. "Be strong in the Lord and in His mighty power. Put on all of God's armor so that you will be able to stand firm against all strategies of the devil" (Ephesians 6:10-11).

When the day of trouble comes, the easiest thing to do is run and hide. We run from the enemy because he can be scary. He taunts the weak, he lies to the naïve, he steals from the poor, he kills the innocent, he shows no mercy. On every level of our journey, we will meet a new devil. The devil will always be stronger than we are. However, the size of the Holy Spirit in us will always be bigger and more powerful than our enemy. We need to learn how to stand, not run. Stand like Mordecai, refusing to bow or cower to the enemy. He did not run from his enemy, he stood firm. Stand, but also press in like David, and cry out to the Lord; under the pressure from that new devil, we will grow in the realm of the Spirit. It is who we are becoming.

If we stand in the mighty power of the Lord, the enemy does not stand a chance. He knows it too. Even Haman's wife knew that Haman was bothering the wrong person. She said, "Since Mordecai—this man who has humiliated you—is of Jewish birth, you will never succeed in your plans against him. It will be fatal to continue opposing him" (Esther 6:13).

Like Jesus did with Judas, Esther knew how to handle her enemy! She needed to be strategic in how she handled the person she knew was out for the blood of her people. In the least likely way, she prepared a banquet for her enemy. She fed her enemy. She showed kindness to her enemy. Esther did not expose the enemy right away. She planned strategically and carefully, and trusted the king to handle it. She didn't take matters into her own hands.

Jesus gives us wisdom on how to handle the Haman in our lives too. He said to love our enemies. He wants us to pray for those who have persecuted us and mistreated us (Matthew 5:44). He wants us to do good to those who hate us, and bless those who curse us (Matthew 5:27-28). This is definitely not the custom of most people in our world today. If someone were to take our coat, we would probably take theirs too. But Jesus tells us to take a bigger step—to not only turn our cheek when they strike, but also give the enemy something more than they take. It is definitely the reverse of what the world would like us to believe and live by. Jesus teaches us to do to others as we would want them to do to us.

One time in particular, I mentioned someone's name, someone who hurt someone very close to me; at the mention of this person's name, I felt anger rising up in me, and I started to say things against him. Immediately, I was convicted that I was slandering my enemy, and Jesus pressed it upon my heart in that moment that I needed to bless those who curse me. I needed to speak life into this situation, rather than follow the anger that would lead to my being an accomplice with the enemy.

God's ways are much higher than ours! When we allow God to handle our enemy, the enemy is always defeated. Moreover, in His unfailing love, He promises to silence and destroy any and all our foes (Psalm 143:12). Let us love our enemies like Jesus did, and live a life of love because He first loved us when we were His enemies.

Hiding from Haman

*T*he classic game of "hide and seek" is a daily metaphor for the life of a Christian. My son, Daniel, and I like to play hide and seek. But the bigger I get, the harder it is for me to hide from him. That was meant to be funny. But in all seriousness, I have run out of places to hide. We play this game in life too. As we hide from trouble, we often seek refuge in places that have holes, making it easy for the enemy to spot us.

There have been times when I've wanted to just get under the covers and hide from the enemy. I might have even hid myself in the refrigerator, seeking the comfort of food. My favorite hide and seek story in the Bible is found in 2 Chronicles 20:1-22. From it I've learned that we can hide from the vast army of our enemies by seeking the Lord. As we seek the Lord, we sing and watch the battle from a distance. That is what Jehoshaphat did as the enemy's forces approached his camp. He was terrified by them; he hid in his prayer closet and began to seek the Lord's guidance. Jehoshaphat declared that God was the Ruler of all kingdoms of the earth, and because He was all powerful and mighty, no one could stand against Him. He reminded God that He was the one who drove out those who occupied the Promised Land—a territory God had set apart and given to His own people. With great faith and assurance, God had established that with any calamity, such as war, plague, or famine, they could come to stand in His presence and cry out to Him to save, and that He would hear and rescue. Jehoshaphat reported to the Lord all that the armies were doing. "Hah, they think they have come to throw us out of Your land which You gave as an inheritance," he basically said to the Lord. Then he acknowledged that he was completely powerless against this great army, that he was putting his trust in the Lord to help them.

At last, the Lord replied, saying, "Do not be afraid! Don't be discouraged by this mighty army, for the battle is not yours, but God's" (2 Chronicles 10:15). He told Jehoshaphat that they wouldn't even need to fight; they would only stand and take their positions to worship and watch. They all stood with their armor in place and sang praises to the Lord. And this is my favorite part of the story. The very moment that they gave praises, the Lord caused the armies to start fighting amongst themselves. We can trust the Lord to handle our battles too. Just pop in a praise CD, and start singing. Our hearts of praise to the Lord will scatter the enemy in every direction; he won't even know what hit him.

This was David's song when the Lord delivered him from the hand of all his enemies and from Saul, "He reached down from heaven and rescued me; he drew me out of deep waters. He rescued me from my powerful enemies, from those who hated me and were too strong for me. They attacked me at a moment when I was in distress, but the Lord supported me. He led me to a place of safety; he rescued me because he delights in me" (Psalm 18:16-19).

When we are abiding in Christ, the enemy cannot touch us. I learned that the enemy is after my treasure, so I must keep it hidden. We must hide our treasure deep within. My heart is hidden in Christ. Is your heart hidden in Christ? "The name of the Lord is a strong fortress; the godly run to him and are safe" (Proverbs 18:10).

There is power in the name of Jesus. Jesus Himself said this to us just before He left earth. He was speaking with His disciples, encouraging them in what they were to do next for Him. He reminded them that there was power in His name.

Not only is there power available in His name, but when we live and work and pray in His name, we have been granted the authority to call upon the same anointing Jesus Himself used to destroy yokes and remove burdens; with the assurance that we too will see the same results. Jesus encouraged us in this way: "Yes, ask me for anything in my name, and I will do it!" (John 14:14). He was saying, ask for anything—anything in line with My will and I will do it in My name! When we operate in His name, we not only have all that He has, but He gives us permission to be used of Him, to speak for Him, to live for Him, and to have resources from Him.

There is safety in the counsel of the godly as well. We can hide in their counsel. Both Eve and Sarai were deceived, and they both convinced their husbands to sin. Because women tend to become so emotionally invested in most aspects of their lives, they allow themselves to be easily deceived. We women must be careful with how we interact

226

with others because we also possess a strong ability to be deceptive ourselves. Because my heart had led me astray before, I wanted to be certain that any decisions I made in regards to opening my heart to a perspective husband were indeed guided by the Lord, and not just my heart being persuaded by another smooth talking man. Human reasoning can be dangerous and deceitful. With that in mind, I was determined that I would be held accountable for any decision I made. I approached both of my pastors, and also Jerry, my favorite janitor, at Calvary Assembly of God and told them that I wanted them to be like my spiritual fathers. I told them that, when my year was up, the enemy would surely try to deceive me; and because I had been so easily deceived before, I was afraid of repeating the cycle. I didn't want to be deceived, so I told them that I needed their approval of any man that might take an interest in me.

They were faithful to do that. Pastor Chad said that if any man were to pursue me, he would think of them as a "weasel" until proven worthy. I knew in my heart that my pastors and Jerry had my best interests at heart. Because of my commitment to serve at my church during my year of personal beauty treatments, Jerry and I had grown close; I shared all that the Lord revealed to me throughout this time. His encouragement and wise counsel was a real blessing to me and a source of great peace and security. When the end came, there was a man that pursued a relationship with me. The pastors took a liking to him; and when he attended an event with me at church, there was an opportunity for Jerry to watch this man in action. The janitors often see what pastors don't. All too often, a mask covers the heart of man and that mask only comes off when he doesn't know someone is looking. I think, because they tend to serve so quietly and without a lot of fanfare, people are not always aware of all that janitors do to keep a church beautiful; therefore they are almost invisible. This is one reason why they often have the advantage of being able to see people for who they really are—behind the mask.

Jerry said to me, "He is not the one; trust me, he is not the one for you." In my heart I knew Jerry was right, and that he was trying to protect me. However, I stepped out of the counsel to test the waters myself. It only took three months before I realized that Jerry was right; he was not the one. Again, I started pouting and thinking, *what now?* I

227

had consecrated my heart to the King of Kings. Surely He would have someone for me by now. Jerry saw me crying at church one day and we talked about the matter. He asked me if I would ever consider going on a blind date. I had honestly never thought about it, but I trusted Jerry and his judgment, so I agreed to meet the man he had in mind.

Still with the thought that I could be deceived, I became friends with a man named Bill. I asked him if he would arrange for a meeting with the pastors. At first he didn't understand why I would want him to do that and he procrastinated. Therefore, we sat down for coffee and I explained to him, with all the force I could muster, that I did not want to play high school games. I gave him the facts: I had been deceived before and I would not be deceived again. I told him that if he did not sit down and meet with my pastors, then I was walking away before I got too attached to him. I needed the protective covering of my pastors to help guard my heart because, as the Bible says, the heart is deceitful above all things (Jeremiah 17:9). I knew myself well enough to realize that, if I wasn't overly cautious, my heart might compel me to fall for someone with hidden secrets and ulterior motives. Bill liked me a lot and he was pursuing me. He had tears in his eyes and felt genuinely sorry that he had not followed through to meet with the pastors—he had no idea that I felt so strongly about it. The next day, he made an appointment to meet with them. Both Pastor Chad and Pastor Bill were present and met with him for about an hour. They were both impressed with Bill and gave me two thumbs up to continue building the friendship. That friendship turned into courtship, which turned into true love, which eventually turned into a beautiful marriage. Now, and for the rest of our lives, we are as one—embracing the journey that lies before us as we travel on the love boat of life.

Bottom Line: I do not want to be deceived, just as Eve was deceived. Just as countless other women are deceived into thinking they have to settle for less than God's perfect will. Our hearts can hide from Haman in the refuge of the Lord's name and His mighty counsel.

Chapter Eight: Meet My Earthly King

One night, my girlfriends and I played a game called "wedding planner." It was a night of fun and laughter, but we also took time to speak sincerely about the desires of our hearts. Many shared their hopes regarding future husbands. One of those friends, who was already married, told us that we should make a list and present it to God and leave it there. She also helped us to see that there are areas in which we need not negotiate. So I made a list of negotiable character traits and non-negotiable traits that I would want in a man. I laid it down at the cross, trusting that God gives good things to those who put their hope in Him. And then I waited, confident that He would give me the desires of my heart as I delighted in Him.

God's Permissible Will

We are ultimately created for God: to worship Him and have relationship with Him. But He created us to do His will together; He doesn't want us to be alone. He made Eve for Adam. He made woman for man. He made man first, and then He made the woman. He designed that the man pursue or hunt, if you will, for the woman.

"The man who finds a wife finds a treasure, and he receives favor from the Lord" (Proverbs 18:22).

Note that it says he who finds a wife, not she who finds her husband. Ladies, I am speaking from experience: when we look for our earthly king, we will not find him. The Lord has someone for each one of us, but He wants to give him to us. We must wait. Having gone through the process of learning this myself, I felt it would be beneficial to many to share with you the conversation that took place between the one I thought was going to be my earthly king and myself.

Two months prior to the start of this journey, I was in a relationship. The man I cared for deeply was a man sold out to God with his whole heart. We both wanted God's best. I have included the conversation that took place between us just prior to the stirrings which prompted me to write this work because I believe it will relate to many of you.

I wrote to him:

"I am concerned that you felt I was luring you into some kind of love trap. I think that you should take some time away from talking to me. I am also going to stop emailing you, texting you, and calling you for a little while. I think that you need a clearer picture and a proper perspective of where our relationship is heading. I do not want my opinion to steer your course. I believe that you are a man who is led by the Holy Spirit; He will persuade you, not me. My opinion doesn't really matter when we are talking about your future. I definitely can't see what will happen in the next two hours, let alone know what God has planned in two years. You have to be certain that I am the one; otherwise, I don't want it. I don't want to be thinking in the back of my head that this man loves me, but he only pursued me because I told him I think I am to be his wife. It is scary to me that you think that I have chased you. I do not want to chase you! I want to be chased!

I desire with all my heart for you to have the very best. If I am not the very best for you, then I pray that you find the very best for you. I want you to know for sure who you are going to spend the rest of your life with. The very fact that you were so honest with me and that you valued my opinion and how I felt, has built my confidence in you. Thank you for asking me how I felt. It felt good that you wanted to be open with me. I think that if you and I backed up a little, then we would see more clearly the direction the Lord is leading us. I see that God is taking you to a place of clarity, and I need to be out of the way. As hard as it is for me to not communicate with you, I believe the Lord is also going to teach me something about moving outside of His perfect will—teaching me to not take matters into my own hands. You seem to have many doubts about us, like where my children fit into the picture, the mission field, etc.

I think (but again it doesn't matter what I think) our callings are completely equal and my children and I are flexible to go and do anything for the Lord; but if you have any doubts whatsoever, then you really need to seek God on this, and with me out of the way. I want you to know for sure! I don't want to be years down the road thinking 'But he didn't know for sure that I was the one.' I need the security that the man who takes me to be his bride is one hundred percent positive that I am the right one. Okay, I think I got it all off my chest. Now I will just wait on the Lord for His timing in everything."

His response to me was:

"My love for you surpasses any form of romantic love. I am not interested in meeting my carnal desires or filling any void of companionship. If the Lord has eternal purposes for us, it will become clear. For now, it will be good to give Him this kind of space. I woke up with the same feeling you did. We need to take some time apart to hear from Him. I am starting a three-day fast today. It is my sole desire to get back into true communion and fellowship with the Holy Spirit. I think we both need to take the time to pursue a greater holiness, seek true purity, and gain a clear understanding as to what the Lord's purposes are for us during this time in our lives. I am searching for, and seeking, answers. Where do I place my adoration? Are my eyes fully resting on Jesus? Am I looking for comfort, affirmation, or significance outside of Christ? Have I kept my heart from the Lord?

I wrote down a statement you made last week. You said, in reference to your joy, 'It doesn't come by circumstance. I am always joyful.' Your unsinkable joy is a beautiful gift from God. Thank God that our joy is found in Him and Him alone. We can bring joy into each other's lives, but only when our hearts are right before Him. I think in some ways we have both taken our eyes off God. It would be good for us to get back in line with His purposes. We must set our eyes fully upon Him. We need to seek His perfect will. As you said, joy does not come by circumstance. So Lord, we ask You to establish us in Your truth. Lead us according to Your purposes and fill us each day with Your perfect love and immeasurable joy. Let us be established in true godliness through the lives we live in Him. We have no righteousness of our own. But in Christ Jesus we are made right before God. Let us preach the gospel through the lives we live each day.

You are a pure, virtuous woman of God. I am grateful to know you and call you friend. You are truly my sister in every way. I want to honor you and treat you as the precious daughter you are. Please forgive me for not honoring you in every way. It is my desire to treat as holy that which the Lord calls sacred. You are a temple for the Most High God. Please forgive me for waking love before it so desired.

Lord, I ask that You bless Jodie and fill her heart with Your love today. Cover her family in Your peace. Let her face be adorned with the smile of heaven. She is precious and beautiful in Your sight. She is truly a gem."

After he and I fasted for three days, I felt it was necessary to communicate with him what the Lord showed me. After careful examination of my own heart, and after weighing out what he had been saying to me. I wrote to him:

"First, I want to apologize for being responsible for causing you to entertain thoughts of us together. I feel like I have too openly shared my feelings and emotions with you, and I am not supposed to do that with my brother and friend. You have clearly stated that friendship is all you want out of our relationship, and

232

I am cool with that. The Lord showed me that I am to be a closed garden, a sealed fountain, not to be opened for just anyone. Not that you are just anyone, but I have to face the fact that you may not be the one for me. The Lord has someone for me who will pursue me; and though I hate to admit it, I need to be honest with myself and acknowledge that I have been the one pursuing you in my heart, and maybe even openly.

I had to come to a place of repentance this morning to return to my first love and remember the heights from which I had fallen. I am so valuable and rare in the kingdom that I will not settle for less than what God has for me. He is the very best! He is the love of my love, and He has rescued me. He loves me sacrificially and the man that He sends my way will completely model that sacrifice. He will pursue me and win my heart, not the other way around.

There is no fear in love; if you are afraid, then it is quite possible that I am not the one for you. I am content to be your very close friend and dear sister in the Lord. I am sealing up all of me in my alabaster jar and I will only pour it out on the one who takes me to be their bride. Forgive me for leading you to a place you were not ready to go. I hope that it has not caused any hurt to your heart. I just can not go any longer entertaining thoughts and giving myself to someone who just needs family. I'm truly sorry for saying words like, 'I am your secret weapon,' or 'I will wait for you,' etc. Those words really must have scared you, and I don't want to cause you to become uncomfortable around me, because we really do have a great friendship."

He replied to me:

"I appreciate you letting the Lord speak to you and through you. You are certainly very valuable and extremely rare in the kingdom. You are not the kind of woman who has to pursue. You are not the kind of woman who has to settle. You are a rare gem, a precious stone. When Jesus found you, you were a diamond in the rough. Others saw a hard rock, covered with the grime of life and endless hardship. You were buried deep in the earth. The world had covered you over. You were simply lost. Clearly this diamond had been buried for some time. The world certainly left its mark. Dirt and small rocks camouflaged the stone laying under the corruption of the hard earth. The stone had been passed up countless times by other miners who could not see its true value. It was tossed to the side repeatedly.

Over time it collected many scrapes, bruises, and cuts. It gave up hope of ever finding its way out of the dark mine. It felt alone, rejected, and unwanted. Each time it was tossed to the side, it felt more abandoned than ever. Eventually the stone began to believe it was just a plain rock, like all the others. Joy was a stranger. Love was a mystery. Hope was an ancient dream. Despair found a home in the heart of the stone and darkness became its dwelling place. The stone grew harder as the cruel days unfolded. The heart of this living stone became hard like a rock. Then one day, something unusual happened. A glimmer of light found its way through the mine shaft and broke through the darkness, eventually settling into the dark corner of the stone's world. A Miner the stone had never seen before approached the stone and bent down to examine it. With gentle hands, He lifted the stone and brought it close to His face, to get a good look at it. The stone immediately noticed something different about this Miner. His eyes were kind and His face radiant. It was not dark and leathery like the others.

The stone also felt a notable difference in the hands of this Miner. They were not cold and rough like the others; His hands were strong and firm, but not brutal. They were warm, soft, and gentle. The stone had gotten use to being cast aside. Normally, fear would grip its heart each time it was snatched off the ground. But this time it was different. This time it felt safe, secure, and protected. When the Miner reached down and lifted the stone up to examine it, He was delighted. He knew He had found it.

This was the stone He had been searching for His whole life. He had finally found it. He had at last discovered what He was looking for—the diamond in the rough. Jesus knew you were a unique diamond from the beginning. When the right time finally arrived, He rescued you. He snatched you out from the mines, before the other miners could steal you away forever. He wanted you for Himself. He grabbed you and hid you securely in His arms. He carried you out of the darkness of the mine and into the broad daylight. As He did, He whispered softly into your ear, 'Rejoice, for it is truly a new day!'

He dusted you off and began to polish you. Slowly, His light began to reflect through you. As He polished, traces of light would occasionally sparkle across your surface. He studied you closely for a while, patiently searching to find the hidden beauty in you. It didn't take long until He saw what He was looking for. He saw your true identity. In that moment, He saw Himself— His nature reflecting back through you. He grabbed His tool of choice—a keen, sharp, trustworthy instrument with a fine tip, He always kept next to His side, called the Holy Spirit. Slowly, with great patience, steady hands, and expert skill, He began to shape you. He cut away excess fragments. Day after day, He worked steadily, with expert patience and great care, gently grinding away all the dross. Now, with great wisdom and mastery, He is bringing forth the precise cut He has been after all along.

With flawless instinct, He is revealing the true diamond. With great skill, He is allowing the true nature of the diamond to emerge. Every cut, every angle, was shaped perfectly to reveal and reflect the light of its Maker. There has never been a diamond like this before. It is flawless in every way. It will not be sold to a conventional jewelry store only to end up adorning the limb of a discarded life. No, this diamond is meant for greatness. This diamond is to be a hallmark display of the Maker's love.

Beauty Treatments

Many diamonds throughout the earth are still buried deep in the recesses of the world's caverns. There are thousands of precious stones that lay dormant, unmoved by the winds of time, unreached by the promise of discovery. Deep in the mines, they are entombed in darkness. The light of day is far from their view. The winds of hope never reach them. Other gems are occasionally unearthed by miners and sold into the marketplace. There are countless jewels lost in the streams of society. Each one finds a home somewhere, but is eventually cast aside, hidden in a small box and left sitting in a dark and remote space. But the Maker has placed this unique diamond in a setting to His liking. It was not created to exalt the huddled masses of the world. This diamond is to be a display of beauty and distinction for His glory. It is to be held high for the entire world to see. This diamond He has selected will be His and His alone.

Every king has a ring, symbolizing power, authority, majesty, and greatness. Now the King finally has a ring of His own, suitable enough to wear upon His royal hand. He is quite pleased. Yes, this diamond is truly fit to adorn the righteous right hand of the noble King. He sits back, quietly admiring the diamond, smiling as He contemplates the beauty of this magnificent gem. He knows it will bring great honor, real glory, and immense joy to Him and His kingdom. As the King reclines in His throne, He is filled with great peace and satisfaction, knowing deep in His heart, that through this little diamond, the world will finally see the genuine light of His kind heart, the full measure of His goodness, and the truth of His perfect, unfailing love. This little diamond will reflect the King's glorious, radiant light throughout the world. It is an eternal light that will never grow faint. The lost gems throughout the world will finally see the true light of the merciful King. The light of discovery will reach the lost stones of time and the world will finally know their kind Maker. They will finally see their beloved King. At last, the world will truly see Jesus."

236

God did close the door on my relationship with this man—not because of impurity, but because it was not God's perfect plan. We were both looking for God's perfect plan, and it was revealed to us that it was not His timing. Nevertheless, this heartbreaking experience led me straight into this year of preparation for the King of Kings. This was my time to heal, learn, apply, and prepare for God's perfect plan. Both of us have remained strong in our friendship and he has continued to be a godly blessing in my life.

During that year, I pondered in my heart all that God had done in my life; it was hard to not wonder who my earthly king would be. I prepared my heart for the King of Kings, but I also knew that God was preparing me for a man that was close to the throne of God himself. In order for me to keep those thoughts at a distance, I wrote them in my journal and went on. As I read back through my journal, I noticed there were quite a few men that I thought God was preparing me for. Now I laugh at myself. I even told God that I wanted my prince charming, whoever he was, to call me or come over at midnight on April 16, when the year of consecration was over. I really believed that when that year was over, I would receive my earthly inheritance. However, God knew best and that was not in His plan. I did receive a call that night at midnight by a dear brother in the Lord, congratulating me on completing my year, and that made my emotions go wild. I automatically started thinking He was my prince charming. He took me out on a date the next night, bought me a couple of dresses, and took me out to dinner. He wondered if He was my prince charming as well. We dated for a few months, but we never really seemed to connect as a couple. He desired to shower gifts on me to show his love for me; however, quality time meant more to me than gifts. He just didn't have the time for me. When I let him know that quality time was what I needed, he realized he couldn't give me that. We stopped dating but remained great friends.

"You say, 'I am allowed to do anything'—but not everything is good for you. You say, 'I am allowed to do anything'—but not everything is beneficial" (1 Corinthians 10:23).

God's Perfect Will

ecause the Lord had spoken clearly to my heart in my solitude, I knew that, although I could settle for His permissible will, if I would just be patient, His Perfect will for me was coming. I just could not settle. I had too much at stake now. I needed to wait.

A few months later at church, I was pouting and the janitor stopped to inquire of my long face. I told him that I was disappointed that God had not provided me with the earthly king I had hoped for. I told him I had laid all my desires down and given my life solely to the Lord; now I was ready to be someone's wife. He looked at me, smiled, agreed that it was time, and asked me if I would ever consider going on a blind date? Normally, my thought would have been no way, but I knew this janitor. Jerry had been someone I had confided in the whole year through. He was excited about all that God was doing, and I somehow trusted that he would not set me up with just anyone. I gave him my number, not thinking much else about it.

Apparently the janitors had wanted to set us up before Jerry and I even talked. Bill Dye Sr. is one of those janitors, and the guy they wanted to set me up with just happened to be his son. The next night, the blind date called me and we talked for about an hour. He had said he lived in Perrysburg, a nice suburb about twenty minutes from where I lived; I said I lived in the projects in Toledo. He didn't call back. Jerry asked me about a month later if we had ever gotten together and I told him that I thought I must have scared him away when I told him I lived in the projects. Jerry got on his back for that. The next night, he called me again and we agreed to meet for the first time at my church. We were wearing similar clothing, almost as though we had planned it like that. We had a nice conversation during Sunday school, and then attended service together.

When he walked me out to my car, I said to him, "I need to be up front with you. I am an old-fashioned kind of girl, so I won't be calling you. I also won't be handing anything out, so if that is what you're interested in, then don't bother calling me." He looked shocked that I

238

had said that, but he called me ten minutes later. That was exactly what he was looking for—an old fashioned woman. He wanted a woman who had high standards, and a woman whom he could trust. I was not that kind of woman before, but after receiving my beauty treatments, I could honestly say that that is the woman I had become. We got to know each other really well through webcam chats, and we both knew it was the right time for us. He started to pursue marriage, but he did not officially ask me until he could get a ring. However, he did tell me a date that he believed in his heart would be a good day to get married. When he said 10-10-10, I was excited because that just so happened to be the same month that Esther was taken into the palace for the king. The tenth month was the month of Tebeth (Esther 2:16). *Tebeth* means "goodness" in the Hebrew language. [39]

Another significant thing to me was that on 7-7-07, the Lord had separated the soul-tie between me and my first husband through a very long fast, and a whole night of crying out in prayer. When I looked up those numbers, I felt it was significant for my story. The number 7 means completion, and the number 10 means completeness. God had completed a chapter in my life with my previous husband, and brought me to a place to receive beauty treatments so that, with my earthly king, I would experience a completeness that I had never before known—one that He desires all marriages to possess. Then, guess what day it fell on when he asked me to marry him? That's right, he asked me on April 16, 2010, the anniversary day of the day I started my sabbatical. In the months to come, as we prepared our hearts for marriage, we encountered many obstacles that only made us stronger. We married on 10-10-10. He made me feel valuable and loved as he never once tried to have sex before our marriage. We waited until we got married to consummate our marriage vows.

"This explains why a man leaves his father and mother and is joined to his wife, and the two are united into one. Now the man and his wife were both naked, but they felt no shame" (Genesis 2:24-25).

39. The Net Bible Study Dictionary Online, http://classic.net.bible.org/dictionary. php?word=Tebeth (accessed July 16,2013). Used by permission.

Two years into our marriage, I can honestly say that he completes me. He does things for me before I even ask. He is truly the other half of me. At times I just have to pick a little bit of "peace" off his tree; his tree, spiritually speaking, is full of that particular fruit. What a wonderful and godly man the Lord put in my life. He is truly sent from above. I am so glad that I did not take matters into my own hands as Sarah did when she gave her husband, Abraham, her maidservant, Hagar, to sleep with so that she could hurry God's promise along. It turned sour when Hagar had Ishmael and brought all kinds of grief. God had told Abraham and Sarah that they were going to have a child, but Sarah thought surely it had to come some other way. She relied on her own understanding. God had spoken gently in my heart that I could settle for Ishmael (meaning less than God's best) or I could wait on the promise that He had an Isaac for me (a promise He kept). My earthly king's name is William, and I say to him, "Sir William, my king, I adore thee." And I do!

Psalm 45

A wedding song to my earthly king, "Sir William Thatcher Dye, Jr."

"Beautiful words stir my heart. I will recite a lovely poem about the king, for my tongue is like the pen of a skillful poet. You are the most handsome of all. Gracious words stream from your lips. God Himself has blessed you forever. Put on your sword, O mighty warrior! You are so glorious, so majestic! In your majesty, ride out to victory, defending truth, humility, and justice. Go forth to perform awe-inspiring deeds! Your arrows are sharp, piercing your enemies' hearts. The nations fall beneath your feet. You love justice and hate evil. Therefore God, your God, has anointed you, pouring out the oil of joy on you more than on anyone else. Myrrh, aloes, and cassia perfume your robes. In ivory palaces, the music of strings entertains you. Kings' daughters are among your noble women. At your right side stands the queen, wearing jewelry of finest gold from Ophir!" (Psalm 45:1-9).

Our Heavenly King knows just what we need. He never designed for us to be alone. Granted, He has called some to walk that road, but the majority of His people are to have helpmates to expand His kingdom. This is not just a romantic story that I tell you. It is a real life marriage that is filled with the vitality of abundant life. This marriage that we have is a picture of what our Heavenly King wants for Himself from the church. He loves you, He chose you, He pursues you, He draws you, He gives you all you need, He waits for you so patiently, and He wants to complete you. And rest assured, He will (Philippians 1:6).

He is not done with us yet while we live in a sinful world, but He promises that He will complete us. And since God is not a man that He should lie, we can trust Him to accomplish what He said He would do. He has ordered beauty treatments on your behalf. He will make you beautiful in His time. He will bring forth His spotless bride at "such a time as this."

Testimonials

My life was over. I was broken down and I felt I would never be whole again. I had lost my children and my home. To get my babies back, I had to change my life—that day. I had no living relatives and the friends I had only helped sink me deeper into the pit. In that despair, I turned to God. I asked Him to be with me and help me. My new church, Calvary Assembly of God, rallied around me. That is when I met Jodie. She brought me into her home, or her "heavenly harem" as she called it. More than that, she brought me into her heart. Jodie comforted me and began to show me how to turn to the Lord to begin my new life.

When I looked at Jodie, I saw a woman who was confident in Jesus and His presence in her life. I wanted to be like her; this light that shined inside of her was undeniable. There was one problem: how to get to that point of happiness in my life was a mystery to me. Jodie was absolutely the right person to show me how to get there. She too had come from a troubled background and understood how I was feeling and how I was living.

Jodie started to peel back the layers of denial and resistance I had developed over the years. We laughed and cried together daily. She showed me Scriptures and we prayed together until we could feel that the Spirit of God was in the room with us. It would dazzle me and astound me as I was filled with hope that I could really begin to live for the first time in my life. Jodie was in the middle of some big changes in her life as well. She had come to believe that she should not be in any relationships with men. She did not wear makeup and did not style her hair; instead she decided to use that energy to worship the Lord. She might not have even realized that she was preaching an amazing message to me: to focus on what is going on in the inside of our hearts and souls. She taught me to focus on inner beauty, grace, and modesty, and to do it all in honor of our Father. In addition to prayer and verbal instruction, Jodie's example brought me closer to God, showing me how to live day-to-day and do what honors the Lord.

Since then, I have continually grown in the Lord; the Lord has given me a new home and I have all my children back home with me. Now I sit back and watch as God continues to do a work in me!

~Heide Higgins
Toledo, OH

Back in 2005, my life was very hard and I was lost. I was a divorced single mother of three in yet again another abusive relationship. I met Jodie, and she told me how much Jesus loves me and how He had a purpose and a plan for me, no matter what I had done. She never judged me; she was there to help me and my children. She spoke the Word and read me Scriptures from the Bible. Jodie encouraged me to remain single and wait on God.

After my daughter was in a terrible car accident, Jodie told me that I needed to trust that Jesus had it all under control. Then we lost everything in a house fire, and Jodie said that Jesus would bring beauty out of the ashes. Again, our Heavenly Father was there helping us in every way. I realized that I have a Father who loves me so much He sent His Son to die for me. I have been healed inside and out because of the love our Father has for us. I have survived every kind of abuse you could imagine, and I have had way more than my share of issues, but I am here alive, living His abundant life and loving others as He has loved

242

me. After a couple of years of waiting on God, now I have someone in my life who loves me and we are planning on getting married soon. So when someone tells you to wait on God, and that He does things in His time, do it and you will see that the best is yet to come. Our Almighty Father will never, ever fail us or leave us. He cares for us. Whether it is just a hang nail or a serious addiction, our Father cares all the same. My children and I are living, breathing proof.

~Shryl Keith
Toledo, OH

Jodie has been very influential in my life. When she told me she was writing a book called *Beauty Treatments* I was very excited. We would have conversations about Gods love for me. I have always struggled with feeling rejection and wanting people's approval and acceptance. Jodie would talk to me about going to God and believing that God loves me no matter what and that I needed to see that God sees me as beautiful from the inside out. Today, I see myself as God sees me, beautiful from the inside out. I am not so focused on what other people think of me. I am going to God more when I don't see myself as being pretty. I see that God is transforming my mind to only think how He views me.

~Dawn Owens
Wixom, MI

When I first heard about *Beauty Treatments* three years ago, I thought, *yes, this will be fabulous; my friend is going to teach all her girlfriends how to apply makeup.* Boy, was I wrong. *Beauty Treatments* found me at a time where I was lonely and not respecting my husband the way God intends wives to do. I was borderline depressed, even though I wore a smile everyday so no one would ever know Ms. Sunshine was down in the dumps. Jesus is not looking for someone who is beautiful on the outside; He is looking for us all to find the queen within ourselves and live up to His expectations. *Beauty Treatments* is a must read because life is short, and we have to be ready for Jesus when He comes back. He is expecting us to look past the ugliness this world has offered and bring our beauty within forward, and shine His light through our lives now, so we can serve Him today. He has already prepared a castle for us, His queens. He has made Jodie's book relevant to today's woman as they compare their life in contrast to women of the Bible, to reflect a mirror image of themselves. Jodie uses her own life experiences, along with firm Scripture to demonstrate God's image and expectations. Apply *Beauty Treatments* to your life and you'll see God's image in your mirror.

~Marcie Woodard
Ormond Beach, Florida

I have known Jodie for about six years. I know that God put her into my life because, right before I met her, I asked God to give me friends that love Him and are devoted and loving toward others and God. Jodie has been such an inspiration to me in so many ways. Her life reflects the love she has for God and her love she has for others. Her character is pure. She sets a very high standard, not in word only, but by the way she lives. I wish the whole world was full of "Jodies." It would be a world of fun, love, excitement, purity, truth, and integrity. I love Jodie. I told her once that she was like sparkling diamonds and that she has high worth, that she is the jewel that someone has to search for and dig deep for; that she is rare and precious. I cannot wait to read the book she has written. I am confident that it is nothing less than a written expression of who she is and the God she loves—amazing.

~Pam Starr
Clawson, MI

I have had the wonderful privilege to serve as one of Jodie's pastors; and have personally observed the spiritual growth that has taken place in her life as a result of her obedience, diligence, and devotion to God and His Word. She is a follower of Christ that I deeply respect and admire.

~Pastor Bill McGinnis
Executive Pastor, Calvary Assembly of God
Toledo, OH

About the Author

Jodie Dye was just a commoner who became a queen. A child without a mother, she grew up, married, and soon found herself a single mother. Raising three children on her own, she could easily relate to Mordecai who was like Esther's single father. And just like Esther, the Lord led Jodie to a quiet place and instructed her to wait there for His wondrous provision. He gave her specific "beauty treatments" to prepare her for that special day when she would be presented to her King. She now has the opportunity to share her Beauty Treatments with you.

Jodie actively hosts Beauty Treatment seminars and events. To contact Jodie about her events or about the book, email:

Jodiedye@ymail.com

More Titles by 5 Fold Media

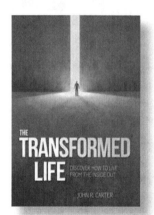

"To Establish and Reveal"
For more information
visit:
www.5foldmedia.com

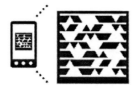

Use your mobile device to scan
the tag above and visit our
website.
Get the free app:
http://gettag.mobi

CPSIA information can be obtained at www.ICGtesting.com
Printed in the USA
LVOW12s1410130514

385605LV00011B/170/P